T0278125

ACTS
for
EVERYONE

PART 1
CHAPTERS 1–12

20TH ANNIVERSARY EDITION WITH STUDY GUIDE

ENLARGED PRINT

NEW TESTAMENT FOR EVERYONE
20TH ANNIVERSARY EDITION WITH STUDY GUIDE
ENLARGED PRINT
N. T. Wright

ACTS
for
EVERYONE

PART 1
CHAPTERS 1–12

20TH ANNIVERSARY EDITION WITH STUDY GUIDE

ENLARGED PRINT

N. T.
WRIGHT

STUDY GUIDE BY MARK PRICE

WESTMINSTER
JOHN KNOX PRESS
LOUISVILLE · KENTUCKY

© 2008, 2023 Nicholas Thomas Wright
Study guide © 2023 Westminster John Knox Press

First published in Great Britain in 2008 by the
Society for Promoting Christian Knowledge
36 Causton Street
London SW1P 4ST
www.spckpublishing.co.uk

and in the United States of America by
Westminster John Knox Press,
100 Witherspoon Street, Louisville, KY 40202

20th Anniversary Edition with Study Guide
Enlarged Print
Published in 2023
by Westminster John Knox Press
Louisville, Kentucky

23 24 25 26 27 28 29 30 31 32—10 9 8 7 6 5 4 3 2 1

Scripture quotations marked NRSV are from the New Revised Standard Version of the Bible, copyright © 1989 by the Division of Christian Education of the National Council of the Churches of Christ in the U.S.A., and are used by permission. Scripture quotations marked RSV are from the Revised Standard Version of the Bible, copyright © 1946, 1952, 1971, and 1973 by the Division of Christian Education of the National Council of the Churches of Christ in the U.S.A., and are used by permission.

Maps by Pantek Arts Ltd., Maidstone, Kent, UK.

Cover design by Allison Taylor

Library of Congress Cataloging-in-Publication Data is on file at the Library of Congress, Washington, DC.

ISBN-13: 978-0-664-26642-4 (U.S. edition)
ISBN-13: 978-0-664-26872-5 (U.S. enlarged print)

Most Westminster John Knox Press books are available at special quantity discounts when purchased in bulk by corporations, organizations and special-interest groups. For more information, please e-mail SpecialSales@wjkbooks.com.

To
John Pritchard and Mark Bryant
Fellow workers for the kingdom of God

CONTENTS

CONTENTS

INTRODUCTION TO THE
ANNIVERSARY EDITION

It took me ten years, but I'm glad I did it. Writing a guide to the books of the New Testament felt at times like trying to climb all the Scottish mountains in quick succession. But the views from the tops were amazing, and discovering new pathways up and down was very rewarding as well. The real reward, though, has come in the messages I've received from around the world, telling me that the books have been helpful and encouraging, opening up new and unexpected vistas.

Perhaps I should say that this series wasn't designed to help with sermon preparation, though many preachers have confessed to me that they've used it that way. The books were meant, as their title suggests, for everyone, particularly for people who would never dream of picking up an academic commentary but who nevertheless want to dig a little deeper.

The New Testament seems intended to provoke all readers, at whatever stage, to fresh thought, understanding and practice. For that, we all need explanation, advice and encouragement. I'm glad these books seem to have had that effect, and I'm delighted that they are now available with study guides in these new editions.

N. T. Wright
2022

INTRODUCTION

On the very first occasion when someone stood up in public to tell people about Jesus, he made it very clear: this message is for *everyone*.

It was a great day – sometimes called the birthday of the church. The great wind of God's spirit had swept through Jesus' followers and filled them with a new joy and a sense of God's presence and power. Their leader, Peter, who only a few weeks before had been crying like a baby because he'd lied and cursed and denied even knowing Jesus, found himself on his feet explaining to a huge crowd that something had happened which had changed the world for ever. What God had done for him, Peter, he was beginning to do for the whole world: new life, forgiveness, new hope and power were opening up like spring flowers after a long winter. A new age had begun in which the living God was going to do new things in the world – beginning then and there with the individuals who were listening to him. 'This promise is for *you*', he said, 'and for your children, and for everyone who is far away' (Acts 2.39). It wasn't just for the person standing next to you. It was for everyone.

Within a remarkably short time this came true to such an extent that the young movement spread throughout much of the known world. And one way in which the *everyone* promise worked out was through the writings of the early Christian leaders. These short works – mostly letters and stories about Jesus – were widely circulated and eagerly read. They were never intended for either a religious or intellectual elite. From the very beginning they were meant for everyone.

That is as true today as it was then. Of course, it matters that some people give time and care to the historical evidence, the meaning of the original words (the early Christians wrote in Greek), and the exact and particular force of what different writers were saying about God, Jesus, the world and themselves. This series is based quite closely on that sort of work. But the point of it all is that the message can get out to everyone, especially to people who wouldn't normally read a book with footnotes and Greek words in it. That's the sort of person for whom these books are written. And that's why there's a glossary, in the back, of the key words that you can't really get along without, with a simple description of what they mean. Whenever you see a word in **bold type** in the text, you can go to the back and remind yourself what's going on.

There are of course many translations of the New Testament available today. The one I offer here is designed for the same kind of reader: one who mightn't necessarily understand the more formal, sometimes even ponderous, tones of some of the standard ones. I have of course tried to keep as close to the original as I can. But my main aim has been to be sure that the words can speak not just to some people, but to everyone.

Let me add a note about the translation the reader will find here of the Greek word *Christos*. Most translations simply say 'Christ', but most modern English speakers assume that that word is simply a proper name (as though 'Jesus' were Jesus 'Christian' name and 'Christ' were his 'surname'). For all sorts of reasons, I disagree; so I have experimented not only with 'Messiah' (which is what the word literally means) but sometimes, too, with 'King'.

The book of Acts, which I quoted a moment ago, is full of the energy and excitement of the early Christians as they found God doing new things all over the place and learned to take the **good news** of Jesus around the world. It's also full of the puzzles and problems that churches faced then and face today – crises over leadership, money, ethnic divisions, theology and ethics, not to mention serious clashes with political and religious authorities. It's comforting to know that 'normal church life', even in the time of the first apostles, was neither trouble-free nor plain sailing, just as it's encouraging to know that even in the midst of all their difficulties the early church was able to take the gospel forward in such dynamic ways. Actually, 'plain sailing' reminds us that this is the book where more journeys take place, including several across the sea, than anywhere else in the Bible – with the last journey, in particular, including a terrific storm and a dramatic shipwreck. There isn't a dull page in Acts. But, equally importantly, the whole book reminds us that whatever 'journey' we are making, in our own lives, our spirituality, our following of Jesus and our work for his kingdom, his spirit will guide us too, and make us fruitful in his service. So here it is: Acts for everyone!

MAPS

Map 1

R. Tiber

Rome
ITALY

Dyrrhachium

Brundisium

MACEDONIA
Thessalonica
Beroea

Messana
Rhegium

Sicily

Syracuse

Corinth
ACHAEA Athens
(GREECE)

Malta

Mediterranean Sea

Lesser
Syrtis

Crete

Phoenix
Fair Havens

Cauda

AFRICA

Greater
Syrtis

Cyrene

CYRENAICA

0	100	200 miles

0	100	200 kms

LIBYA

The Eastern Mediterranean in the First Century AD

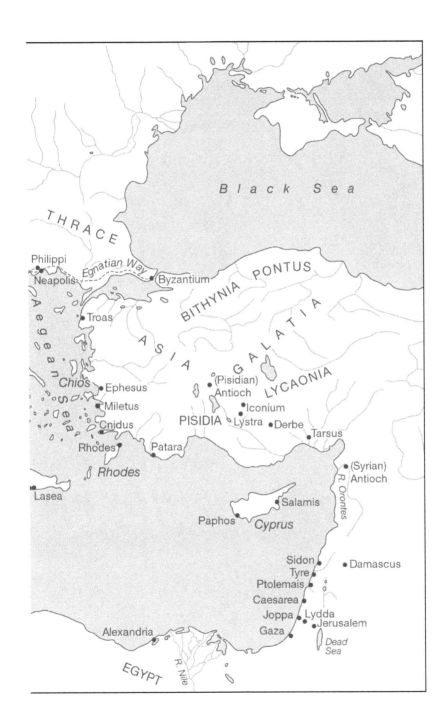

THRACE

Philippi

Neapolis

Egnatian Way

Byzantium

Black Sea

BITHYNIA

PONTUS

A e g e a n   S e a

Troas

A S I A

GALATIA

LYCAONIA

Chios

Ephesus

(Pisidian)
Antioch

Miletus

Iconium

Cnidus

PISIDIA

Lystra

Derbe

Tarsus

Rhodes

Patara

Rhodes

(Syrian)
Antioch

Lasea

R. Orontes

Cyprus

Salamis

Paphos

Sidon

Damascus

Tyre

Ptolemais

Caesarea

Joppa

Lydda

Gaza

Jerusalem

Alexandria

*Dead
Sea*

EGYPT

R. Nile

Map 2

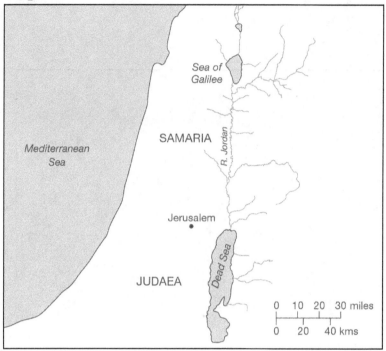

Acts 1.6–8

Map 3

Acts 2.5–13

Map 4

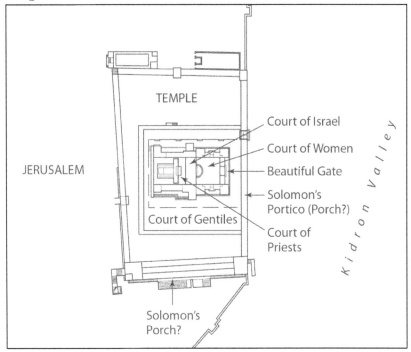

TEMPLE

JERUSALEM

Court of Israel

Court of Women

Beautiful Gate

Solomon's Portico (Porch?)

Court of Gentiles

Court of Priests

Kidron Valley

Solomon's Porch?

Acts 3.1–10, 11–16

Map 5

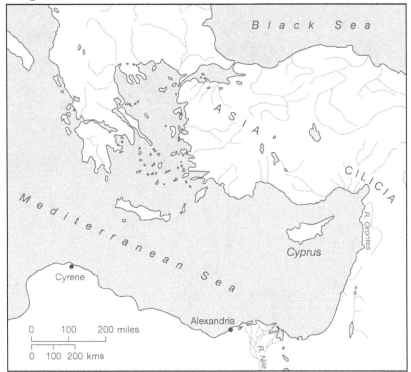

Black Sea

ASIA

CILICIA

R. Orontes

Mediterranean Sea

Cyprus

Cyrene

Alexandria

R. Nile

| 0 | 100 | 200 miles |

| 0 | 100 | 200 kms |

Acts 6.9

Map 6

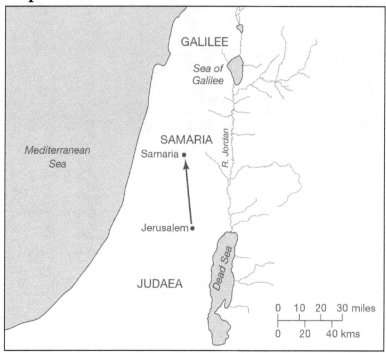

Acts 8.4–25

Map 7

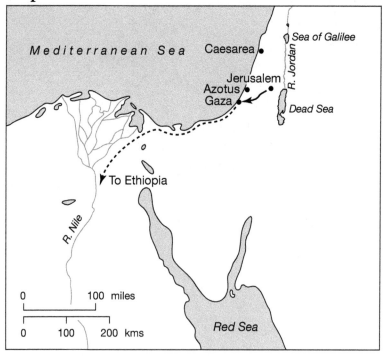

Acts 8.26–40

Map 8

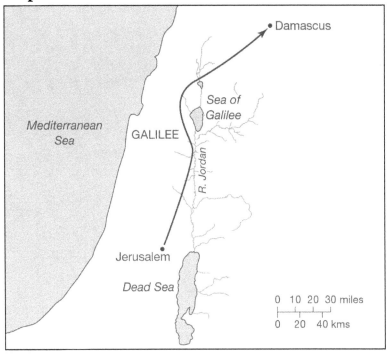

Acts 9.1–9

Map 9

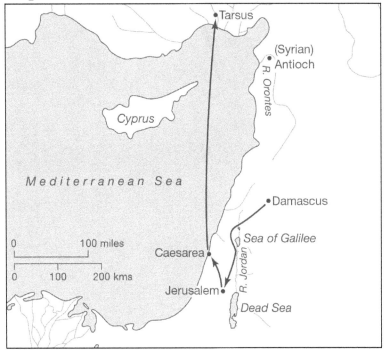

Acts 9.19b–26, 30

Map 10

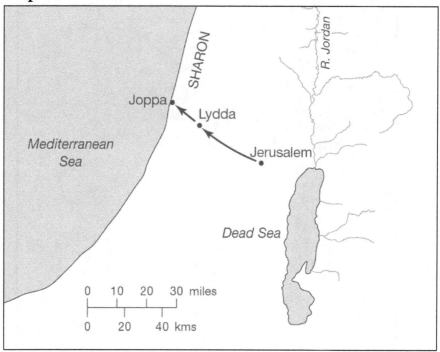

Acts 9.32, 35, 36

Map 11

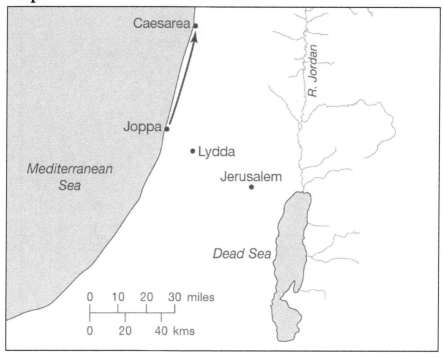

Acts 10.1–16

Map 12

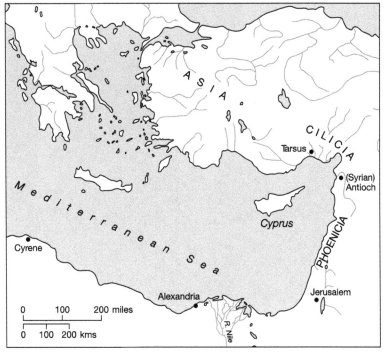

Acts 11.19–30

Map 13

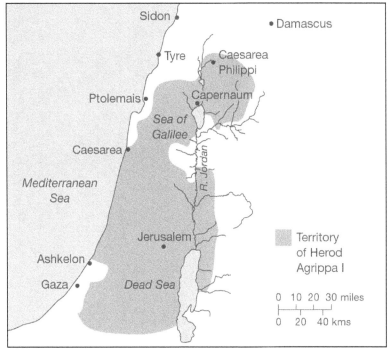

Acts 12.20–25

ACTS 1.1–5

Here Comes the Sequel!

¹Dear Theophilus,
  The previous book which I wrote was about everything Jesus began to do and teach. ²I took the story as far as the day when he was taken up, once he had given instructions through the holy spirit to his chosen apostles.
  ³He showed himself to them alive, after his suffering, by many proofs. He was seen by them for forty days, during which he spoke about God's kingdom. ⁴As they were having a meal together, he told them not to go away from Jerusalem, but to wait, as he put it, 'for the father's promise, which I was telling you about earlier. ⁵John baptized with water, you see; but in a few days from now you will be baptized with the holy spirit.'

The English playwright Alan Bennett wrote a famous play about the equally famous madness of a well-known king. In the eighteenth and nineteenth centuries, England had four kings in succession all called 'George', and the third of them – George III, in other words – suffered for a fair amount of his reign from some kind of mental illness, probably porphyria. So Bennett called his play *The Madness of George III*.

But when they came to make a movie of the play, the movie-makers faced a problem. Moviegoers were used to sequels: *Spiderman II*, *Superman III*, and so on. A title like that meant that there had been an earlier film of the same name. So they were worried that if people saw a title like *The Madness of George III* they would assume they had missed the first two films in the sequence – and perhaps they wouldn't go to see what they took to be the third. So the filmmakers just called the movie *The Madness of King George*.

The opening paragraph of the book we are now going to read declares, clearly and solidly, that, unlike Bennett's play and film, it is indeed a sequel. There has been a previous book, and this one continues the story. In fact, it even suggests a kind of title: *The Deeds and Teaching of King Jesus II* – not *Jesus the Second*, of course, because there is only one King Jesus, but the second book about what the one and only Jesus did and taught.

At first sight, this is a strange title, since Jesus himself only appears on stage, as it were, during the first nine verses of this first chapter. But Luke, whose first volume we know as the **gospel** which bears his name, is telling us with his opening sentence one of the most important things about the whole book which is now beginning. *It is all about what Jesus is continuing to do and to teach.* The mysterious presence of Jesus haunts the whole story. He is announced as King and Lord, not as an increasingly distant memory but as a living and powerful reality, a person who can be known and loved, obeyed and followed, a person who continues to act within the real world. That, Luke is telling us, is what this book is going to be all about. We call it 'The Acts of the Apostles', but in truth we should really think of it as 'The Acts of Jesus (II)'.

Luke is already warning us, then, that this is an unusual type of book. At one level, it shares a good deal with some of the literature of the day. It has quite a lot in common, for instance, with the work of the great first-century Jewish historian Josephus. Some of the New Testament writers are cheerfully innocent of any pretensions to literary style, but Luke knows what he's doing with his language, with the structure of the book, and with his entire presentation in his pair of volumes. He is not, like Mark, aiming for the first-century equivalent of the airport bookstall. He is aiming for what today we call 'the intelligent reader'. One would expect to see a review of this book, not necessarily in the tabloid newspapers, but in *The Times Literary Supplement* or *The New York Review of Books*. Not that Luke is snooty or highfalutin. He doesn't talk down to his readers; his book is such a page-turner that anyone who enjoys a good story will be drawn along with excitement the whole way – even if he then leaves them with something of a puzzle at the end, which corresponds as we shall see to the puzzle we've just encountered at the beginning . . .

But the unusual nature of the book is that we are supposed (so Luke is telling us) to read it on at least two levels. At one level, it is of course the story of the early church – told very selectively, of course, like all history (if you wrote down every single thing that happened in a single day you would already fill a library), and told with an eye, as we shall see, to particular concerns and interests. But Luke wants us to read it, all the way through, as a book about Jesus, a book indeed with Jesus as the principal actor, rather like some of the plays by another great playwright of recent years, Samuel Beckett, where the action on stage sometimes crucially depends on a person whom the audience never actually sees.

If this is so, one of the results is that there is a third level as well on which Luke wants us to read his work. *This is a play in which we are invited to become actors ourselves.* The stage opens up and we discover we're in the middle of the action. That is part of the point of the 'ending' which isn't really an ending: the story continues, and we are part of it! What we are reading, from this moment on, is the opening scene, or set of scenes, in a play whose action we ourselves are called to continue. As they say, it ain't over yet. We need to refresh our minds as to how the opening scenes worked so that we can play our parts properly, 'in character', in line with the inner nature of the unfolding drama.

As we do so, Luke is keen that we latch on to two things which are fundamental to his whole book and indeed his whole view of the world. First, it is all based on the resurrection of Jesus. In the last chapter of his gospel, Luke described some of the scenes in which Jesus met his followers after being raised from the dead: it really was him, he really was alive, richly alive, in a transformed body that could eat and drink as well as walk and talk, but which seemed to have . . . some different properties. His body could, for instance, appear and disappear, and come and go through locked doors.

To us, that sounds as if he was a ghost, someone less than properly embodied. What Luke and the other writers who describe the risen body of Jesus are saying, rather, is that Jesus is *more* than ordinarily embodied, not less. His transformed body is now the beginning of God's new creation; and in God's new creation, as we know from passages like Revelation 21 and Ephesians 1, **heaven** and earth will come together in a new way. Jesus' risen body is the beginning of that, the beginning of a heavenly reality which is fully at home on, and in, this physical world ('earth'), and the beginning of a transformed physical world which is fully at home in God's sphere ('heaven'). This, indeed, will help us in the next scene. But the point of the resurrection itself is that without it there is no gospel, no *Deeds and Teachings of King Jesus II*. There would only be the sad and glorious memory of a great, but failed, teacher and would-be **Messiah**. The resurrection of the Jesus who died under the weight of the world's evil is the foundation of the new world, God's new world, whose opening scenes Luke is describing.

The second thing he wants us to latch onto, indeed is so eager to get to that he puts it here, right up front, is the presence and power of the **holy spirit**. He will have much more to say about this in due course, but already here he insists that the spirit is present when Jesus is teaching his followers about what is to come and, above all, that they are about to discover the spirit as a new and powerful reality in their own lives. Jesus, Luke says, pointed them back to the beginning of his own **kingdom**-work, the time when **John the Baptist** summoned all Israel to a **baptism** of **repentance** and renewal. It's going to be like that, he said, only much more so. Instead of being plunged into water, you'll be plunged into the holy spirit. Instead of a renewal which would form them as the restored Israel, waiting for God to become their king as so many Jews of the day had hoped, they would experience a renewal which would form them as the restored humanity, celebrating the fact that God was becoming king of the whole world, *and knowing that as a reality inside their own selves*. That is the very heart of the spirituality, and indeed the theology, of 'The Acts of the Apostles'. God is at work to do a new thing in the whole world. And it catches up, within its powerful movement, every child, woman and man who comes within its orbit.

Jesus told his followers to wait for this to happen before they tried to do anything too much. That is important advice. Far too often, to this day, people blunder ahead, assuming that if they know a little about Jesus, and about God's kingdom, they can just go off and put things into action in whatever way occurs to them. Luke would tell us to wait: to pray for the presence and power of the holy spirit, and to find our calling and our energy from that source. If this is a play in which we are all called to take different parts, it is a play in which the only true acting is what happens when the spirit of the playwright himself takes charge.

ACTS 1.6-8

When, What and How? (See map 2, page xvi.)

⁶So when the apostles came together, they put this question to Jesus.

'Master,' they said, 'is this the time when you are going to restore the kingdom to Israel?'

⁷'It's not your business to know about times and dates', he replied. 'The father has placed all that under his own direct authority. ⁸What will happen, though, is that you will receive power when the holy spirit comes upon you. Then you will be my witnesses in Jerusalem, in all Judaea and Samaria, and to the very ends of the earth.'

'Are we nearly there yet?'

Any parent who has been on a car journey with small children will know the question – and the tone of voice in which it's usually asked. Sometimes the child is so eager (or so bored), so quickly, that the question gets asked before you have even left your own street.

And of course it all depends what you mean by 'nearly'. If I drive from my home in the north of England all the way to London, I could reasonably say that I was 'nearly' there when we had got to within an hour of the capital. But if I am driving from my home to the town where my parents live, which takes about an hour, I would only say I was 'nearly' there when I was a few minutes away. It's all relative.

Jesus must have had similar reflections when faced with the question the **apostles** were eager to ask him. 'Apostle', by the way, is one of the words Luke regularly uses to describe the **Twelve** – or, as they now were, the Eleven, following Judas' death – whom Jesus had chosen as special witnesses. The reason why there were twelve of them is obvious

4

to anyone who understands Jewish culture and history. There had been twelve tribes of Israel, and Jesus was signalling, in his choice of twelve close followers to be around him, that God had called him to renew and restore the people of Israel. So it isn't surprising that they of all people were keen to ask the question, 'Are we nearly there yet? Is this the time? Is it going to happen at last?'

They must, after all, have been very puzzled. Nothing that had happened in the previous few weeks had corresponded at all to their game plan. As far as they were concerned, when Jesus called them and taught them in Galilee during the previous three years or so, they were signing on for some kind of Jewish renewal movement. They believed that God had appointed Jesus to be the true King of Israel, even though most of their contemporaries were still (to say the least) suspicious of him. They had seen Jesus rather like King David in the Old Testament, who for several years was a kind of king-in-waiting, standing in the wings with a ragtag group of followers wondering when their turn would come. Jesus' motley band of followers had imagined that he would be king in some quite ordinary sense, which was why some of them had asked if they could have the top jobs in his government. Jesus, with his extraordinary healing power and visionary teaching, would rule in Jerusalem, and would restore God's people Israel.

The result of this, as many Jews of the time believed, was that, when God restored Israel, the whole world would be turned around at last. Israel would be the top nation, ruling over the rest of the world. That's what had been promised, more or less, in the Psalms (look at Psalm 72, or Psalm 89) and the prophets (read Isaiah 40—55). Of course, the nations of the world would then be judged for their wickedness. But there might also be the possibility that the blessing God gave to Israel would come at last upon the whole creation.

All of this could be summed up in the phrase: 'restore the kingdom to Israel'. That's what they were hoping for, and the question was natural: 'Are we nearly there yet?' They hadn't been expecting that Jesus would die a violent death. His crucifixion made it look as though they were wrong: he wasn't the **Messiah**, they weren't heading for the top jobs, Israel wasn't being renewed, and the world was carrying on in its wicked way, with the rich and powerful oppressing the poor and needy. Business as usual. And then he had risen from the dead, again confounding their own and everyone else's expectations. What did it mean? Did it mean that their dreams of 'restoring the kingdom to Israel' were now back on track?

Well, it did and it didn't. Like everything else, the dream of the **kingdom** had been transformed through Jesus' death and **resurrection**. Just as Jesus had told them they would have to lose their lives to save

5

them, so now he had to explain that they had to lose their kingdom-dreams – of an earthly kingdom with ordinary administrative and governmental power, in charge of subject states – in order to gain them. But at this point many people, reading Acts, have gone badly wrong.

It would be easy to imagine that what Jesus (and Luke) meant at this point was something like this: 'No, no, you're dreaming of an earthly kingdom, but I'm telling you about a heavenly one. You think what matters is reorganizing this world, but I'm preparing you for the next one. What counts is not what happens in this world of space and time, but where you're going to spend eternity. I'm going off to heaven, and you must tell people how they can follow me there.' From that point of view, the answer to 'Are we nearly there yet?' is 'No, we're not going there at all, actually.'

That certainly isn't what Luke means. But, like the children in the car, we ourselves are going to have to wait, as his book unfolds, to see just what he does mean. We know enough from his first volume, though, to see where it's all going. God's kingdom is coming in and through the work of Jesus, not by taking people away from this world but by transforming things within this world, bringing the sphere of earth into the presence, and under the rule, of heaven itself. So when is this all happening? Again, many people, reading this passage, have assumed that Jesus' basic answer is 'No': No, this isn't the time, all of those things will happen a long way off in the future. No, we're not nearly there yet; you have a lot of things to do, tasks to perform, and only when you're finished all of them will I 'restore the kingdom to Israel'. And, actually, there is a sense in which all that is indeed true. There is a 'still-future' dimension to everything that happens in this book, as we shall see. But wait a minute. Is that really what Jesus' answer means?

I don't think it is. Jesus does indeed warn them that they won't be given a timetable. In terms of the children in the car, he is telling them that they simply aren't going to have a sense of where they are on the calendar of God's unfolding purposes. But what he goes on to say hints at something different. 'You will receive power. . . . Then you will be my witnesses in Jerusalem . . . and to the very ends of the earth.'

'My witnesses'? What does that mean? Quite simply this: in the resurrection (and the **ascension**, which is about to happen), Jesus is indeed being enthroned as Israel's Messiah and therefore king of the whole world. He is the one at whose name every knee shall bow, as Paul puts it in Philippians 2.10. In the world of the first century, when someone was enthroned as king, that new authority would take effect through heralds going off throughout the territory in question with the news, 'We have a king!' That was always proclaimed as good news, because everyone in the ancient world (unlike many in the modern world) knew that anarchy is always worse than authorized government. Governments may be bad, but chaos is worse. So the heralds, the messengers, would go off to the far reaches of the kingdom (imagine, for instance, a new Roman emperor coming to the throne, and heralds going off as far as Spain to the west, Britain to the north, and Egypt to the south-east), to announce that Claudius, or Nero, or whoever, was now the rightful king, and to demand glad allegiance from supposedly grateful subjects.

And that is what Jesus is telling them they must now do. You're asking about the kingdom? You're asking when it will come about, when Israel will be exalted as the top nation, with the nations of the world being subject to God through his vindicated people? Well, in one sense it has already happened, Jesus is saying, because in my own death and resurrection I have already been exalted as Israel's representative. In another sense it is yet to happen, because we still await the time when the whole world is visibly and clearly living under God's just and healing rule. But we are now living in between those two points, *and you must be my witnesses from here to the ends of the world.* The apostles are to go out as heralds, not of someone who may become king at some point in the future, but of the one who has *already* been appointed and enthroned.

Notice the subtle difference, in verses 7 and 8, between the words 'authority' and 'power'. God has all authority, and it is through him and from him that all 'authorized' rule in the world must flow. We don't have that ultimate authority; no human, in whatever task or role, ever does. It all comes from God. But what God's people are promised is *power*; the word used here is *dynamis*, from which we get 'dynamite'. We need that power, just as Jesus' first followers did, if we or they are to be his witnesses, to find ways of announcing to the world that he is already its rightful king and lord. And in the next chapters of Acts we see what that witness, and that power, are going to mean.

But for the moment we notice one thing in particular, which will help us as we read into the rest of the book. Jesus gives the apostles an agenda: Jerusalem first, then Judaea (the surrounding countryside), then Samaria (the hated semi-foreigners living right next door) and to the ends of the earth. Sit back and watch, Luke says. That's exactly the journey we're about to take. And, like the child who stops asking the question because suddenly the journey itself has become so interesting, we find there's so much to see that we won't worry so much about the 'when'. Jesus is already appointed and enthroned as the world's true king. One day that kingdom will come, fully and finally. In the meantime, we have a job to do.

ACTS 1.9–14

Ascension!

⁹As Jesus said this, he was lifted up while they were watching, and a cloud took him out of their sight. ¹⁰They were gazing into heaven as he disappeared. Then, lo and behold, two men appeared, dressed in white, standing beside them.

¹¹'Galileans,' they said, 'why are you standing here staring into heaven? This Jesus, who has been taken from you into heaven, will come back in the same way you saw him go into heaven.'

¹²Then they went back to Jerusalem from the hill called the Mount of Olives, which is close to Jerusalem, about the distance you could travel on a sabbath. ¹³They then entered the city ('they' here means Peter, John, James, Andrew, Philip, Thomas, Bartholomew, Matthew, James the son of Alphaeus, Simon the zealot, and Judas the son of James) and went to the upstairs room where they were staying. ¹⁴They all gave themselves single-heartedly to prayer, with the women, including Mary, Jesus' mother, and his brothers.

We were having supper with some friends who had recently moved to western Canada.

'So,' my wife began, 'does Vancouver feel like home?'

'It's not home,' replied the wife energetically. 'It's **heaven**!'

'Well, my dear,' commented her husband, a theologian, reproachfully and perhaps over-piously, 'if you knew your business, you would know that heaven is your true home.'

'No,' she replied. 'Home is where there's hard work, and hassle, and all kinds of difficulties. Here I'm free from all that. This is heaven!'

I have often pondered that conversation, and I want to take issue with the theologian-husband. Though many hymns and prayers (mostly from the nineteenth and early twentieth century) speak of heaven as our home, that isn't how the Bible normally puts it. In the Bible, heaven and earth are the two halves of God's created world. They aren't so much like the two halves of an orange, more or less identical but occupying different space. They are more like the weight of an object and the stuff it's made of, or perhaps the meaning of a flag and the cloth or paper it's made of: two (related) ways of looking at the same thing, two different and interlocking dimensions, the one perhaps explaining the other. Talking about 'heaven and earth' is a way, in the Bible, of talking about the fact, as many people and many cultures have perceived it to be, that everything in our world (call it 'earth' for the sake of argument, though that can be confusing because that is also the name we give to our particular planet within our particular solar system, whereas 'earth' in the Bible really means the entire cosmos of space, time and matter) has another dimension, another sort of reality, that goes with it as well.

You could call this other reality, this other dimension, the 'inner' reality, if you like, thinking perhaps of a golf ball which has an outer reality (the hard, mottled surface) and an inner reality (the tightly packed, springy interior). But you could just as easily think of earth as the 'inner' reality, the dense material of the world where we live at the moment, and 'heaven' as the outer reality, the 'side' of our reality that is open to all kinds of other things, to meanings and possibilities which our 'inner' reality, our busy little world of space, time and matter sometimes seems to exclude.

If these illustrations don't help, leave them to one side and concentrate on the reality. The reality is this: 'heaven' in the Bible is God's space, and 'earth' is our space. 'Heaven' isn't just 'the happy place where God's people go when they die', and it certainly isn't our 'home' if by that you mean (as some Christians, sadly, have meant) that our eventual destiny is to leave 'earth' altogether and go to 'heaven' instead. God's plan, as we see again and again in the Bible, is for 'new heavens and new earth', and for them to be joined together in that renewal once and for all. 'Heaven' may well be our *temporary* home, after this present life; but the whole new world, united and transformed, is our eventual destination.

Part of the point about Jesus' **resurrection** is that it was the beginning of precisely that astonishing and world-shattering renewal. It wasn't just that he happened to be alive again, as though by some quirk of previously unsuspected 'nature', or by some extraordinary '**miracle**' in which God did the impossible just to show how powerful he was, death suddenly worked backwards in his particular case. It was, rather, that because on the cross he had indeed dealt with the main force of evil, decay and death itself, the creative power of God, no longer thwarted as it had been by human rebellion, could at last burst forth and produce the beginning, the pilot project, of that joined-up heaven-and-earth reality which is God's plan for the whole world. This is part at least of the explanation of the sheer strangeness of Jesus' risen body, which hits us in all the Easter stories. At the very point where they're explaining that it really is him, that he isn't a ghost, that he can eat and drink, just at that moment he appears and disappears at will. It seems as though the first disciples really didn't know what to make of it either, and were simply doing their best to tell it like they had seen it.

But once we grasp that 'heaven and earth' mean what they mean in the Bible, and that 'heaven' is not, repeat *not*, a location within our own cosmos of space, time and matter, situated somewhere up in the sky ('up' from whose point of view? Europe? Brazil? Australia?), then

9

we are ready, or as ready as we are likely to be, to understand the **ascension**, described here quite simply and briefly by Luke. Neither Luke nor the other early Christians thought Jesus had suddenly become a primitive spaceman, heading off into orbit or beyond, so that if you searched throughout the far reaches of what we call 'space' you would eventually find him. They believed that 'heaven' and 'earth' are the two interlocking spheres of God's reality, and that the risen body of Jesus is the first (and so far the only) object which is fully at home in both and hence in either, anticipating the time when everything will be renewed and joined together. And so, since as T. S. Eliot said, 'humankind cannot bear very much reality', the new, overwhelming reality of a heaven-and-earth creature will not just yet live in both dimensions together, but will make itself – himself – at home within the 'heavenly' dimension for the moment, until the time comes for heaven and earth to be finally renewed and united. At that point, of course, this renewed Jesus himself will be the central figure.

That is the point of the event, and its explanation, as we find them in verses 9–11. Jesus is 'lifted up', indicating to the disciples not that he was heading out somewhere beyond the moon, beyond Mars, or wherever, but that he was going into 'God's space', God's dimension. The cloud, as so often in the Bible, is the sign of God's presence (think of the pillar of cloud and fire as the children of Israel wandered through the desert, or the cloud and smoke that filled the **Temple** when God became suddenly present in a new way). Jesus has gone into God's dimension of reality; but he'll be back on the day when that dimension and our present one are brought together once and for all. That promise hangs in the air over the whole of Christian history from that day to this. That is what we mean by the '**second coming**'.

There are two other things which are, as we say, 'going on' in this passage. Some first-century readers would have picked up one of these, some the other, some perhaps both. First, one of the central Old Testament promises for the early Christians was in Daniel 7, where 'one like a **son of man**' is brought up, on the clouds of heaven, to the 'Ancient of Days', and is presented before him and given kingly power over the nations, and particularly over the 'beasts', the monsters representing the forces of evil and chaos. For someone who had long pondered that passage – and there are plenty of signs that the early Christians did just that – the story of Jesus' ascension would indicate that Daniel 7 had been fulfilled in a dramatic and unexpected way, with the human figure who had suffered at the hands of the evil powers of the world now being exalted into the very presence of God himself, there to receive kingly power. This fits so well with the previous passage (verses 6–8) that it is hard to suppose that Luke did not intend it.

Second, many of Luke's readers would know that when a Roman emperor died, it had become customary to declare that someone had seen his soul escaping from his body and going up to heaven. If you go to the top end of the Forum in Rome, stand under the Arch of Titus, and look up, you will see a carving of the soul of Titus, who was emperor in the 80s of the first century, ascending to heaven. The message of this was clear: the emperor was becoming a god (thus enabling his son and heir to style himself 'son of god', which is a useful title if you want to run the world). The parallel is not so close this time, since Luke is clear that it was not Jesus' soul that ascended into heaven, leaving his body behind somewhere, but his whole, renewed, bodily, complete self. But there is then a sense that Jesus is *upstaging* anything the Roman emperors might imagine for themselves. He is the reality, and they are the parody – a theme we will notice more than once as Luke's story unfolds. And when, at the end of Luke's book, the good news of Jesus is being preached in Rome itself, openly and unhindered, we have a sense of 'Of course! That's how it had to be.' He is the world's true and rightful king, sharing the very throne, and somehow even, so it seems, the identity, of the one true God.

The first and most important response to this extraordinary, unprecedented and still hard-to-describe event is of course worship. Luke often tells us about the early Christians devoting themselves to prayer. As we go back with them on this occasion from the Mount of Olives to the house where they were staying, and look round the room and see these puzzled but excited men and women – including Jesus' own mother – giving themselves to prayer, we ought to feel a strong identification with them. All those who name the name of Jesus, who worship him, who study his **word**, are called to be people of worship and prayer. Why?

Well, it's obvious, isn't it? It is precisely in worship and prayer that we, while still on 'earth' in the sense I've explored already, find ourselves sharing in the life of 'heaven', which is where Jesus is. The constant references to prayer in Acts are a sign that this is how these very ordinary, frequently muddled, deeply human beings, the **apostles** and the others with them, found that their story was being bound up with the story of 'what Jesus was continuing to do and to teach'. From the ascension onwards, the story of Jesus' followers takes place in both dimensions. That, by the way, is why there was an inevitable head-on clash with the Temple, because the Temple was thought to be the key spot where heaven and earth overlapped. The resurrection and ascension of Jesus are launching a claim to the contrary, and Jesus' followers had to work out what that would mean. As we in our own day not only read Acts but try to follow Jesus and witness to his lordship over the world, it is through prayer and worship that we, too, can know, enjoy and be energized by the life of heaven, right here on earth, and work out what that will mean in terms of other claims, other lords, other ways of **life**.

ACTS 1.15–26

Restoring the Twelve

[15]Around that time Peter stood up in the middle of the gathering, which by this stage numbered about a hundred and twenty.

[16]'My dear family,' he said, 'the holy spirit spoke long ago, through the mouth of David, about Judas, who became a guide to the people who arrested Jesus. There it is in the Bible, and it had to come true. [17]He was counted along with us, and he had his own share in the work we've been given.'

([18]Judas, you see, had bought a field with the money his wickedness had brought him, where he fell headlong and burst open, with all his innards gushing out. [19]This became known to everyone who lived in Jerusalem, so that the field was called, in their local language, 'Akeldamach', which means 'Blood-place'.)

[20]'For this is what it says in the book of Psalms:

Let his home become desolate
and let nobody live in it;

and again,

Let someone else receive his overseeing task.

[21]'So this is what has to be done. There are plenty of people who have gone about with us all the time that our master Jesus was coming and going among us, [22]starting from John's baptism until the day he was taken from us. Let one of them be chosen to be alongside us as a special witness of his resurrection.'

[23]So they chose two: Joseph who was called Barsabbas, with the surname Justus, and Matthias.

[24]'Lord,' they prayed, 'you know the hearts of all people. Show us which one of these two you have chosen [25]to receive this particular place of service and apostleship, from which Judas went away to go to his own place.'

[26]So they cast lots for them. The lot fell on Matthias, and he was enrolled along with the eleven apostles.

The older I get, the more I dislike trying to follow the complicated instructions that come with new technology. I'm not what they call technophobic. On the desk where I am working there is a computer.

It is linked to a cell phone which includes addresses, diary details and so on. Beside me there is an iPod containing hundreds of hours of music. On another desk there is a microphone connecting me to radio stations, and a broadcast-quality pocket-sized voice recorder. I've had to learn how to use all of them, and I get there eventually. But there is always the awful moment when the new toy comes out of its box, and I stare at it in horror, realizing that I have to learn a whole new language, to figure out which complex buttons and switches do what, how to plug different cables into their proper sockets, and so on. At times like that the written instructions had better be good. I'm in uncharted territory and I need someone to hold my hand.

That must have been exactly how the **apostles** felt in the very early days. What are we supposed to *do*? You might suppose that they would want to rush out and tell everyone about Jesus right away, but they didn't do that. (Perhaps, along with their enormous excitement at his **resurrection**, and now his **ascension**, there may have been a realistic awareness that those who brought about Jesus' death would have no compunction about attacking them as well. Perhaps, too, they were careful to remember Jesus' instructions about waiting for God's power to come on them before going off to do what had to be done.) Was there a set of instructions and, if so, how could they get access to it?

They faced a particular problem right at the start, rather like the sort of problem I had the other day when one of the cables I'd been sent for a new piece of equipment simply didn't fit the socket it was supposed to. There they were, the spearhead of Jesus' plan to renew and restore God's people – and there were supposed to be twelve of them. Only eleven were left. How could they model, and symbolize, God's plan for Israel (and therefore for the world) if they were, so to speak, one patriarch short of a true Israel? Did they just have to stay like that, and if not what should they do about it?

As with everything else that happened in the early church – and Luke is probably already hinting at this in the present passage – they went to two sources for instructions: to the **word** of God, and to prayer. By 'the word of God' I mean, as they seemed to have meant, something more than scripture but not less. For them, the Jewish Bible (what we call the Old Testament) was not just a record of what God had said to his people of old. It was a huge and vital story, the story of the earlier part of God's purposes, full of signposts pointing forward to the time when, further forward within the same story, the plans God was nurturing would come to fruition. Prophets and kings had listened to what the **spirit** had been saying to them, and had written things which, like seeds sown in the dark earth and long watered, would eventually emerge as plants and would bear fruit.

So it was that, from within the life of constant prayer to which Jesus' followers had given themselves after his ascension, they pondered the Psalms which spoke, as several Psalms speak, of a time when God's people, and God's true king, would be opposed by a traitor from within their midst, betrayed by one who had been counted a close friend and colleague. Here they found, not indeed a road map for exactly where they were – scripture seldom supplies exactly that – but the hints and clues to enable them to see how to feel their way forward in this new and unprecedented dilemma. The Psalms made it quite clear: it is not only all right for someone else to take the place of the one who has gone, it is the proper thing to do. It doesn't mean, in other words, that God's plan, or their obedience to it, has gone worryingly wrong. The tragedy of Judas is held within the strange, dark, overarching purpose of God.

We had better get used to this theme of God's plan, over-ruling complex and problematic circumstances; because for Luke, as for his near-contemporary Josephus, the idea of God's providence, still at work even though things may seem sad and dark, is extremely important. And the defection of Judas must have seemed like that in a high degree to the apostles. Judas had been their friend. Until a few short weeks before, he had been one of them in every possible sense. They had known him intimately, and he them. The tragic story of his untimely death is told in quite a different form here from what we find in Matthew 27.3–10, and since nobody in the early church attempted to tidy things up we probably shouldn't try either. One way or another – whether it was actual suicide, as Matthew says, or whether it was the sudden and violent onset of a fatal disease, as Luke suggests – Judas was no longer among them. Insofar as they could make any sense of this, it was a scriptural sense. Insofar as they could see what to do as a result, it was a scripturally rooted sense of direction. That is the main point Luke wants us to grasp here.

And so they chose Matthias. Or rather, they would say, God chose Matthias. They used the well-known method of drawing lots (having already chosen a very brief short list of candidates!). Some have seen this as rather arbitrary, and have suggested that, had the choice been delayed until after the **day of Pentecost** and the arrival of the **holy spirit** in power, they might have done it differently. Luke doesn't seem to think so, since part of his point is precisely to show how, from the beginning, the apostles did what they did in the light of the scriptures and in the context of prayer. Part of his point, too, is to insist that what the apostles go on to do really is, in the proper sense, 'the restoration of the kingdom to Israel', even though it didn't look like they, or anyone else at the time, would have thought such an event would look like. And for that they needed the powerful symbol of **the Twelve** to be restored.

Nor does Luke imagine that the choice of people for particular offices (as in this case) and tasks (as in many others to come) is always plain or straightforward. There is at least one tragic story later in the book where serious disagreement over the choice of someone for a particular job leads to a major row. What concerns Luke most, in the present case, is the fact that God 'knows the hearts' (verse 24), and that it is therefore up to God who gets chosen for a role, and a task, in which the particular disposition of the particular heart matters very much indeed. And the role itself, and task itself, are important as well. The person to take Judas' place must be someone who had gone about with them all since the time of John's baptism right through, and who was, along with the Eleven, a witness to Jesus' **resurrection**.

This 'person specification' in verses 21 and 22 is extremely interesting. It shows that from the beginning the early Christians saw themselves as being the continuation (just as Luke indicates in the first verse of the book) of the **kingdom**-work of Jesus which had begun with John's baptism. And it shows that those roots were important for how they understood themselves. Because of that, in fact, one possible candidate who was not considered was James the brother of the Lord, who quickly became a prominent leader even though he wasn't one of the Twelve. He had not, it seems, been a believer until the Lord appeared to him personally (John 7.5; 1 Corinthians 15.7). And it shows that the primary apostolic task was to bear witness to the resurrection of Jesus himself. As we shall see, if you take that away from Acts you are left with nothing. The resurrection defines the church, from that day to this. The church is either the movement which announces God's new creation, or it is just another irrelevant religious sect.

I always feel both sorry for, and curious about, Joseph called Barsabbas, also known as Justus, who was the candidate not chosen. There is no suggestion that his heart was not right with God, or that he was otherwise unsuited for the task. He was, after all, one of the 'last two' in the consideration of the Eleven. They would have trusted him. We have no idea what happened to him after this, just as we have no idea, for that matter, what happened to Matthias himself. Part of Christian obedience, right from the beginning, was the call to play (apparently) great parts without pride and (apparently) small parts without shame. There are, of course, no passengers in the kingdom of God, and actually no 'great' and 'small' parts either. The different tasks and roles to which God assigns us are his business, not ours.

ACTS 2.1–4

Here Comes the Power

¹When the day of Pentecost had finally arrived, they were all together in the same place. ²Suddenly there came from heaven a noise like the sound of a strong, blowing wind, and it filled the whole house where they were sitting. ³Then tongues, seemingly made of fire, appeared to them, moving apart and coming to rest on each one of them. ⁴They were all filled with the holy spirit, and began to speak in other languages, as the spirit gave them the words to say.

Sometimes a name, belonging to one particular person, becomes so attached to a particular object or product that we forget where it originally came from. The obvious example is 'Hoover': in England at least we speak of 'the Hoover' when we mean 'the vacuum cleaner', happily ignoring the fact that quite a lot of vacuum cleaners are made by other companies which owe nothing to the original Mr Hoover. It is as though Henry Ford had been so successful in car production that people said 'the Ford' when they meant 'the car', even if in fact it was a Volvo.

Something similar has happened with the word 'Pentecost'. If 'Pentecost' means anything at all to most people today, it is probably something to do with 'Pentecostalism'. And that – again, if it means anything to people at all – probably signifies a somewhat wild form of Christian religious experience and practice, outside the main stream of church life, involving a lot of noise and waving of arms, and (of course) **speaking in tongues**. We often forget that all Christians, not only those who call themselves 'Pentecostalists', derive their meaning from the first Pentecost. We often forget, too, perhaps equally importantly, just what 'Pentecost' itself originally was and meant.

For a first-century Jew, Pentecost was the fiftieth day after Passover. It was an agricultural festival. It was the day when farmers brought the first sheaf of wheat from the crop, and offered it to God, partly as a sign of gratitude and partly as a prayer that all the rest of the crop, too, would be safely gathered in. But, for the Jew, neither Passover nor Pentecost were simply agricultural festivals. These festivals awakened echoes of the great story which dominated the long memories of the Jewish people, the story of the **Exodus** from Egypt, when God fulfilled his promises to Abraham by rescuing his people. Passover was the time when the lambs were **sacrificed,** and the Israelites were saved from the avenging angel who slew the firstborn of the Egyptians. Off went the Israelites that very night, and passed through the Red Sea into the Sinai desert. Then, 50 days after Passover, they came to Mount Sinai, where

Moses received the **law**. Pentecost, the fiftieth day, isn't (in other words) just about the 'first fruits', the sheaf which says the harvest has begun. It's about God giving to his redeemed people the way of life by which they must now carry out his purposes.

All of that, and more besides, keeps peeping out from behind what the New Testament says about the **spirit**, and about Pentecost in particular. For Luke there is a kind of easy assumption that people would know about the first fruits. He can more or less take it for granted that readers will see this story, of the **apostles** being filled with the spirit and then going on to bear powerful witness to Jesus and his **resurrection** and to win converts from the very first day, as a sign that this is like the sheaf which is offered to God as the sign of the great harvest to come. And, when we look closely at the way some Jews told the story of the giving of the law on Mount Sinai, we can see some parallels there, too. When the Israelites arrived at Mount Sinai, Moses went up the mountain, and then came down again with the law. Here, Jesus has gone up into heaven in the **ascension**, and – so Luke wants us to understand – he is now coming down again, not with a written law carved on tablets of stone, but with the dynamic energy of the law, designed to be written on human hearts.

'Pentecost', then, is a word with very particular meaning, which Luke is keen that we should grasp. But of course the first **day of Pentecost**, and the experience of God's spirit from that day to this, can no more be reduced to theological formulae and interesting Old Testament echoes than you can reduce a hurricane to a list of diagrams on a meteorologist's chart. It's important that someone somewhere is tracking the hurricane and telling us what it's doing, but when it comes to Pentecost it's far more important that you're out there in the wind, letting it sweep through your life, your heart, your imagination, your powers of speech, and transform you from a listless or lifeless believer into someone whose heart is on fire with the love of God. Those images of wind and fire are of course what Luke says it was like on the first day. Many Christians in many traditions have used similar images to describe what it is sometimes like when the spirit comes to do new things in the lives of individuals and communities.

It is most significant, in the light of what we said before about the ascension, that the wind came 'from heaven' (verse 2). The whole point is that, through the spirit, some of the creative power of God himself comes from heaven to earth and does its work there. The aim is not to give people a 'spirituality' which will make the things of earth irrelevant. The point is to transform earth with the power of heaven, starting with those parts of 'earth' which consist of the bodies, minds, hearts and lives of the followers of Jesus – as a community: notice that, in

17

verse 1, Luke stresses the fact that they were all together in one place; the spirit comes, not to divide, but to unite. The coming of the spirit at Pentecost, in other words, is the complementary fact to the ascension of Jesus into heaven. The risen Jesus in heaven is the presence, in God's sphere, of the first part of 'earth' to be transformed into 'new creation' in which heaven and earth are joined; the pouring out of the spirit on earth is the presence, in our sphere, of the sheer energy of heaven itself. The gift of the spirit is thus the direct result of the ascension of Jesus. Because he is the Lord of all, his energy, the power to be and do something quite new, is available through the spirit to all who call on him, all who follow him, all who trust him.

The wind and the fire are wild, untameable forces, and the experience of the wind rushing through the house with a great roar, and the fire coming to rest on each person present, must have been both terrifying and exhilarating. Of course, there are many times later in this book, as there are many times in the life of the church, when the spirit works softly and secretly, quietly transforming people's lives and situations without any big noise or fuss. People sometimes suppose that this is the norm, and that the noise, the force and the fire are the exception – just as some have supposed, within 'Pentecostal' and similar circles, that without the noise and the fire, and particularly the speaking in tongues, something is seriously lacking or deficient. We should beware of drawing either conclusion. Luke clearly intends to describe something new, something that launched a great movement, as a fleet of ships is launched by the strong wind that drives them out to sea or a forest fire is started by a few small flames. He intends to explain how it was that a small group of frightened, puzzled and largely uneducated men and women could so quickly become, as they undoubtedly did, a force to be reckoned with right across the known world.

In particular, Luke highlights this strange phenomenon of 'speaking in tongues'. This has been a prominent feature of some parts of church life in the last century or so, though for many previous generations and in many parts of church history it has been virtually unknown. It occurs, it seems, in other religions, as Paul was aware (1 Corinthians 12.2–3). Some people try to sweep 'tongues' aside as if it was a peculiar thing which happened early on and which, fortunately, doesn't need to happen any more. Sometimes this is combined with a sense of the need to control the emotions, both one's own and other people's. But 'speaking in tongues' and similar phenomena are, very often, a way of getting in touch with deeply buried emotions and bringing them to the surface in praise, celebration, grief or sorrow, or urgent desire turned into prayer. It is hard, seeing the importance of 'tongues' in the New Testament, and their manifest usefulness in these and other ways, to go along with the idea that they should be ruled out for today's church.

In particular, it is precisely part of being a genuine human being, made and renewed in God's image, that people should do that most characteristic thing, using words and language, in quite a new way. We are called to be people of God's **word**, and God's word can never be controlled by rationalistic schemes, or contained within the tight little frameworks that we invent to keep everything tidy and under control.

People sometimes feel guilty if they think they haven't had such wonderful experiences as the **apostles** had on the first Pentecost. Or they feel jealous of those who seem to have had things like this happen to them. About this there are two things to say. First, as we saw in the first chapter, God moves mysteriously among his people, dealing with each individual in a different way. Some people are allowed remarkable experiences, perhaps (we can't always tell) because they are going to have to go into difficult situations and need to know very directly just how dramatically powerful and life-transforming God can be. Other people have to work in quiet and patient ways and not rely on a sudden burst of extra power to fix all the problems which in fact need a much more steady, and perhaps much deeper, work. There is no room for pride or jealousy in a well-ordered **fellowship**, where everybody is as delighted with the gifts given to others as with those given to themselves.

Second, it is clear from words of Jesus himself (Luke 11.13) that God longs to give the holy spirit to people, and that all we have to do is ask. What the spirit will do when he comes is anybody's guess. Be prepared for wind and fire, for some fairly drastic spring-cleaning of the dusty and cold rooms of one's life. But we should not doubt that God will give his spirit to all who seek him, and that the form and direction that any particular spirit-led life will take will be (ultimately, and assuming obedience and **faith**) the one that will enable that person, uniquely, to bring glory to God.

ACTS 2.5–13

New Words for New News (See map 3, page xvi.)

[5]There were devout Jews from every nation under heaven staying in Jerusalem at that time. [6]When they heard this noise they came together in a crowd. They were deeply puzzled, because every single one of them could hear them speaking in his or her own native language. [7]They were astonished and amazed.

'These men who are doing the speaking are all Galileans, aren't they?' they said. [8]'So how is it that each of us can hear them in our own mother tongues? [9]There are Parthians here, and Medians, Elamites, people from Mesopotamia, Judaea, Cappadocia, Pontus, Asia, [10]Phrygia and Pamphylia, Egypt and the parts of Libya that belong to Cyrene; there are people from Rome, [11]proselytes as well as Jews; there are Cretans and Arabs. We can hear them speaking about the powerful things God has done – *in our own languages!*'

[12]Everyone was astonished and perplexed.

'What does it all mean?' they were asking each other.

[13]But some sneered.

'They're full of new wine!' they said.

I once went to an international conference for Christian students, where I had to give some lectures – on Luke, as it happens. There were students there from all over Eastern Europe: Poles, Russians, Romanians, Hungarians, as well as people from the Czech Republic, Germany, France and elsewhere. I was excited by what I was going to say, and I set off talking at a good pace. Meanwhile, behind soundproof screens, the translators worked to keep up and to put my words into the languages of the various students who were listening through headphones.

When it came to coffee time, the young woman from Hungary who had been doing her best with my enthusiastic lecture came up. She was almost in tears.

'Dr Wright,' she said, 'you are going to have to go much, much slower. You see, the average word in Hungarian is two or three times as long as its equivalent in English. Even if your English was easy to translate all the time, it is physically impossible to speak the Hungarian words at the same pace as the English ones. There are just too many syllables.'

I learnt my lesson, and spent the week talking (for me) very, very slowly, keeping my eye on the glass screens and watching for signs of distress among the hard-working translators. But my mind kept jumping across – not least because I was talking about Luke's theology – to this scene at the start of Acts. Somehow, on the **day of Pentecost**, they didn't need translators. Everybody understood in their own language.

What language would they have been expecting? At that time, all around the Mediterranean world, everybody's second language was Greek. Ever since the conquests of Alexander the Great, 400 years earlier, Greek had been to much of that world what English is for many people in the world today. People who travelled, as the people in this story seem to have done, would pretty certainly be able to get by in Greek, while probably speaking at least one other language, if not two or three. Jews in Palestine would know, and usually speak, Aramaic, but some might well know some classical Hebrew as well. Many people would know at least some Latin, as the Roman Empire gradually imposed itself on many of the countries originally conquered by Greece.

But on the day of Pentecost they didn't need to switch languages, or to worry about translation. It was all done for them. People are often surprised by this, because many have seen 'the gift of tongues' not as the gift of being able to speak other specific languages, but rather as the gift of a kind of heavenly babble, a succession of syllables and sounds which, though they may sound like a language, do not appear to be so in fact, either to the speaker or to any listeners. For many devout Christians who '**speak in tongues**' as part of their regular life of prayer, either in public or private or both, there is no expectation that anyone will 'understand' in the same way as, if I suddenly spoke Arabic in a crowded bus in Jerusalem, many people would understand what I was saying.

But there are well-attested instances, in modern as well as ancient times, of people 'speaking in tongues' suddenly, at the **spirit**'s bidding, in particular situations where they have no idea that someone from a particular language and culture is present, and indeed without themselves knowing a single word of that language in the ordinary sense – and discovering that someone present can understand them. I have met people to whom this has happened, and I have no reason to think they were deceiving either themselves or me. I have no explanation for this other than that God can do whatever God wants to do, and that it isn't up to us to set bounds to the ways in which God can and does reach out, either when the **gospel** needs to make an impact on someone, or some group, that is otherwise peculiarly difficult to penetrate, or when someone is present in special need or distress. Or whatever.

But this phenomenon, strange though it is to most of us, highlights something else that is going on in the narrative at this point, and to which Luke wants to draw our attention. The whole question of Acts 1, you remember, was of how God would fulfil the promise to extend his **kingdom**, his saving, sovereign rule, not only in Israel but *through* Israel, to reach the rest of the world. In other words, the question had to do with the challenge to see how God was going to fulfil what he had said to Abraham in Genesis 12.3: 'In you, and in your family, all the families of the earth will be blessed.' And this promise to Abraham comes directly after the dramatic and comic chapter in which the people of Babel are building a tower, thinking arrogantly to make a name for themselves. God's response, as always, to human pride and arrogance is to overturn the project and ridicule the people, which he accomplishes by confusing their languages so that they cannot understand one another and cannot therefore work together on creating a human society which would have no need of the creator God.

Now, Luke is implying, with the day of Pentecost this curse is itself overturned; in other words, God is dramatically signalling that his promises to Abraham are being fulfilled, and the whole human race is going to be addressed with the **good news** of what has happened in and through Jesus. (The summary of the message in verse 11 is that it concerned 'God's powerful deeds'; in other words, the dramatic and extra-ordinary things God had done in and through Jesus, as in 10.38–43.) Granted, all the people present were Jewish or at least proselytes (**Gentiles** who had converted to Judaism), since the reason they were in Jerusalem was to attend the Jewish festival. But they had come from all over, from countries each of which would have its own native language and local dialects. Luke gives the list of where they came from in a great sprawling sweep, covering tens of thousands of square miles, from Parthia and Mesopotamia in the north and east to Rome in the west and Egypt and Arabia in the south, together with the island of Crete. The point is not to give an exact list of precisely where everyone came from in the crowded city of Jerusalem that day, but to splash across the page the sense of a great polyglot company all hearing words spoken in their own language.

Hardly surprisingly, to some it sounded simply like the slurred and babbling speech of people who have had too much to drink. Again and again in Acts we find opposition, incredulity, scoffing and sneering at what the **apostles** say and do, at the same time as great success and conviction. And again and again in the work of the church, to this day, there are always plenty who declare that we are wasting our time and talking incomprehensible nonsense. Equally, some Christians have been so concerned to keep up safe appearances and to make sure they are looking like ordinary, normal people that they would never, under any circumstances, have been accused of being drunk, at nine o'clock in the morning or any other time. Part of the challenge of this passage is the question: have our churches today got enough energy, enough spirit-driven new life, to make onlookers pass any comment at all? Has anything happened which might make people think we were drunk? If not, is it because the spirit is simply at work in other ways, or because we have so successfully quenched the spirit that there is actually nothing happening at all?

ACTS 2.14–21

It's All Coming True at Last!

[14]Then Peter got up, with the eleven. He spoke to them in a loud voice.

'People of Judaea!' he began. 'All of you staying here in Jerusalem! There's something you have to know! Listen to what I'm saying! [15]These people aren't drunk, as you imagine. It's only nine o'clock in the morning! [16]No, this is what the prophet Joel was talking about, when he said,

> [17]In the last days, declares God, I will pour out my spirit on all
>   people.
> Your sons and your daughters will prophesy;
> your young men will see visions, your old men will dream dreams;
> [18]yes, even on slaves, men and women alike, will I pour out my
>   spirit in those days, and they shall prophesy.
> [19]And I will give signs in the heavens above, and portents on earth
>   beneath,
> blood and fire and clouds of smoke.
> [20]The sun will be turned into darkness, and the moon into blood,
> before the day of the Lord comes, the great and glorious day.
> [21]And then everyone who calls on the name of the Lord will be
>   saved.'

We don't always plan our holidays very carefully, but on this occasion we had. We had read the brochures. We had worked through the alternative places to stay. We had looked at the special things we could do when we got there. And, in particular, we had planned the travel.

Or so we thought. Of course, once you set off on a journey involving trains and planes and buses and cars, there are many hidden snags. We got to the airport all right, but the flight was delayed, and we spent half a day playing cards in the airport lounge. Then we had to get a different train at the other end, going a different route. It was dark by the time we reached . . . but was this our destination? Was it the right town, the right station? How would we know? It didn't look like we'd thought it would.

Then, a sigh of relief. There, just as we had been told weeks before, was the man with the sign, collecting us tired stragglers and putting us on the bus to the hotel. We had arrived. It was the end of the journey; the promises had come true; now the holiday could really begin.

Project the journey on to a larger timescale, 2,000 years long. And, instead of a holiday, imagine a moment, long promised, dreamed of, planned for, mulled over, prayed for, ached for, agonized over: a moment when things would work out right at last, when hopes would be realized and good times would begin. A moment when a huge sigh of relief would give way to a huge sense of new possibilities: now, at last, things could really start!

That is how the Jews of the first century read their scriptures. They saw themselves as the generation for whom it should all come true. In the book of Daniel, one of the Old Testament books people studied most carefully in the first century, there was a prophecy of an **exile** that would last for 490 years, starting with the Babylonian exile. And the Babylonian exile had taken place . . . well, somewhere between 400 and 500 years before, depending on how you calculated it (and plenty of people did it different ways). That was, if you like, the travel brochure that kept them moving forwards: if only they kept going long enough, they would surely, eventually, arrive at the destination! But at the same time they studied, memorized, prayed over and puzzled over many other old texts, texts which spoke of terrible things that would happen but of a time when it would all be reversed, when God would bring them to a new place and do quite new things with them. And some of the texts spoke of the signs that they would see when they arrived at that new moment, the signals that would say, 'You're here! This is where you were going!'

It's only by imagining that world, a world where people were puzzling and praying over ancient texts to try to find urgently needed meanings in times of great stress and sorrow, that we can understand how Peter could even think of launching in to a great long quotation from the prophet Joel in order to explain the apparently confused babbling and shouting that was going on. If I was asked by a crowd to explain why my friends and I appeared to be behaving in a drunken fashion I don't somehow think I would at once start quoting chunks of the Bible, even the New Testament. But Jerusalem was full of people who were eager for signs that maybe the people of Israel had at last arrived at their destination, even if it didn't look like they thought it was going to. Yes, says Peter. We've got to the point where all that the brochures said is starting to come true. These are indeed 'the **last days**'.

What did that mean, 'the last days'? It was a general term for the time to come, the time when promises would be fulfilled. The story would arrive at its climax, the journey would reach its destination, and so all sorts of new things would start to happen. So what Peter was offering wasn't simply an explanation for strange behaviour, even for strange religious phenomena (always a dangerous thing in a crowded city at the time of a big religious and national festival). It was a challenge: we've arrived! The journey's over! Here are the signs of the destination! Time to have a fresh look around and see where we are!

But, though Peter declares that these are indeed 'the last days' which the prophet Joel had spoken of, they are not 'the last day' itself. There remains another 'day' (not necessarily a period of 24 hours, but 'a moment', 'a coming time') which the prophets referred to as 'the day of the Lord'. (We remind ourselves that 'the Lord' is the way they would speak to avoid saying the name of Israel's covenant God, YHWH.) The early Christians, breathtakingly, took that idea of 'the day of the Lord', and went on using it – only now with 'the Lord' referring to Jesus. They seem to have made this transition apparently without effort or problem, as we can see frequently in Paul and elsewhere. The early Christians believed, in other words, that they were living in a period of time between the moment when 'the last days' had been launched and the moment when even those 'last days' would come to an end on 'the day of the Lord', the moment when, with Jesus' final reappearance (already promised in Acts 1.11), **heaven** and earth would be joined together in the great coming renewal of all things (see 3.21).

In the light of this hope, we shouldn't be surprised that among the signs of things coming true there would be 'signs in heaven and earth'. But nor should we imagine that people in the first century would necessarily have taken these, as we say, 'literally'. Mention of 'blood and fire and clouds of smoke', and of 'the sun . . . turned into darkness, and the moon into blood' could refer to a great eclipse or other natural phenomena. But those who were used to the language of biblical prophecy knew well enough that these were regular ways of referring to what we would call 'earth-shattering' events, things in society and global politics that would shake to the foundations what we call 'the fabric of society'. Terrifying times, in other words; times of great instability and uncertainty.

But the prophet didn't just warn of times of fear and trembling. Part of the point of 'the last days' was that they were the time of new creation – and the new creation would start with God's own people! This is where the quotation from Joel functions as a direct explanation of the otherwise bizarre behaviour of the **apostles**, shouting out in several different languages the powerful things that God had done. Peter connects it directly with the promise of Joel that God would pour out his **spirit** in a new way. Up to this moment, God has acted by his spirit among his people, but it's always been by inspiring one person here, one or two there – kings and prophets and **priests** and righteous men and women. Now, in a sudden burst of fresh divine energy released through the death and **resurrection** of Jesus, God's spirit has been poured out upon a lot of people all at once. There is no discrimination between slaves and free, male and female, young and old. They are all marked out, side by side, as the nucleus of God's true people.

This itself is striking, when you think about it. If the prophecies of Joel are coming true, the spirit is available for all God's people . . . so why is the spirit not being poured out on the chief priests, on the official religious leaders and teachers? The answer, as politically uncomfortable in the first century as anywhere else, is that the spirit seems to be indicating that the work of new creation is beginning here, in this upper room, where Jesus' friends and family have gathered: not in the **Temple**, not in the rabbinic schools, not in the back rooms where

25

the revolutionaries plot violence, but here, where those who had been with Jesus, and had seen him alive again after his resurrection, find themselves overwhelmed with the fresh wind of the spirit and unable to stop speaking about what they have seen and heard.

This work of God is wonderfully inclusive, because there is no category of people which is left out: both genders, all ages, all social classes. But it is wonderfully focused, because it happens to all 'who call on the name of the Lord' (verse 21). Here, once more, 'the Lord', which in Joel meant Israel's God, YHWH, now seems to mean Jesus himself. And with this Luke introduces a vital and complex theme in his work: '**salvation**'. All who call on the Lord's name will be *saved*.

'Being saved' doesn't just mean, as it does for many today, 'going to heaven when they die'. It means 'knowing God's rescuing power, the power revealed in Jesus, which anticipates, in the present, God's final great act of deliverance'. Peter will now go on to encourage his hearers to 'call on the Lord's name', and so to know that 'salvation', that rescue, as a present reality as well as a future hope. If these really are 'the last days', then 'salvation' has already begun. Anyone who knows they need rescuing, whatever from, can 'call on the Lord' and discover how it can happen.

ACTS 2.22–36

David Speaks of Jesus' Resurrection

[22]'You people of Israel,' Peter continued, 'listen to this. The man Jesus of Nazareth was marked out for you by God through the mighty works, signs and portents which God performed through him right here among you, as you all know. [23]He was handed over in accordance with God's determined purpose and foreknowledge – and you used people outside the law to nail him up and kill him.

[24]'But God raised him from the dead! Death had its painful grip on him; but God released him from it, because it wasn't possible for him to be mastered by it. [25]This, you see, is how David speaks of him:

'I set the Lord before me always;
because he is at my right hand, I won't be shaken.
[26]So my heart was happy, and my tongue rejoiced,
and my flesh, too, will rest in hope.
[27]For you will not leave my soul in Hades,
nor will you allow your Holy One to see corruption.
[28]You showed me the path of life,
you filled me with gladness in your presence.

[29]'My dear family, I can surely speak freely to you about the patriarch David. He died and was buried, and his tomb is here with us to

this day. [30]He was of course a prophet, and he knew that God had sworn an oath to him to set one of his own physical offspring on his throne. [31]He foresaw the Messiah's resurrection, and spoke about him 'not being left in Hades', and about his flesh 'not seeing corruption'. [32]This is the Jesus we're talking about! God raised him from the dead, and all of us here are witnesses to the fact! [33]Now he's been exalted to God's right hand; and what you see and hear is the result of the fact that he is pouring out the holy spirit, which had been promised, and which he has received from the father.

[34]'David, after all, did not ascend into the heavens. This is what he says:

'The Lord said to my Lord,
sit at my right hand,
[35]until I place your enemies
underneath your feet.

[36]'So the whole house of Israel must know this for a fact: God has made him Lord and Messiah – this Jesus, the one you crucified.'

I watched the Press Gallery during the speech. For most of the time, the journalists looked bored. One was sharpening his pencil; another was varnishing her nails. Then, quite suddenly, all that changed. Notebooks were seized, shorthand phrases flew onto the paper. One began sending text messages back to base. The speech which, up to that point, had been important but not that important, had instantly turned into something that would make tomorrow's headlines. The speaker had suddenly given a broad hint that he wasn't just commenting about important issues that were happening that day. He was launching his campaign to be leader of his party, which meant he hoped to be Prime Minister within the next year or two.

That is the impression we get from the move which Peter makes at this point in his speech. Up to now, he has been showing that the extraordinary phenomenon of the wind, the fire and the babbling **tongues** are best explained by claiming that the '**last days**' have arrived, the time which the prophet Joel had spoken of. But now he changes tack. The reason the 'last days' are here is because of the **resurrection** of Jesus, nothing more nor less. But the resurrection of Jesus demands to be explained, not as an odd, isolated '**miracle**', as though God suddenly thought of doing something totally bizarre to show how powerful he is. The resurrection of Jesus is best explained as the fulfilment of specific promises made by God through King David. And they show that the one who has been raised from the dead is the true son and heir of David. He, in other words, is *the rightful king of Israel*. This is the point where the journalists go scurrying off to file their reports: revolution is in the air!

Note how Luke insists that, for him as for all the early Christians, 'resurrection' wasn't about a disembodied spirit going off to **heaven**, leaving a body behind in a tomb. That is precisely what the word 'resurrection' did *not* mean. 'Resurrection' was and is about a physical body being very thoroughly dead, but then being very thoroughly alive again, so that the normal corruption and decay which follows death wouldn't even begin. This point is made graphically through Peter's quoting from Psalm 16 in verses 25–28, and returning to it again in verse 31. The Psalm – which both Luke and Peter take as having been written by David himself – speaks of a 'way of life' in which one who dies will not be abandoned, and will not suffer the usual fate of the dissolution of the flesh. Instead, because of God's utter and faithful reliability, the person in question will somehow come through death and out the other side.

Now, says Peter to rub the point in (verses 29 and 30): we know that David cannot have been referring to himself when he wrote this. After all, he died and was buried, and his flesh decayed and corrupted in the normal way. The only sense we can make of the Psalm is to read it prophetically; that is, to see it as expressing a deep 'Davidic' truth which would remain mysterious until, one day, a **son of David** would appear to whom it would actually happen. Then we would know that he was the one in whom the strange, dark prophecies had come true. Then we would know that 'the last days' had indeed arrived. *And then we would know that he was indeed the rightful king.* Peter has worked back, from the babbling of tongues being a sign of 'the last days' and the outpouring of God's **spirit**, to the resurrection of Jesus as the sure and certain sign that he is the **Messiah**, the one Israel had been waiting for.

He ties the two points together in verse 33. Jesus has now been exalted at God's right hand (as in Daniel 7, and as in Psalm 110, which he is about to quote). That is why he has been able to pour out the holy spirit with such dramatic effect. The extraordinary phenomena of Pentecost were the signpost. But Easter was the reality to which they pointed. And the meaning of Easter is: 'God has made him Lord and Messiah – this Jesus, the one you crucified.'

What does the word 'Lord' add to 'Messiah'? It seems to refer to Psalm 110, quoted in verses 34 and 35: 'The Lord said to my Lord, sit at my right hand, until I place your enemies underneath your feet.' Here, as in several '**messianic**' Psalms, we find that Israel's true king is the world's true Lord; that's how the logic of messiahship, if we can put it like that, works out. Israel is God's chosen people for the sake of the world; so Israel's true and final king, when he arrives, will be the world's rightful sovereign. The early Christians, following Jesus himself (see Luke 20.41–44), went back to Psalm 110 again and again to make this point. They saw it tying together Jesus' Davidic ancestry with God's fresh action in raising and exalting him, and thus declaring him to be the true Messiah. And they saw in this Psalm, too, the massive sense, looming up behind even the exalted title of Messiah, that in Jesus they had been looking at the human face of God himself.

It is only in the light of this that we can begin to understand verse 27, which summarizes, in a sharp and difficult way, the point of view of the whole New Testament. On the one hand, Jesus' shameful and horrible death was the act of wicked, unscrupulous, lawless people. The leaders of the Jewish people had handed Jesus over to the pagans, in full knowledge of the brutally effective torture and death they would inflict on him. At every stage of the process – Judas' betrayal, Peter's denial, the trumped-up charge, the kangaroo court, the cynicism of the Jewish leaders, Pilate's vacillation, cowardice and indifference to justice, the crowd baying for blood, the mocking of the soldiers and one at least of those crucified alongside him – Jesus' path to his death had been marked by all kinds of evil, doing its worst to him. But the early Christians quickly came to see, in the light of the resurrection and the gift of the spirit, that even this, all this, was what Israel's God, the creator God, had determined must take place.

God's plan of **salvation**, Peter is saying, was always intended to reach its climax with Israel's Messiah undertaking his ultimate rescuing task. The anointed king would come to the place where evil was reaching its height, where the greatest human systems would reveal their greatest corruption (Rome, with its much-vaunted system of justice revealing itself rotten at the core; Israel, with its celebrated **Temple** and hierarchy, revealing itself hollow at its heart), and where this accumulated evil would blow itself out in one great act of unwarranted violence against the person who, of all, had done nothing to deserve it. That, the early Christians believed, was what God had always intended.

Acts does not, at this point, offer a developed 'theology of the cross' such as we find in Paul, Hebrews and other writers later on. What it does is simply to say: (a) God intended Jesus to die as the climax of his rescue operation; (b) the intentions and actions that sent Jesus to his death were desperately wicked. This doesn't for a moment justify the wickedness. Rather, it declares that God, knowing how powerful that wickedness was, had long planned to nullify its power by taking its full force *upon himself, in the person of his Messiah, the man in whom God himself would be embodied.*

There is much, much more to be said about the meaning of the cross than this. Acts will introduce it step by step. But this is a powerful point to begin with. Peter has launched the early Christians on a double collision course with the authorities. Jesus is the true King, which means that his followers need no longer regard the current authorities as absolute. What is more, the authorities themselves were responsible, along with the pagans, for Jesus' death. Their power was called into question: all they could do now would be to repent.

That is, of course, the call to all who have bought into, and perpetrated, systems of evil. The **good news**, the great news, of Jesus is that with his resurrection it becomes clear not only that he is Messiah and Lord, but that in his death he has dealt evil itself a blow from which, though it still retains some real power, it will never recover.

ACTS 2.37–41

God's Rescue Plan

[37]When they heard this, the people in the crowd were cut to the heart.

'Brothers,' they said to Peter and the other apostles, 'what shall we do?'

[38]'Turn back!' replied Peter. 'Be baptized – every single one of you – in the name of Jesus the Messiah, so that your sins can be forgiven, and you will receive the gift of the holy spirit. [39]The promise is for you and for your children, and for everyone who is far away, as many as the Lord our God will call.'

[40]He carried on explaining things to them with many other words.

'Let God rescue you,' he was urging them, 'from this wicked generation!'

Those who welcomed his word were baptized. About three thousand people were added to the community that day.

It's one thing to discover you are driving along the wrong road. It may be frustrating, and even embarrassing if you have people in the car who thought you knew where you were going. But you can at least admit the mistake, turn round and set off again, this time in the right direction.

But it's quite another thing if you are sliding down a steep slope – say, on a toboggan, or on skis, or (as we sometimes used to do) on tin trays over grass – and suddenly realize you are heading for a sheer drop. You seem to be accelerating towards it, and the slope is too steep for you to check your speed, let alone to stop, turn round, and go back up again out of danger. What are you going to do?

The answer may well be that there's nothing you can do. You need to be rescued.

You need, in fact, someone to stand in the way: someone who has managed to get a fixed foothold on the slope, and who will catch you, stop you, and help you to safety. And if you were lucky enough to see someone offering to do that, you'd have to steer towards them and be ready for the shock of a sudden stop. Better that than plunging over a cliff.

The key thing to realize, in reading the early chapters of Acts, is that Jesus himself had warned his fellow Jews that they were precisely in danger of accelerating towards a cliff. If you read Luke's **gospel** straight through, you will notice how the warnings which Jesus gave seem to increase in quantity and volume all the way to chapters 19, 20 and 21, where he solemnly declares that if the nation as a whole, and the city of Jerusalem in particular, don't stop their headlong flight into ruin, their enemies will come and destroy them. The warnings are very specific. Israel (so Jesus declares) has bought into a way of life which is directly opposite to what God wants: a way which ignores the plight of the poor, which embraces violence, which denies God's call to his people to become the light of the world. Again and again Jesus warns, 'Unless you repent, you will all be destroyed in the same way' (Luke 13.5). When he arrives in Jerusalem he bursts into tears as he describes, in a prophetic vision, a great military force laying siege to the city and leaving no stone on top of another. This will happen, he says, because you didn't know 'what peace meant', and 'because you didn't know the moment when God was visiting you' (Luke 19.41, 44).

But then we watch in amazement – horror, even – at a new twist in the plot. Jesus has announced God's judgment on the nation that has gone its own way, the way of violence. But then we realize that Jesus himself has, again and again, taken Israel's identity upon himself. He is the representative Israelite, the **Messiah** who sums up his people in himself. And we realize that he believes it's his calling to go to the place where the judgment is about to fall on rebellious Israel, and to take that judgment – the one he himself had announced – onto himself. He speaks of himself as the 'green tree', the one you wouldn't expect to see thrown onto the fire, while all around him are the dry twigs ready for burning (Luke 23.31). He warns that, though he is bearing Israel's judgment, dying on a charge of which he was innocent but thousands around him were guilty (Luke 23.2–5, 18–25), those who nevertheless persisted in their headlong rush towards the sheer drop of violence would reap the consequences.

And, of course, when the crowds, the chief **priests** and the other leaders rejected Jesus at that Passover, Jesus himself saw that as the culmination of their rejection of his way of peace, his **kingdom**-way, the way he had been urging them to follow all along. It wasn't that their sending of Jesus to his death was an isolated act of folly or sin. It was the symptom of their rejection of God's way. It was the sign of what Jesus had said many times: this generation is wicked and corrupt, heading for disaster.

But now, with Jesus' **resurrection**, Peter and the others can unpack the meaning of the crucifixion for the benefit of the crowds. This is, perhaps, the first beginning, the first small glimpse, of the church's developing understanding of the purpose of the cross. That understanding doesn't begin as an abstract theory about 'sin' or 'judgment'. It begins as the very concrete and specific awareness: 'this corrupt generation' is heading for disaster, but Jesus stands in the way and can stop them from falling over the cliff. The message is then clear: 'Be rescued' – in other words, let God rescue you, let Jesus rescue you – from the ruin that will come upon the city and the nation, not as a specific punishment for rejecting Jesus, but as the necessary consequence of that entire way of life of which rejecting Jesus was a key, telltale sign.

But how do you steer towards Jesus? How does he catch you, stop you, and rescue you? Peter and the others are quite clear – and the message of the Christian **gospel** fans out from this point to all people and all times. You need to turn back. But the way to do that is to become part of the kingdom-movement that is identified with Jesus, part of the people who claim his life, death and resurrection as the centre and foundation of their own. You need, in other words, to be baptized, to join the company marked out with the sign of the 'new **Exodus**', coming through the water to leave behind slavery and sin and to find the way to freedom and **life**. You need to allow Jesus himself to grasp hold of you, to save you from the consequences of the way you were going ('**forgiveness** of sins') and to give you new energy to go in the right way instead ('the gift of the **holy spirit**'). To do all that is to 'turn back' from the way you were going, and to go in the other direction instead. That is what is meant by the word 'repent'.

All this was very concrete and specific for the crowd in Jerusalem on that first Pentecost. Join this movement, allow the death and resurrection of Jesus to become the badge you wear, the sign of your identity, with you and your children (verse 39) sharing in the new life of the baptized community, the life which has the stamp of Jesus upon it, the life which is defined in terms of turning away from the course you were on and embracing Jesus' way instead. And, though circumstances change, we can see how the same **message** translates without difficulty to everyone in every society and at every moment in time. 'The promise is for you, and for your children, *and for everyone who is far away, as many as the Lord our God will call.*' That means all the rest of us.

What we are witnessing, in this passage, is the beginning of the Christian theme called '**salvation**'. It isn't simply about 'going to **heaven**', though of course it includes the promise, not only of heaven after death but, beyond that, of resurrection into God's new creation. 'Salvation' is therefore pointing towards a very concrete and particular reality in the future. If God's ultimate intention was to 'save' only disembodied 'souls', that wouldn't be *rescue from* death. It would simply allow the death of the body to have the last word. 'Salvation' regularly refers constantly, not least in Luke and Acts, to specific acts of 'rescue' within the present life: being 'saved' from *this* potential disaster, here and now.

That, of course, is something Luke stresses throughout his work. What God has promised for the ultimate future has come forward to meet us in Jesus Christ. We should expect signs of that future to appear in the present. And, whenever we are in a mess, of whatever sort and for whatever reason, we should remember this: we are 'turn-back-and-be-rescued' people. We are 'repent-and-be-baptized' people. We have the right, the birthright, to cash in that promise at any place and any time.

No wonder 3,000 people signed up that very day.

ACTS 2.42–47

The New Family

⁴²They all gave full attention to the teaching of the apostles and to the common life, to the breaking of bread and the prayers. ⁴³Great awe fell on everyone, and many remarkable deeds and signs were performed by the apostles.

⁴⁴All of those who believed came together, and held everything in common. ⁴⁵They sold their possessions and belongings and divided them up to everyone in proportion to their various needs. ⁴⁶Day by day they were all together attending the Temple. They broke bread in their various houses, and ate their food with glad and sincere hearts, ⁴⁷praising God and standing in favour with all the people. And every day the Lord added to their number those who were being rescued.

A couple of years ago I took part in a charity walk. It was a sunny day, there were thousands of people taking part, and we went through some breathtaking scenery. We were put in several groups, with a few hundred setting off every few minutes. I was in the first group, and it was enormously exciting; though it wasn't a race, there was a sense of trailblazing, of leading the way for thousands to follow. We went off at a cracking pace, too fast perhaps but thoroughly enjoying ourselves.

It was only after a couple of miles that those of us in the leading pack paused for breath. We knew we were more or less on the right track, but it was as well to be sure. Yes, there were the landmarks: the river, the hill, the wood behind the village. And there, up ahead, was a tiny flag fluttering in the breeze. A moment's pause, admiring the view, allowing some others to catch up, and then off we went again.

That is the mood Luke creates at the end of chapter 2. His book has got off to a flying start, with the extraordinary conversation between the risen Jesus and the **apostles**, and then the spectacular events of the **day of Pentecost**. Peter's address to the puzzled crowds, the first public statement of the **good news** about Jesus and his **resurrection** and about God's rescue operation through him, now in full swing, is dramatic, full of energy and possibility and hope. And now, at the end of that first Pentecost, we pause for breath, look around, and see where we've got to.

Luke is careful to point out the landmarks. In fact, Acts 2.42 is often regarded as laying down 'the four marks of the church'. The apostles' teaching; the common life of those who believed; the breaking of bread; and the prayers. These four go together. You can't separate them, or leave one out, without damage to the whole thing. Where no attention is given to teaching, and to constant, lifelong Christian learning, people quickly revert to the worldview or mindset of the surrounding culture, and end up with their minds shaped by whichever social pressures are most persuasive, with Jesus somewhere around as a pale influence or memory. Where people ignore the common life of the Christian family (the technical term often used is '**fellowship**', which is more than friendship but not less), they become isolated, and often find it difficult to sustain a living **faith**. Where people no longer share regularly in 'the breaking of bread' (the early Christian term for the simple meal that took them back to the Upper Room 'in remembrance of Jesus'), they are failing to raise the flag which says 'Jesus' death and resurrection are the centre of everything' (see 1 Corinthians 11.26). And whenever people do all these things but neglect prayer, they are quite simply forgetting that Christians are supposed to be **heaven**-and-earth people. Prayer makes no sense whatever – unless heaven and earth are designed to be joined together, and we can share in that already.

Those of us who grew up in Christian families, with 'going to church' as a habit of life from our earliest days, may sometimes think of all this as quite humdrum and ordinary. In some churches, of course, it does feel that way. But imagine a world without this astonishing teaching! Imagine a society where there was no 'common life' built around a shared belief in Jesus! Imagine a world without 'the bread-breaking', or a world without prayer! Life would be bleak indeed – as it often is for many people, not least those who embrace a relentlessly secularist lifestyle, shutting the door on any of these possibilities. And if you lived in such a world, and then suddenly found yourself swept up in this pattern of teaching, fellowship, bread-breaking and prayer, you would know that new dimensions had opened up before you, and new vistas of how the world might be had suddenly become visible. You would be awestruck. That, says Luke, is how it was at the beginning (verse 43). And that awe was only increased as the power of the **spirit** was at work through the apostles, as it had been with Jesus, power to heal and transform people's lives.

This shared life quickly developed in one particular direction, which is both fascinating and controversial. The earliest Christians lived *as a single family*. When you live together as a family under one roof, you don't see *this* chair, *this* table, *this* bottle of milk, *this* loaf of bread, as 'mine' rather than 'yours'. The breadwinners in the household don't see the money they bring in as 'theirs' rather than belonging to the whole household. That's part of what it means to be a family. In the ancient world this was often highlighted by members of a family all working in the same trade or business together, so that you might have three generations, including cousins, working alongside one another, trusting each other, sharing a common purse out of which everyone got what they needed.

The early Christian impulse was to see things exactly like that. We are 'family'! We are brothers and sisters! Our **baptism**, our shared faith, our fellowship at 'the bread-breaking', all point in this direction. When the **Twelve** (with their larger company of friends and followers, as in Luke 8.1–3) were going about with Jesus, they had a common purse; various people contributed to it out of their resources; they behaved as a single family. How do you continue with that when, quite suddenly, several thousand join the movement?

With difficulty, it seems. But they were determined to do it. Not to do it would be to deny something basic about who they were. (They didn't, at this stage, seem to have a word for 'who they were'; that developed gradually, as we shall see; but they were, at least, 'the people who had been with Jesus' (4.13), 'the people who bore witness to his resurrection', 'the people who were filled with the holy spirit', 'those who believed' (verse 44), 'those who were being rescued' (verse 47).) They seem not to have sold the houses in which they lived, since they went on meeting in individual houses (verse 46). Rather, they sold extra property they possessed – a highly significant thing for a people for whom land was not just an economic asset but part of their ancestral heritage, part of God's promised inheritance.

And they had a word for this way of ordering their life, a word which we have often taken to refer to feelings inside you but which, for them, was primarily about what you do with your possessions when you're part of this big, extended family. The word is 'love', *agapē* in Greek. When Paul tells the Thessalonians that, since they already love one another, they must do so more and more, he doesn't primarily mean that since they already have warm feelings for one another, they must have even warmer ones. He means that, since they already care practically for one another, they must work at making that more and more of a reality (1 Thessalonians 4.9–12). The challenge remains for every generation in the church, especially now that Jesus' followers number several million all around the world. Many Christians and agencies give themselves tirelessly to the work of making this practical sharing of resources a reality in all the complexities of our contemporary world.

When Jesus' followers behave like this, they sometimes find, to their surprise, that they have a new spring in their step. There is an attractiveness, an energy about a life in which we stop clinging on to everything we can get and start sharing it, giving it away, celebrating God's generosity by being generous ourselves. And that attractiveness is one of the things that draws other people in. They were praising God, says Luke (verse 47), and stood in favour with the people; and day by day the Lord was adding to their number those who were being rescued. Of course they were, and of course he did. That's how it works. Where the church today finds itself stagnant, unattractive, humdrum and shrinking – and, sadly, there are many churches, in the Western world at least, of which that has to be admitted – it's time to read Acts 2.42–47 again, get down on our knees, and ask what isn't happening that should be happening. The **gospel** hasn't changed. God's power hasn't diminished. People still need rescuing. What are we doing about it?

ACTS 3.1–10

More than He Bargained For (See map 4, page xvii.)

[1]One day, Peter and John were going up to the Temple at three o'clock in the afternoon, the time for prayer. [2]There was a man being carried in who had been lame since birth. People used to bring him every day to the Temple gate called 'Beautiful', so that he could ask for alms from folk on their way in to the Temple. [3]When he saw Peter and John going in to the Temple, he asked them to give him some money. [4]Peter, with John, looked hard at him.

'Look at us', he said.

[5]The man stared at them, expecting to get something from them.

[6]'I haven't got any silver or gold', Peter said, 'but I'll give you what I have got. In the name of the Messiah, Jesus of Nazareth, get up and walk!'

[7]He grabbed the man by his right hand and lifted him up. At once his feet and ankles became strong, [8]and he leaped to his feet and began to walk. He went in with them into the Temple, walking and jumping up and down and praising God. [9]All the people saw him walking and praising God, [10]and they recognized him as the man who had been

sitting begging for alms by the Beautiful Gate of the Temple. They were filled with amazement and astonishment at what had happened to him.

There was once a young man who sneaked into church hoping nobody would notice him. The only reason he'd come was because he was keen on a girl who sang in the choir, and he hoped that if he was in the service he'd be able to see her at the end of the service and ask her out. He wasn't quite sure what to do, but he saw people going in and sitting down, so he did the same. Just as the service was beginning, an usher came up to him.

'Excuse me', he said. 'The person who's supposed to do the reading hasn't turned up. Could you possibly do it?'

The young man was horrified for a moment, but then thought quickly. The girl he had his eye on was there, in the choir. She would be most impressed if she heard him reading in the service.

'All right', he said. He took the Bible and looked through the reading the usher had showed him.

It came to the moment. He went up, opened the Bible, and began to read. It was from John's **gospel** and he vaguely recognized it.

'Anyone who doesn't enter the sheepfold by the gate,' he heard his own voice say, 'but climbs in by another way, is a thief and a bandit.'

He was thunderstruck. This was what he'd done! He was standing here, pretending to be a regular Bible-reader, when in fact he'd only come in to meet a girl. He forced himself to go on, aware of his heart beating loudly. If he was a bandit, coming in under false pretences, what was the alternative?

'I am the gate for the sheep', said Jesus. 'The bandit only comes to steal, kill and destroy. I came that they might have life, and have it full to overflowing.'

Suddenly, something happened inside the young man. He stopped thinking about himself. He stopped thinking about the girl, about the congregation, about the fact that he'd just done a ridiculous and hypocritical thing. He thought about Jesus. Unaware of the shock he was causing, he swung round to the clergyman leading the service.

'Is it true?' he asked. 'Did he really come so that we could have real life, full life like that?'

The clergyman smiled.

'Of course it is', he replied, quite unfazed by this non-liturgical outburst. 'That's why we're all here. Come and join in this next song and see what happens if you really mean it.'

And the young man found himself swept off his feet by the presence and the love of Jesus, filling him, changing him, calling him to follow, like a grateful sheep, after the shepherd who can be trusted to lead the way to good pasture by day and safe rest at night. He got more, much more, than he bargained for.

Something like that happened to the man who was sitting by the Beautiful Gate of the **Temple** in Jerusalem. You can see similar sights in many parts of the world today, not least in the Middle East. People often sit or stand in the same place each day, begging from passers-by. If you go that way, you get to know them. In the fall of 1999 I taught at Harvard, and walked most days through Harvard Square past two or three beggars who each had their own regular pitch. Sometimes I gave them money. About five years later I went back for a short visit, and walked down the same street. They were still there; I suppose I shouldn't have been surprised.

Certainly the people who went into the Temple by that gate day after day and week after week wouldn't have been surprised to see the disabled man. His friends brought him there every day. He would beg what he could, and at night they would take him back home.

So his request to Peter and John was what he asked everybody, every hour of every day. 'Have pity on me! Have pity on me!' – in other words, 'Give me some money!'

And of course he got far more than he bargained for. Peter's response is all the more interesting in view of what we heard at the end of the previous chapter about the believers sharing their property. Money had stopped being the most important thing for them. There was a new power, a new kind of life, which they had discovered. So what Peter said was the natural response. He didn't have any money, but he had something much better, something of a different order entirely. He didn't even ask the lame man if he would like to be healed. He just went ahead and healed him in the name of Jesus.

This story is the first occurrence in Acts of two interesting phenomena. First, Luke emphasizes that Peter and John looked hard at the man. They stared intently at him. What were they looking for? A sincere spirit, ready to receive more than he'd asked for? A heart full of pain and sorrow, ready to be touched by God's healing love? Somehow there is something important about that deep, face-to-face contact: not only did Peter and John stare at him, but they told him to look hard at them, too. No good turning your face away in embarrassment, as often happens with beggars who are ashamed to catch your eye, and of passers-by who are equally ashamed to look at beggars. What is about to happen is something that involves a deep human contact as well as a deep work of God.

Second, what Peter says will resonate through the next chapters and on into the wider story which Luke is telling. He doesn't just say, 'Stand up and walk', as Jesus himself would probably have done. He makes it quite clear where the healing power resides.

'In the name of the **Messiah**, Jesus of Nazareth', he says, 'get up and walk!'

It is the power of the name of Jesus that counts, here and everywhere. The idea of names having power is strange to those of us who live in the modern Western world (though we sometimes catch a dim echo of it when some important person, a civic or business leader, or perhaps a senior politician, says, 'Just mention my name and they'll let you in'). But most people in the first-century world, and many people in non-Western countries today, know exactly what's going on here. Of course names carry power: the power of magic, the invocation of hidden forces, the summoning up of new possibilities beyond normal human ability. And the point which resonates through the narrative from now on is this: the name 'Jesus' now carries that power. Mention his name, and new things will happen. This is as true now as ever it was. In this story, it turned a disabled man who sat outside the Temple into a worshipper who went all the way in. There's something to ponder.

This points us to something else that's going on here. Up to now, in Acts, the whole story has taken place in Jerusalem, but not in or around the Temple. Now we find that the believers were regularly going to worship in the Temple, even though (as we saw at the end of the previous chapter) the most important things they did (their teaching, **fellowship**, bread-breaking and prayer) happened elsewhere. But the demonstration of the power of Jesus' name took place, not in the Temple, but outside the gate. God is on the move, not confined within the institution, breaking out into new worlds, leaving behind the shrine which had become a place of worldly power and resistance to his purposes. This theme will come to a head four chapters from now. Whereas Luke's gospel began and ended in the Temple, what he is telling us now is that the good news of Jesus, though beginning in Jerusalem, is starting to reach outside to anyone and everyone who needs it.

ACTS 3.11-16

An Explanation Is Called For

> [11]All the people ran together in astonishment towards Peter and John, and the man who was clinging onto them. They were in the part of the Temple known as 'Solomon's Porch'. [12]Peter saw them all and began to speak.
>
> 'Fellow Israelites,' he said, 'why are you amazed at this? Why are you staring at us as though it was our own power or piety that made this man walk? [13]"The God of Abraham, the God of Isaac, the God of

Jacob – the God of our ancestors" – he has glorified his child Jesus, the one you handed over and denied in the presence of Pilate, although he had decided to let him go. [14]But you denied the Holy One, the Just One, and requested instead to have a murderer given to you; [15]and so you killed the Prince of Life. But God raised him from the dead, and we are witnesses to the fact. [16]And it is his name, working through faith in his name, that has given strength to this man, whom you see and know. It is faith which comes through him that has given him this new complete wholeness in front of all of you.'

'How did you do that?'

I stood beside the car as it spluttered into life. I had fiddled and jiggled with everything I could, and hadn't been able to make it start. (This, I should say, was a long time ago, in the days when you could poke around in car engines more easily than you can today.) My next-door neighbour, who was coming by, had offered to lend a hand. He had leant over the engine, done something I couldn't see, and suddenly the car had come back to life.

'Oh,' he said, 'don't thank me. It's a trick I learned from Jim down at the garage. He got fed up with me asking him what was wrong with my car and he showed me one of the most common faults and the easy way to sort it out.'

Now of course a disabled man isn't the same as a lifeless car engine. And the healing power of the name of Jesus isn't the same as a trick you learned in a garage. But the underlying point is still valid: it isn't that Peter or John were anyone special, just as it wasn't that my friend was a trained or clever mechanic. He simply trusted someone who knew how, who did have the power to make things happen. Peter and John, surrounded by an amazed crowd, were able to say the same.

'It wasn't us; it was Jesus!'

Or rather, it was the God who was at work in and through Jesus and is at work through him still. Peter, launching into an impromptu address, and eager perhaps to deflect attention from himself in such a prominent place as the **Temple** (where Jesus himself had taught great crowds only a few weeks before), takes care to refer to God in rather a dramatic, almost formal way: 'The God of Abraham, of Isaac, and of Jacob – the God of our ancestors'. Why does he do it like that?

This way of referring to God is actually a quotation. It comes from the book of Exodus (3.6). It's a famous passage, and Peter and his hearers would know it and would understand the point of the reference. Jesus himself had quoted it when debating with the **Sadducees** in the Temple a few weeks earlier (Luke 20.37), and he certainly intended that people should pick up the whole context of the passage. The point is this: Exodus 3 is the moment when God calls Moses, at the burning bush, and tells him to go back from the desert into Egypt and to lead his people out from slavery into freedom. God assures Moses that this isn't just some odd experience he's having; this really is Israel's God speaking, Abraham's God, the God who made promises to the ancestors of the presently enslaved Israelites and is now about to make those promises come true. Peter, quoting this passage, is saying, 'It's happening again!'

Peter, in other words, is doing what all the early Christians did all the time. Faced with a question to which the answer is something to do with Jesus, he goes back in his mind to the **Exodus**. That was when God acted spectacularly to fulfil his promises and rescue his people. That was when they **sacrificed** the Passover lamb, when they came through the water, when they were given the **law**, when they went off in search of their inheritance. All these themes jostle together in the New Testament, clustering around the question of who Jesus is and how it is that God acts through him. And, again and again, we get the sense: when we look at Jesus, and see what happens through his name, it is as though, like Moses, we are standing by the burning bush, seeing something spectacular, which ought to say to us that the creator God, the God of Abraham, is living and active and keeping his promises once again.

In particular, this sets Peter up to say some extraordinary things about Jesus, things which again will be picked up by Luke as the story moves forwards.

First, Jesus was the innocent 'servant'. The word 'servant' in verse 13 could equally be translated 'child', but 'servant' was a regular meaning of the word. In the Greek translation of Genesis 24, Abraham sends his servant to find a wife for Isaac, and the word used for 'servant' is the same as the word here, even though the servant in question wasn't Abraham's own child and certainly wasn't young. So the meaning 'servant' is probably uppermost. As we shall see more fully in due course, the idea of an 'innocent servant' should send our minds back to Isaiah 53, one of the all-time central passages in early Christian understanding of who Jesus was and why he died.

This points on to another theme. Just as in his account of Jesus' trial and death, Luke emphasizes that Jesus was innocent of the crimes of which he was charged – and that people who were released instead, like Barabbas (Luke 23.25), were guilty. That, as we saw earlier, is central to Luke's interpretation of the cross: Jesus dies on a charge of which he was innocent but plenty of other people were guilty. It is a matter of literal historic truth, as well as of theological interpretation, that 'the one bore the sins of the many' (Isaiah 53.12).

41

Second, Jesus was the 'Holy One, the Just One'. Jesus is referred to like this again in Acts (4.27, 30; 7.52; 22.14), and it's worth reflecting on these titles. Of course, the main point is that Jesus *was* 'holy'. His closest followers and friends had had ample opportunity to see his life close up at first-hand, and they continued to be astonished at the sheer God-centredness, the utter integrity and total love which Jesus always displayed. And certainly, in terms of Pilate's initial, and official, verdict (verse 13), Jesus was 'innocent' or 'just' in contrast to Barabbas, the murderer released in his place. But both words, 'holy' and 'just', carry echoes once more of Isaiah. They serve to strengthen the impression that Peter is insisting that if his hearers want to know why and how the lame man has been healed, they should think first of the Exodus (God freeing those who had been enslaved), second of Isaiah (God's servant bearing the sins and infirmities of his people), and finally of Jesus in the middle of both those stories, making them come true in a new way.

That is why, third, Jesus is also 'the prince of life'. The word 'prince' here can also mean 'the one who initiates something': he is not so much the ruler *over* 'life', as the sovereign one who brings life, who *initiates* new life, who pioneers the way through death, decay and corruption and out the other side into a kind of 'life' that nobody had imagined before. And the point is that Jesus was already doing this during his public career. Wherever he went, he brought new life, the life which indicated that God was now in charge. This makes it all the more ridiculous, paradoxical even, that his own people rejected him and sent him to his death: they *killed* the prince of *life*! But, of course, God raised him up – the **resurrection** continues to be at the heart of the proclamation of the church and the explanation of why new life is now happening – so that his work of bringing new life continues unchecked.

With all this, it's not surprising that Peter goes on to insist on the central explanation for how the disabled man was healed. He adds just one new note, which is enormously important in early Christianity. It is the name of Jesus, *through faith in his name*, which has done this. He repeats the point to rub it in. Using the name of Jesus isn't a matter of a new kind of magic, mumbling a secret word, a kind of abracadabra, which will make things happen automatically. There has to be faith, faith in the one who speaks the name, faith in the one who hears it. Other names, used in magic, keep people enslaved to the power of the name itself and the one who invokes it. The name of Jesus makes people grow up, become whole people, rinsed out and renewed, standing on their own feet literally (as the lame man now was), morally, spiritually and personally. That's what we find in verse 16, where Luke uses an unusual word to mean 'complete wholeness'. That's what is on offer through the **gospel** message which announces the powerful name of Jesus. Believing in him and in the power of his name is the way to wholeness, in the twenty-first century just as in the first.

ACTS 3.17–26

Restoration and Refreshment

> [17]'Now, my dear family,' Peter continued, 'I know that you acted in ignorance, just as your rulers did. [18]But this is how God has fulfilled what he promised through the mouth of all the prophets, that his Messiah would suffer. [19]So now repent, and turn back, so that your sins may be blotted out, [20]so that times of refreshment may come from the presence of the Lord, and so that he will send you Jesus, the one he chose and appointed to be his Messiah. [21]He must be received in heaven, you see, until the time which God spoke about through the mouth of his holy prophets from ancient days, the time when God will restore all things. [22]Moses said, "The Lord your God will raise up for you a prophet like me, one from among your own brothers; whatever he says to you, you must pay attention to him. [23]And everyone who does not listen to that prophet will be cut off from the people." [24]All the prophets who have spoken, from Samuel and his successors, told us about these days too. [25]You are the children of the prophets, the children of the covenant which God established with your ancestors when he said to Abraham, "In your seed shall all the families of the earth be blessed." [26]When God raised up his servant he sent him to you first, to bless you by turning each of you away from your wicked deeds.'

I remember a hot, hot walk in the Scottish highlands. (It's true: there are times, even at altitudes of 4,000 feet, when you can be just as hot in Scotland as anywhere in Europe.) We climbed Braeriach and Cairn Toul, the third and fourth highest mountains in the British Isles, on a cloudless and windless day, and walking at a good pace, too.

For the last few miles back down the path we fantasized about how it would be when we got back to camp. There would be water to wash in, a stream where we could cool down our feet after we'd taken our boots off; there would be tea and food . . . but most of all we wanted something cold to drink. (We'd long since gone through the water we'd brought with us.) Only a few more miles . . . and then, what was this? A Land Rover was coming up the track towards us. It was one of the camp staff.

'I reckoned you'd be hotter than you thought you were going to be', he said. 'So I put a couple of crates of this and that in the car and brought it up.'

We stared in amazement, and then, gratefully, got stuck in to the various soft drinks he'd brought. It tasted good, good as it only tastes when you are tired and dry. It was still good to get back to the camp, but the refreshment had come to meet us before we even finished the walk.

That is the image we need to have in mind in reading this passage. Like some other bits of the New Testament, even good stories like the ones in Acts can get a little dense, and we can miss the big things that are going on. The point to watch for here is verse 21. There is coming a time *when God will restore all things*. And, though that final day will be truly wonderful, *it can be anticipated with 'times of refreshment' in the present*.

This is one way of putting a central truth for which the early Christians had a wide variety of expressions. God would 'sum up all things in Christ' (Ephesians 1.10); through Christ, he would 'reconcile all things to himself, making peace by his blood, shed on the cross' (Colossians 1.20); he will make 'new heavens and new earth, in which justice will dwell' (Revelation 21.1 and 2 Peter 3.13); he will overcome every power which destroys and corrupts his good creation, so that eventually God will be 'all in all' (1 Corinthians 15.28); the whole creation will be 'set free from its slavery to decay, to share the liberty of the glory of God's children' (Romans 8.21). Like so much early Christian belief, this is basically a Jewish belief about the future, based on the solid rock of belief in God as both creator and judge, but rethought now around the events to do with Jesus. In this present passage we can actually watch this process going on.

The ultimate promise of verse 21, that there will be a final restoration of all things, is firmly rooted in the Jewish prophets. What has changed now is that the final restoration has already happened to Jesus himself: what God is going to do to the whole of creation, he has done for Jesus in raising him from the dead. That is why Jesus now remains 'in **heaven**', in other words (as we have already seen) in God's sphere. Heaven is the place where God's purposes for the future are stored up, like pieces of a stage set waiting in the wings until they are needed for the final great act of the play. When Jesus finally reappears, heaven and earth will come together as one. That will be the great renewal of all things.

But we don't have to wait, so to speak, until we get back to camp. When people turn away from the life they have led, and the wicked things they may have done, and turn back to God – the technical term for all that is the solid old word 'repent' – then 'times of refreshment' can come from the very presence of the Lord himself, a kind of advance anticipation of the full and final 'refreshment' that we can expect when God completes the work at last. This notion of 'refreshment', though itself unusual in the New Testament, is by no means unusual in Christian experience, as again and again, in worship and sacrament, in reading the scriptures, in Christian **fellowship** and prayer, we taste in advance just a little bit of the coming together of heaven and earth, the sense that this is what we were made for, the new world which we shall finally enjoy. It is there, available, ready for all who seriously seek it.

In case anyone should suppose he was just making all this up, or just tossing out empty promises, Peter again insists, in more detail this time, that all this has happened in direct fulfilment of what the prophets had said. He goes for the big names: not just Isaiah, whom he referred to earlier, but Moses himself, the greatest prophet of them all; Samuel, who anointed the first kings of Israel; and Abraham too, who though not normally thought of as a prophet is on one occasion designated as such (Genesis 20.7). It was Abraham who received the first and perhaps the greatest promise of all, which dominates the very structure of biblical thought: in you, and in your family, all earth's families are to be blessed (verse 25, quoting Genesis 12.3 – and compare Genesis 18.18; 22.18; 26.4; 28.14).

Peter, you see, is claiming much more than simply a few random proof-texts which, if you shut one eye and concentrate hard, can be made to sound a bit like things that had happened to Jesus. He is understanding the Old Testament as a single great story which was constantly pointing forwards to something that God was going to do through Abraham and his family, something that Moses, Samuel, Isaiah and the rest were pointing on towards as well. This great Something was the restoration of all things, the time when everything would be put right at last. And now, he says, it's happened! It's happened in Jesus! *And you can be part of it.*

This is the point of the appeal at the start and the finish of this passage. When the **good news** of Jesus is announced, it is, of course, about God the creator setting everything right. But part of the point of saying that this final restoration can come forward into the present is that God longs to see it happen to individual men, women and children, right now, in anticipation. Because of Jesus' death and **resurrection**, anyone who turns away from the life they've been leading and turns to God instead – anyone, including the crowds who bayed for Jesus' blood and the Jewish rulers who sent him off to Pilate to be crucified – anyone at all can know in advance the joy of being forgiven, of being refreshed by the love and mercy of God, of discovering new life and purpose in following Jesus.

The description of **forgiveness** here is particularly striking. In another echo of Isaiah (43.25), Peter speaks of sins being 'blotted out' as one might wipe a blackboard clean of chalk marks. Something that was written up as an accusation against us is simply wiped out when we turn away – when we not only say 'sorry', but actually, in mind and action, turn round in the opposite direction. And all this happens because of Jesus.

Already, with the quotation of the promise to Abraham in verse 25, Peter is hinting at something quite new which is yet to appear, but which will become a major theme in Acts, namely, the time when non-Jews will discover that the Jewish promise fulfilled in Jesus is available equally to them. But Peter explains (and Luke, writing up the speech, stresses) that what is going on at the present moment is the main chance for those Jewish people who had opposed Jesus, rejected him and sent him to his death, to say 'sorry' and to discover God's forgiveness. Tragically, Christians have sometimes taken passages like this and suggested that they meant that the Jewish people were somehow always to be blamed for what had happened. The reverse is the case. Not only is there no sense, in Acts or elsewhere, that the Jewish people somehow bear guilt or blame beyond the initial people who rejected Jesus himself. There is, on the contrary, the extended invitation, rooted in God's covenant faithfulness, for them to receive forgiveness and refreshment as much as anyone else. The promise of the restoration of all things is, after all, a deeply Jewish promise. None of the first Christians, who were of course all themselves Jewish, would have imagined that God would turn his back on the very people who had carried that promise through so many generations.

ACTS 4.1–12

Resurrection Plus the Name of Jesus Equals Trouble

[1]As they were speaking to the people, along came the priests, the chief of the Temple police, and the Sadducees. [2]They were thoroughly annoyed that they were teaching the people and proclaiming that 'the resurrection of the dead' had begun to happen in Jesus. [3]They seized them and put them under guard until the next day, since it was already evening. [4]But a large number of the people who had heard the message believed it, and the number of men grew to five thousand.

[5]On the next day their rulers, the elders and the scribes gathered in Jerusalem, [6]along with Annas the high priest, Caiaphas, John, Alexander and all the members of the high-priestly family. [7]They stood them in the midst.

'How did you do this?' they asked them. 'What power did you use? What name did you invoke?'

[8]Peter was filled with the holy spirit. 'Rulers of the people and elders,' he said, [9]'if the question we're being asked today is about a good deed done for a sick man, and whose power it was that rescued him, [10]let it be known to all of you, and to all the people of Israel, that this man stands before you fit and well because of the name of the Messiah, Jesus of Nazareth, whom you crucified, but whom God raised from the dead. [11]He is the stone which you builders rejected, but which has become the head cornerstone. [12]Rescue won't come from anybody else! There is no other name given under heaven and among humans by which we must be rescued.'

I cherish the remark attributed to a bishop who complained that he didn't seem to be having the same impact as the first **apostles**.

'Everywhere St Paul went,' he said, 'there was a riot. Everywhere I go they serve tea.'

Well, it wasn't just St Paul, either. We shall indeed watch in the later chapters of Acts as Paul goes from place to place and all kinds of trouble gets stirred up. But the **message** about Jesus as **Messiah** and rescuer meant trouble long before Paul started preaching it; indeed, as we shall see before too long, Paul was himself one of the leaders in making trouble for the people who were calling on the name of Jesus and declaring that God had raised him from the dead. So what was it about this early message which got the authorities, and others too, so alarmed and angry? Wouldn't it be simply great news to know that God was alive and well and was providing a wonderful rescue operation through his chosen Messiah?

Answer: not if you were already in power. Not if you were one of the people who had rejected and condemned that Messiah. And not, particularly, if you were in charge of the central institution that administered God's **law**, God's justice and the life of God's people, and if you strongly suspected that this new movement was trying to upstage you, to diminish or overturn that power and prestige and take it for itself. To understand all this – and opposition to the Christian message, which begins here in Acts, continues as a major theme all through from this point – we need to get inside what these people believed on the one hand and what the news of Jesus' **resurrection** actually meant on the other.

It is significant that it was the leaders of the **Temple** hierarchy, not least the **Sadducees**, who were so angry with Peter and John. As we know from other passages, the Sadducees were Jewish aristocrats, including the **high priest** and his family, who for some years had wielded great power in Jerusalem and among the Jewish people generally. They guarded the central shrine, the most holy place in Judaism, the place where for a thousand years the one true God had promised to meet with his people. They oversaw the sacrificial system by which this God had promised to maintain and restore **fellowship** with his people. And – just as a spin-off, of course! – they exercised great power economically, socially and politically. It was with the high priest and his entourage that the Roman governor would normally do business. They had the troops and the Temple police, and they had the whip-hand over the people. They could get things done, or stop things being done.

And that is why they strongly disapproved of the idea of 'resurrection'. This comes as a surprise to many people today. For at least the last 200 years in the Western world people have laughed at 'resurrection', whether that of Jesus or that of anyone else. Those who have stuck out against this mockery, and declared that they do believe in resurrection anyway, have been thought of as 'conservatives' rather than the modern 'liberals'. But resurrection always was a radical, dangerous doctrine, an attack on the status quo and a threat to existing power structures. Resurrection, you see, is the belief which declares that the living God is going to put everything right once and for all, is going (as we saw in the previous chapter) to 'restore all things', to turn the world the right way up at last.

And those who are in power, within the world the way it is, are quite right to suspect that, if God suddenly does such a drastic thing, they (to put it mildly) cannot guarantee that they will end up in power in the new world that God is going to make. What's more, people who believe in resurrection – as did the **Pharisees**, a radical populist group at the time – tend to be more ready than others to cause trouble for the authorities in the present. They believe, after all, that the God who will eventually put the world the right way up is likely to bring about some advance signs of that final judgment. They believe, too, that if they themselves try to produce such advance signs, but die in the process, God will raise them from the dead at the end anyway. Resurrection, whichever way you looked at it, was not what the authorities wanted to hear about.

So what made them angry wasn't just Peter's announcement that God had raised Jesus from the dead. It was, as Luke puts it, a much larger thing: that Peter *was preaching the resurrection of the dead*, and announcing this revolutionary doctrine 'in Jesus'. In other words, Peter was saying not only that Jesus himself had been raised, but that this was the start and the sign of God's eventual restoration of everything (3.21). That was bound to be bad news for the chief priests and the Sadducees, however much it was exactly what plenty of others wanted to hear (Luke notes a further 5,000 coming to **faith** on the spot).

But the really sinister thing about this section is the further question the authorities ask. 'What name did you use to do this?' Our minds go back to the accusations that were hurled at Jesus himself: was he, after all, in league with Beelzebul? Was he using some kind of black magic? (See Luke 11.14–23.) Was Jesus – and were the disciples, now – the kind of people Deuteronomy 13 had warned about, people who were leading Israel astray to worship false gods?

Just as Jesus answered that question by reference to the **holy spirit**, at work in and through him to launch God's **kingdom**-project, so Peter, himself filled with the holy spirit, announces boldly that the 'name' in question is that of 'Jesus, the Messiah, from Nazareth'. He continues, in words that would hardly endear him to the authorities: 'You crucified him' (not that they did, as Luke knows; it was the Romans who did so; but the chief priests had precipitated it by handing him over on a capital charge and by pressing Pilate for a verdict of condemnation). The name of Jesus, in other words, isn't just the name through which healing power can flow into people. It is a name which is already a sign of contradiction.

In particular, Jesus is the place where God is building . . . the new Temple! This is a new level of subversion, which will burst out dramatically in Stephen's speech in Acts 7. As Jesus himself had hinted, he is the one prophesied in Psalm 118, which speaks of a stone that has been rejected by the builders but has become the head cornerstone of the whole building. When builders are searching around for ordinary stones to put up a wall or a house, they reject the one with the odd shape, because it won't fit. But they may then find, when they get to the top of the building, that the one with the strange angles is the very one they want. This passage in Psalm 118 already came to the early Christians full of hints about the Temple itself. God will build a new Temple, thus declaring the present one redundant.

For first-century Jews who were part of regular discussions about who the Messiah might be and what he might do, the 'stone' in this text would carry echoes of other passages as well. In particular, there is Daniel 2, which speaks of the 'stone' cut out of a mountain, which would smash to pieces the blasphemous statue of pagan empire and would itself become a kingdom filling the whole world. The implication is clear. God is indeed turning the world the right way up. He is doing so through the powerful name of Jesus. And, since this will involve the replacement of the present Temple with a new organization based on Jesus himself, the chief priests (who have the present Temple as their power base) hold no terrors for those who follow this Jesus.

Actually, Psalm 118 is full of meaning which would be directly relevant to what Peter and John were saying. It's a Psalm of the Temple, of people going up to it to celebrate God's new day and to claim his **salvation** (verses 21, 24, 25). It's a Psalm about God's life-giving power (verses 15–18), including in particular the way in which God brings his people through trouble and rescues them from danger. And it's a Psalm which, relying on God's mercy (verse 4), celebrates God's victory over all the powers of the world (verses 10, 14). 'It is better to trust in the Lord', sings the Psalm (verses 8–9), 'than to put any confidence in mortals, or in princes.' In other words, this was exactly the Psalm the apostles needed as they stood before the authorities.

All this gives us reason to ask, rather carefully, just why it is that Acts 4.12 has been so unpopular within the politically correct climate of the last few generations in the Western world. 'No other name'? People say this is arrogant, or exclusive, or triumphalist. So, indeed, it can be, if Christians use the name of Jesus to further their own power or prestige. But for many years now, in the Western world at least, the boot has been on the other foot. It is the secularists and the relativists who have acted the part of the chief priests, protecting their cherished temple of modernist thought, within which there can be no mention of resurrection, no naming of a name like that of Jesus. And the apostles, in any case, would answer: Well, who else is there that can rescue people in this fashion?

ACTS 4.13–22

The Clash of Loyalties

[13]When they saw how boldly Peter and John were speaking, and realized that they were untrained, ordinary men, they were astonished, and they recognized them as people who had been with Jesus. [14]And when they saw the man who had been healed standing with them, they had nothing to say in reply. [15]They ordered them to be put out of the assembly while they conferred among themselves.

[16]'What can we do to these men?' they said. 'This is a spectacular sign that has happened through them. All Jerusalem knows it, and we can't deny it! [17]But we certainly don't want it to spread any further among the people. So let's threaten them with awful consequences if they speak any more in this name to anybody.'

[18]So they called them in and gave them orders not to speak at all, or to teach, in the name of Jesus.

[19]But Peter and John gave them this reply.

'You judge', they said, 'whether it's right before God to listen to you rather than to God! [20]As far as we're concerned, we can't stop speaking about what we have seen and heard.'

²¹Then they threatened them some more, and let them go. They couldn't find any way to punish them because of the people, since everyone was glorifying God for what had happened. ²²After all, the man to whom this sign of healing had happened was over forty years old.

Jennifer was teaching some basic geography to a class of eight-year-olds. They were studying Australia. They had just drawn a rough map together, and had worked out where the main cities were. Then Jennifer asked the class if anyone could say what sort of things most people in Australia did.

'Swimming!' shouted several voices.

'Yes,' replied Jennifer, 'but most people don't make a living by swimming.'

'Barbecuing!' said several more.

'Yes, they do a lot of that,' said Jennifer, 'but that's just how people cook their food. First they have to buy it, and for that they need money. What do they do to earn the money in the first place?'

'Well,' said a little girl at the back, 'a long time ago, nearly all Australians worked on farms. They looked after sheep and cattle and they grew all sorts of crops. Nowadays people in the big cities do all sorts of other things too, of course, like business and making cars and building houses and all the other things people get up to. But still a large number of Australians are farmers, and the further you go inland the more likely you are to find them running farms.'

The whole class stared at the little girl who had spoken so confidently.

'How did you learn all that?' asked Jennifer. 'We've only just started studying Australia today! Did you read a book about it?'

'No', said the girl, tossing her head with a mixture of pride and embarrassment. 'It's just that we used to live there. My dad used to run a cattle farm with several thousand cows. I knew all about it from as soon as I could talk.'

There are, in other words, more ways of learning things than studying them in books. Book-learning, in fact, is often a poor substitute for first-hand experience if you want really to get inside a subject or have it inside you. And that was what was so striking about Peter and John.

The authorities were no doubt used to rounding up troublemakers and teaching them a lesson. Normally such people, rabble-rousers of one sort or another, wouldn't have been able to string together more than a few sentences once they were put on the spot and received a direct challenge. But with Peter and John it was different. Clearly they hadn't been to rabbinical school to study the scriptures. In the small society of ancient Judaism people would know who the up-and-coming bright young students were; these men certainly weren't that type. They were 'untrained, ordinary men'. What's more, they had come out with a shrewd use of a Psalm, such as you might expect to get only if someone had sat in class and learned about various types of biblical interpretation. But they hadn't. What on earth was going on?

Like the little girl who used to live in Australia, Peter and John had a secret – a secret that enabled them to run rings round the book-learning of the authorities. They had been with Jesus. They had been with him night and day. They had seen and heard him pray. They knew how he read the scriptures, in his fresh, creative way, drawing out their inner **message** and finding his own vocation in the middle of it. Now that he had died and had then been astonishingly raised, and had then been exalted into the heavenly realm, all Peter and John had to do to explain what they were about was to develop the lines of thought they had heard him use over and over again. This didn't just give them 'boldness' in the sense of courage to stand up and say what they thought. Sometimes people can be bold even when they're muddled. It gave them something more: a clarity, a sharp edge, a definite point at which to stand. And the authorities knew it.

They were therefore at a loss. They couldn't deny that the disabled man had been healed. But nor could they simply shrug their shoulders and say nothing, as though it was of no concern to them that people were going around saying that **resurrection** had begun to happen, that Jesus of Nazareth was the **Messiah**, and that his name was so powerful that invoking it would cure chronically sick people. As we shall see in later chapters, they would soon find plenty of ways of punishing Jesus' followers, but for the moment they were stuck. And so, in what must have been an embarrassing climb-down, all they could do was to tell Peter and John not to speak any more in the name of Jesus.

They must have known, in issuing this order, that they were trying to shut a door when a howling gale was already blowing through it. After all, anyone who has found any word, any name, that will enable sick people to be healed is very unlikely to stop using it just because the authorities forbid it. But Peter's answer to them is more than merely pragmatic. It is theological, and forms the basis of all Christian resistance to the powers of this world from that day to this. We could paraphrase it like this: 'You're the judges around here? Very well, give me your legal judgment on this one! If we're standing here in God's presence, should we obey God, or should we obey you?'

Peter answers his own question. They can actually answer it how they like, but he and his friends are not going to stop speaking in the name of Jesus, and about all the things which God has done through him.

Now of course it is always possible for anyone to claim the name of Jesus, and the right to speak in his name, and to use this as justification for any sort of rebellion against authority that they choose. Such claims have a right to be heard, though they must then be judged on their merits. But the point about this one, which distinguishes it from many claims that might be made which simply borrow the name of Jesus as an excuse for running with an agenda someone has reached on quite different grounds, is that the people making the claim have already shown that they are living by it, and that it has power, kingdom-power, healing power. It makes the lame walk, just like Jesus did. Paul put it crisply: the **kingdom of God** is not about talk, but about power (1 Corinthians 4.20). Where God's power is at work to bring real change, real healing, real new life, there the people who are naming the name of Jesus to bring it about can stand up before judges, whether political or religious, and say with integrity that they are speaking for God. It will be costly; that's part of the deal. But it will be true.

ACTS 4.23–31

Look upon Their Threats

[23]When they had been released, they went back to their own people, and told them everything that the chief priests and the elders had said. [24]When they heard it, they all together lifted up their voices to God.

'Sovereign Master,' they said, 'you made heaven and earth, and the sea, and everything in them. [25]And you said through the holy spirit, by the mouth of our ancestor David, your servant,

'Why did the nations fly into a rage,
and why did the peoples think empty thoughts?
[26]The kings of the earth arose
and the rulers gathered themselves together
against the Lord and against his anointed Messiah.

[27]'It's true: Herod and Pontius Pilate, together with the nations and the peoples of Israel, gathered themselves together in this very city against your holy child Jesus, the one you anointed, [28]to do whatever your hand and your plan had foreordained to take place. [29]So now, Master, look on their threats; and grant that we, your servants, may speak your word with all boldness, [30]while you stretch out your hand for healing, so that signs and wonders may come about through the name of your holy child Jesus.'

[31]When they had prayed, the place where they were gathered was shaken. They were all filled with the holy spirit, and they boldly spoke the word of God.

In the early summer of 1989, I went to Jerusalem to teach, and to work on a couple of books, one of which was about Jesus himself. One day, sitting in my borrowed room at St George's Cathedral, I was struggling with a few pages I was trying to write, concerning the battles Jesus had over his exorcisms – the battles, that is, both with the **demons** themselves and with the people who were accusing him of being, himself, in league with the devil. I was conscious, as I was struggling with this material, that it was not only difficult to say what had to be said historically, but that it was difficult to get it straight theologically, and that in attempting both tasks I was myself straying into a field of forces which I would have preferred to avoid.

Suddenly, just as I had got down onto the computer a few paragraphs in which I had at last said what I wanted to say, there was a loud bang. All the electric systems in the building went dead. A workman downstairs, trying to fix something else, had put a nail straight through a main cable. He was lucky to be alive. And I had lost my morning's work.

It was such a shock, after my hours of silent struggle with the text, the history and the meanings, that I almost burst into tears. I went next door, sat down at the piano, and played for a few minutes to calm myself down and clear my head. Then I came back into my room and knelt down at the prayer desk. For some reason (perhaps I had heard them in the cathedral earlier that day, or that week) the words of Acts 4.29 came straight into my head.

'Now, Lord,' I prayed, 'look upon their threats; and grant to your servant to speak your **word** with all boldness, while you stretch out your hand to heal, and signs and wonders are performed in the name of your holy child Jesus.' I went back to the desk and reconstructed the morning's work.

I have prayed that prayer many times, not usually in such dramatic circumstances, but often with a sense that today, just as much as in the **apostles**' time, there is a battle going on. Sometimes it is with actual, official authorities, as in Acts 4. Sometimes it is with the spirit of the age, with the implied mood of an organization, a family or a club, where certain things are done and said and certain other things are emphatically 'not done' or 'not said' – including, it may be, a definite statement of Christian truth, which bursts upon a room in such circumstances like someone saying a rude word. Sometimes the battle is internal, where things I badly want to do, say or think conflict with what the text really is saying, and I have to recognize my own bias, repent and allow the text to reform my outlook and behaviour. Whatever, the battle is real. I do not say it is always necessarily with actual dark powers, though I would never rule that out. I just know that when you come to speak or write about Jesus, about his cross, about his **resurrection**, about the new life which can break chains and set people free, there seem to be powers around the place which do their best to oppose what you are doing.

The previous passage included a reference to Psalm 118, and we saw just how important that Psalm was for the early church faced with opposition from the authorities. Now we find the apostles at prayer, returning to their friends after a trip to the **Temple** which, against expectations, had gone on from one afternoon to the next morning. And this time the Psalm they focus on is Psalm 2. Another spectacular poem, full of meaning relevant for exactly this situation.

Psalm 2 begins by questioning, before God, why the nations are in such an uproar, and the rulers scheming and plotting. This question stands within a long Jewish tradition in which God places his chosen people amidst the warring and violent nations of the earth, as a sign of his coming **kingdom**, the sovereign rule by which he will eventually bring peace and justice to the world. And on this occasion the means by which God will do this is through his anointed King, the one who will be hailed as '**son of God**'. To this 'son of God', declares the Psalm, God will give not just the promised land as his inheritance, but all the nations of the world. The promises to Abraham have been extended, rather as in Psalm 72 or Psalm 89, and now they embrace the whole world.

So when the apostles quote Psalm 2 in their confident, exhilarated prayer in verses 25 and 26 they are not just finding a vague proof-text to help them anchor a general sense that all the world is against them. They are calling up a very specific text which speaks graphically and powerfully of the **Messiah** as the son of God, destined to rule the whole world. Woven deep into the heart of early Christian belief was exactly this note, as we find in a passage in Paul. In Romans 1.3–5, where he may be drawing on an early Christian confession of **faith**, he declares that in the resurrection God demonstrated that Jesus really was his son, the Messiah from the seed of David, and that this Jesus was therefore the Lord of the whole world, claiming allegiance from all people.

Praying like this is confident praying, not because people necessarily feel more devout than at other times, but because they are rooting themselves firmly in the ancient tradition of scripture. They start their prayer by invoking God as the creator of heaven, earth, the sea and everything else – the God, in other words, of the Old Testament, the God who can be appealed to for all that takes place within his domains. Then follows the quote from the Psalm. Then the present situation is placed firmly on the map of the scriptural story which has already been celebrated. As a result, the prayer can acknowledge, as

Acts already has, the strong theological point that even the apparently disastrous things that took place as Jesus went to the cross were not outside God's will (verse 28). The wickedness of rulers is held in check by, and contained within, the overall purpose of God, who makes even human wrath turn to his praise.

With the ground thus prepared, the main triple thrust of the prayer is quite straightforward. Not 'Lord, please cause them to die horribly' or 'Please stop them being so unpleasant.' Not 'Lord, let this persecution stop', or even 'Please convert the authorities, so that your work can go forward.' Rather, quite simply, 'Now, Lord, look on their threats; let us go on speaking boldly; and will you please continue to work powerfully.' The opposition are there, and God knows about them. We are here, and we need to be faithful, to continue to speak of Jesus boldly and confidently. And here is the power of God, which is not in our possession but which, because of Jesus, will continue to be at work to set up signposts pointing people to the new thing which is happening through him.

The church needs to learn, in every generation, what it means to pray with confidence like this. We do not go looking for persecution. But when it comes, in whatever form, it certainly concentrates the mind, sends us back to the scriptures, and casts us on God's mercy and power. The church needs, again and again, that sense of God's powerful presence, shaking us up, blowing away the cobwebs, filling us with the **spirit**, and giving us that same boldness.

ACTS 4.32–37

Signs of the New Covenant

[32]The company of those who believed had one heart and soul. Nobody said that they owned their property; instead, they had everything in common. [33]The apostles gave their testimony to the resurrection of the Lord Jesus with great power, and great grace was upon all of them. [34]For there was no needy person among them, since any who possessed lands or houses sold them, brought the money from the sale, [35]and placed it at the feet of the apostles, who then gave to each according to their need.

[36]Joseph, a Levite from Cyprus, to whom the apostles gave the surname 'Barnabas' (which means 'son of encouragement'), [37]sold some land which belonged to him, brought the money, and laid it at the apostles' feet.

Some politicians' phrases pass into folk legend. I am old enough (just) to remember Harold Macmillan saying, 'You've never had it so good.'

Some Americans can remember Roosevelt talking about the 'New Deal'. And generations to come will still talk about Margaret Thatcher as the 'Iron Lady'.

Other phrases from other sources stick in people's minds. People speak of 'killing the fatted calf' when they mean 'laying on a great party', even though most of them probably couldn't tell you that it came from Jesus' **parable** of the prodigal son in Luke 15. Many people will quote 'conscience doth make cowards of us all' and speak of 'slings and arrows of outrageous fortune' without knowing that they come from Shakespeare's *Hamlet*. And so on.

We are blessed, of course, with an abundance of literary sources to quote from, even though these days people often prefer electronic entertainment to reading. But it's not so long ago that in many homes the only real, solid book would be the Bible. In fact, the weekend I am writing this, a newspaper article is bemoaning the fact that new translations of the Bible have now deprived many devout people of that sense of familiar resonance you get when you hear a phrase and instinctively know that it's part of your world.

We have to remind ourselves of this whenever we try to track how the New Testament uses the Old. As we have seen in the last few passages in relation to the Psalms, frequently a short quotation will carry with it an entire passage, maybe even an entire world and an entire worldview, from the larger context from which it comes. And many careful readers have pointed out that something similar is going on here, in verse 34 in particular. Luke has already told us that the first Christians, living in Jerusalem, sold property and distributed it to those who were in need. Why does he repeat the point here? What is he adding?

The early Christians were by no means the first Jews of their day to try their hand at communal living. The best-known other example is in the **Dead Sea Scrolls**, where we find a description of the 'covenant community' that formed itself around a character called 'the Teacher of Righteousness', who probably lived in the first century BC or a little earlier. This Teacher claimed (or his followers claimed on his behalf) that through his work God had established the 'new covenant' spoken of by the prophets, especially Jeremiah and Ezekiel. He, the Teacher, had been opposed by the priestly hierarchy of the day, based in the **Temple**. Indeed, the Teacher may himself have been a **priest**, perhaps a rival claimant for the title of **high priest**. Scholars discuss all this at great length. But the point here is this: in making the claims they did, the group who wrote and studied the scrolls (which include large chunks of the Old Testament and several books of commentary upon it) saw themselves as the community in which the ancient ideal of Israel as God's covenant people was coming true. So *they shared* *their possessions.* First they gave them in trust to the community; then, when they were clear they wanted to join irrevocably, they signed them away for good.

It looks as though the early Christians did something very similar, and for a very similar reason. They believed that God had established the 'new covenant', not through the Teacher of Righteousness, but through Jesus of Nazareth. They therefore saw themselves as the 'covenant community' in whom God's promises were coming true. And among these promises we find Deuteronomy, which speaks of what life will be like when God finally establishes his people. And in Deuteronomy we find chapter 15, which gives commands for how, every seven years, there must be a remission of debts: everyone who is owed money must remit the claim. However, the passage goes on (verse 4), 'there will be no needy person among you, because the Lord is sure to bless you in the land that the Lord your God is giving you.'

And now at last we see what Luke is up to.

He is making the striking, controversial claim that the early Christian movement was, in effect, the true covenant community that God had always intended to set up. It had been achieved by the massive and total **forgiveness** of sins and debts accomplished by Jesus in his death; Jesus had, after all, announced as his agenda (in Luke 4) the programme of '**jubilee**' set out in Isaiah 61, and had gone around talking about forgiveness both of sins and of debts. Now his followers were, in the most practical way possible, making real the implied promise of covenant renewal. Not only would they forgive debts every seven years; they would not keep their own private property to themselves, but would share it in common. As we noticed before, this didn't mean that they sold the roofs over their own heads, because then they would have had nowhere to meet or indeed to live. And later on, when Paul is going around the world talking about Jesus, it is assumed that people still have houses to live and eat in (1 Corinthians 11.22), even though Paul makes it quite clear that the gift of love given by God in Christ must be matched by the sharing of money, not just within the believing community in a single city, but across large distances and cultural barriers (Romans 15.25–29; 2 Corinthians 8—9). So strong is this principle in the churches Paul founded that within a very short time he has to write to the Thessalonians warning against the danger of people sponging off the community when they are quite capable of earning their own living. That danger would only have emerged in a community where the sharing of property was a foundation principle.

Luke has used this repeated description of the church to round off the two chapters which describe the healing of the disabled man, the hearing of Peter and John before the authorities, and the powerful prayer which followed. This has given him a chance to introduce several themes which will be important as the book progresses. Now he emphasizes the way in which the early church was living as the true people of God – not least, we may suspect, in order to highlight an emerging paradox. The Temple authorities thought *they* were the guardians of the official traditions of Israel; but, in the very same city, there was a community which was practising the life of the true covenant people of God, and thereby quietly upstaging all that went on in the Temple. What you do with money and possessions declares loudly what sort of a community you are, and the statement made by the early church's practice was clear and definite. No wonder they were able to give such powerful testimony to the **resurrection** of Jesus. They were demonstrating that it was a reality in ways that many Christians today, who often sadly balk at even giving a tithe of their income to the church, can only dream of.

In particular, this paragraph shows us what is meant when, in various early Christian writings (e.g. Philippians 2.1–4; Ephesians 4.1–4), people talk about being of one heart and mind. No doubt there is always a call to try to think alike with one another, to reach a deep, heart-level agreement on all key matters. But the early Christians, being Jewish, did not make as sharp a distinction as we do between heart and mind on the one hand and practical life on the other. 'Being of one heart and soul' in this passage seems to mean not just 'agreeing on all disputed matters' but also 'ready to regard each other's needs as one's own'. Here again there is an important Old Testament echo, and again in a covenantal context: 'I will give them', promises God to Jeremiah, 'one heart and one way' (Jeremiah 32.39; similarly, Ezekiel 11.19). Yes, says Luke; and it's happened through Jesus. This is the 'new covenant' community, right here, where all this is going on. And this establishes the claim of Jesus' people to be the true assembly of God's people, while those who run the Temple are just a sham. This in turn increases the tension that is starting to build between Jesus' followers and the Temple authorities, a tension which comes to the boil in just a few chapters' time.

Meanwhile, Luke uses this note about property-sharing in the community to introduce us to a character who will be important as the book progresses. A man named Joseph was given the nickname, by the **apostles**, of 'Barnabas', which means 'son of encouragement'. He was a 'Levite', that is, a member of the Israelite tribe of Levi, which provided the minor officials who worked in the Temple. (The priests themselves were the descendants of Aaron, one family within the tribe of Levi.) Barnabas provides a concrete example for Luke of someone who sold property and brought the proceeds to the apostles.

It may be that the property in question was on the island of Cyprus, where he came from, and where, with Paul, he would go as part of the first overseas missionary journey (Acts 13). But Barnabas, as we shall see, lived up to his nickname, not only in the matter of his own property but also when it came to taking risks to help people in a difficult spot (9.27; 11.22–26). As in his **gospel**, so here in Acts, Luke keeps popping people like this into his story, not only making it more vivid but helping us to get a sense of what following Jesus looks like in practice.

ACTS 5.1–11

Disaster

[1]There was, however, a man named Ananias, married to a woman called Sapphira. He sold some property, [2]and, with his wife's knowledge, kept back part of the price. He brought the rest and laid it at the apostles' feet.

[3]'Ananias!' said Peter. 'Why did satan fill your heart, to make you tell a lie to the holy spirit and to keep back part of the price of the land? [4]While it was still yours, it belonged to you, didn't it? And, when you sold it, it was still in your power! Why did you get such an idea in your heart? It isn't humans that you've lied to: it's God!'

[5]When Ananias heard these words, he fell down and died. Everyone who heard about it was scared out of their wits. [6]The young men got up, took him away, wrapped up his body and buried him.

[7]After an interval of about three hours, his wife came in, not knowing what had happened.

[8]Peter spoke to her.

'Tell me,' he said, 'did you sell the land for this much?'

'Yes,' she replied, 'that was the price.'

[9]'So why', Peter answered, 'did you agree together to put the holy spirit to the test? Look: the feet of those who have buried your husband are at the door – and they will carry you out too!'

[10]At once she fell down at his feet and died. The young men were just coming in, and they found her dead, so they took her out and buried her beside her husband. [11]Great fear came upon the whole gathering, and on all who heard about these things.

Charles Haddon Spurgeon, the great Victorian Baptist preacher, recounted the story of how, on one occasion, he was preaching as usual when he found himself denouncing someone in the congregation whom he didn't know. Words came into his mouth describing how this man was cheating his employer, stealing from him, and apparently getting away with it. But, he found himself saying, this man should repent at once, or he would be found out.

At the time Spurgeon was surprised and somewhat anxious: where had this come from? Who was he talking about? Why had it happened?

But, after the service, a young man came up to him in great consterna-tion. 'Please', he said, 'don't tell my master. I'll give it all back.' The man repented, made full restitution, and the situation was saved. And Spur-geon was left pondering the strange reality that, without asking for it or seeking it, he had been given a 'word of knowledge' about someone he didn't know.

Stories like that, which crop up relatively frequently in contempo-rary accounts of great preaching movements and other similar reviv-als, help to set the context for grappling with Acts 5, but they hardly make it much easier for us today. Let's face it: most of us would have been relieved if Ananias and Sapphira had been confronted with their cheating, had confessed and repented, and had either gone back to the beginning and decided what they really wanted to do or had simply given the rest of the money over, as they said they already had. Instead, swift judgment falls on them, judgment of a sort which (despite popu-lar impressions to the contrary) is highly unusual in the Bible. Mostly, nations and individuals who do wrong seem to get away with it for a long time, and even if judgment comes eventually it's not always in the form people expect. What is different here? What is Luke trying to tell us in and through it all?

Part of what he is trying to tell us, whether we like it or not (and many of course don't), is that the early Christian community, without even trying, was functioning somewhat like the **Temple** itself. It was a place of holiness, a holiness so dramatic and acute that every blemish was magnified. Remember how, when the Ark of the **Covenant** was brought to Jerusalem in the first place, carried on an ox cart, one of its guardians put out his hand to steady it when it wobbled and was at once struck dead, much to King David's annoyance (2 Samuel 6.6–9). The Temple itself contained warnings against anyone approaching who was unfit to do so. **Gentiles** were kept well out of it (see Acts 21.28–29); Jewish women could only go in as far as a certain point; only the **priests** could go into the inner court; and only the **high priest** himself could go into the central shrine, the 'holy of holies', and then only once a year, taking all kinds of precautions.

This sense of dangerous holiness emanates from some of Israel's ancient traditions, not just about the Temple but about the behaviour of the whole community. Leviticus 10 tells of two sons of Aaron who infringed the holiness of the sanctuary and suffered the consequences. Joshua 7 carries a story which is, in its way, not unlike our story of Ananias and Sapphira: following the destruction of Jericho, a man named Achan takes some of the things that should have been devoted to the Lord, and when trouble comes on the community as a result he is found out, and swift and supernatural judgment is visited on him.

Similarly, 2 Chronicles 26 tells of King Uzziah infringing the sanctuary and being struck down with leprosy.

We don't like those stories, of course, any more than we like Acts 5, but we can't have it both ways. If we watch with excited fascination as the early church does wonderful healings, stands up to the bullying authorities, makes converts right and left, and lives a life of astonishing property-sharing, we may have to face the fact that if you want to be a community which seems to be taking the place of the Temple of the living God you mustn't be surprised if the living God takes you seriously, seriously enough to make it clear that there is no such thing as cheap grace. If you invoke the power of the holy one, the one who will eventually right all wrongs and sort out all cheating and lying, he may just decide to do some of that work already, in advance. God is not mocked, as Paul puts it (Galatians 6.7). Though we sincerely hope he will not normally act with such sudden and swift judgment, leaving no room for the possibility of **repentance** and restoration (and we note that this sort of thing never seems to happen again in the early church, with the possible exception of 1 Corinthians 11.30, and the warning of 1 Corinthians 5.1–5), we either choose to live in the presence of the God who made the world, and who longs passionately for it to be set right, or we lapse back into some variety or other of easy-going paganism, even if it has a Christian veneer to it. Holiness, in other words, is not an optional extra. How God chooses to make that point is in the last analysis up to him, since he is the only one who knows the human heart. But the earliest Christians were quite clear. To name the name of Jesus, and to invoke the **holy spirit**, is to claim to be the Temple of the living God, and that is bound to have consequences.

In particular, this passage puts down a very clear marker about lying. Some of the greatest theologians have agonized over this question (is it right, for instance, to tell a murderer the truth about where his intended victim is hiding?) and have come up with various answers. But however we address the hard cases, our culture, which today is notoriously full of spin and smear, of people who hardly even bother any more to disguise the fact that they are telling half-truths to force their point across, and of politicians and other famous people who lie massively, publicly and dramatically – our culture is due a sharp dose of the warning which a story like this can provide. Ananias didn't have to lie. He could, had he wished, have sold the property, kept back part of the money, and said, 'I choose to give this part.' Had he been embarrassed to do that, he could simply have refrained from selling the property in the first place. Peter implies in verse 4 that there was no actual compulsion about doing what was described at the end of the previous chapter, and Barnabas is held up there not as an example of what everybody was doing but as a striking and special occurrence. The key thing was the lie.

The real, deep-level problem about lying is that it misuses, or abuses, the highest faculty we possess: the gift of expressing in clear speech the reality of who we are, what we think, and how we feel. It is, as it were, the opposite of the gift of **tongues**. Instead of allowing God's **spirit** to have free rein through our faculties, so that we praise God in words or sounds which enable us to stand (however briefly) at the intersection of heaven and earth, when we tell lies we not only hold heaven and earth apart; we twist earth itself, so that it serves our own interests. Lying is, ultimately, a way of declaring that we don't like the world the way it is and we will pretend that it is somehow more the way we want it to be. At that level, it is a way of saying that we don't trust God the creator to look after his world and sort it out in his own time and way. And it is precisely the claim of the early church that God the creator has acted in Jesus Christ to sort the world out and set it right. Those who make that claim, and live by that claim, must expect to be judged by that claim. This is a terrifying prospect. But if we took the underlying message of Acts 5 more seriously, we might perhaps expect to see more of the other bits of Acts, the bits we all prefer, coming true in our communities as well. Like the next section, for instance.

ACTS 5.12–16

Healed by Peter's Shadow

> [12]Many signs and wonders were performed by the apostles among the people. They were all together in Solomon's Porch, [13]while none of the others dared join them, though the people spoke highly of them. [14]But more people, a crowd both of men and women, believed in the Lord, and were added to their number. [15]They used to bring the sick into the streets, and place them on beds and mats so that at least Peter's shadow might fall on them as he went by. [16]Crowds gathered from the towns around Jerusalem, bringing people who were sick, or infested with unclean spirits. All of them were cured.

Imagine you are the manager of a great concert hall or opera house – the Metropolitan in New York, say, or the Albert Hall in London. For generations now this has been the place to which concert-goers have flocked in their thousands, week after week, year after year. All the glittering international stars have played and sung here. Every performance is reported in the national press. A grateful public subscribes for whole seasons of concerts all at once.

And then, quite suddenly, in the middle of your busy season, a small informal group begins to perform, day after day and night after night, right outside the main door of the concert hall. It's a motley collection of musicians, and they're playing a strange mixture of ancient classical music and rowdy new songs, sometimes putting them together in an unprecedented fashion.

Well, you think, people come and people go, strange things happen, there's probably no harm in it. But then you realize that a lot of the people who ought to be coming into the concert hall are coming to see and hear this little ragtag group of musicians. Crowds gather, and stay outside listening to the new music rather than coming inside to hear the advertised programme. And soon the leaders of the new band become well known. People are talking about *them*, and writing news-paper articles about them, rather than paying attention to the 'proper' stars. Now, as manager, you become seriously worried. Perhaps it's time to call the police and have them moved on, or even arrested for disturbing the peace . . .

And now we see why it was that things began to escalate in Jerusalem in the days and weeks after Pentecost. It might not have mattered so much if Peter, John and the rest had met, and drawn crowds, far away – in Galilee, say, or out in one of the villages. When Jesus had done that, he caught people's attention all right, but he was able to establish a large following without the Jerusalem authorities worrying particularly about it. (The **Pharisees**, who did keep checking up on Jesus in Galilee, were not the 'official' authorities; they were a self-appointed pressure group.)

But Peter and the others were continuing to meet in one of the great porches of the **Temple**. To understand this, you need to remember that the Temple in Jerusalem was not a single building, like a great church or cathedral. It was more like an entire area of the city, covering doz-ens of acres, walled off and with several gates and porches. There were trees and shrubs and various buildings, houses where the **priests** on duty would lodge during their days of service and, in the middle, the Temple proper, with its sequence of courts leading in towards the holy of holies. So the **apostles** had taken up the habit of worshipping in the Temple and then staying around beside one of the porches where there would be plenty of room for crowds to gather around them. The crowds were coming, as they came to Jesus, for healing, but of course for teaching as well. And we would be right to assume that the teaching continued down the lines of Peter's opening address in Acts 2, drawing together the ancient scriptures, not least the Psalms and the prophets, and the extraordinary new events concerning Jesus.

This was, as we say, 'in your face' as far as the authorities were con-cerned. And this explains what happened next. It also explains why

Luke says that 'none of the others dared to join them', except of course for those who actually became believers themselves. It was a bold gesture, and was bound to draw comment and resentment from the authorities.

But this is where part of the point of the healings comes in. As with Jesus' ministry, so with his followers. The healings were not simply a matter of providing urgent medical care for people who needed it, though that was of course enfolded within the larger purpose. It was a matter of God's power going out and doing new things: a work of new creation, in deep continuity with the original creation, and indeed mending bodies and lives within that original creation, but demonstrating by its power and character that something new was afoot, something in the light of which believing in Jesus' **resurrection** didn't seem such a strange thing after all. (I well remember a conversation with a leading biblical scholar, much older than myself, who told me that for most of his career he had accepted the view that 'the resurrection' was, basically, an event that happened within the minds and hearts of the disciples rather than something that happened to the body of Jesus – until, in his own family and his own body, he had experienced remarkable healing as an answer to the prayers of the church. Suddenly it dawned on him that maybe God really was not only *interested in* restoring creation but actually *capable of doing it*. That is sometimes how it works.) And where new power is at work, even if its results are a matter for celebration – who could resent people being healed, we may ask? – then those who currently hold power are bound to be alarmed. Consider the reaction of the mainstream medical profession to the rise, in our day, of 'alternative' therapies; and imagine how a great modern hospital would react if a clinic offering a quite different style of treatment opened up right outside its front door.

One of the peculiar things about both Jesus' healings and those of the apostles is the way in which, at certain times and places, things seem to happen which don't happen anywhere else. I have no idea why it might be that in Jerusalem, at that time, Peter's shadow falling on people might cause them to be healed, and why we don't hear any more about that kind of thing; just as I have no idea why it should be that in Ephesus, later in the story (19.12), handkerchiefs were taken from Paul's body and laid on the sick to make them well, which again doesn't seem to have happened anywhere else. There is always a strange unknown quality about God's healing. In our 'democratic' age we tend to suppose that if God is going to do anything at all it would only be fair that he would do it all the same for everybody, but things just don't seem to work like that. I have no idea (if it comes to that) why, in a few chapters' time, James is killed and Peter escapes.

All of that is part of the mystery of living at the overlap between the **present age**, with its griefs and sorrows and decay and death, and the **age to come**, with its new **life** and energy and restorative power. I don't think it has anything much to do with the devotion or holiness of those involved. In the apostolic age they seem simply to have accepted that God can do whatever he pleases and that, when people pray and trust him, he will often do much more than we dare to imagine – while accepting also that frequently things don't work out as we would like, that people still get sick and die (nobody imagined that the healing offered by Peter, any more than that offered by Jesus, made people immortal!), and that many sad and tragic things continue to happen for which we have no particular explanation.

Thus the fact of so many people coming to Jerusalem and being cured was not simply a matter of a sudden burst of healing energy. It was about (and everyone there knew it was about) the establishment of a new reality in a dangerous place: the power of the living God becoming concrete, definite, undeniable, not simply a matter of a few people telling a very strange story and behaving from time to time as if they were drunk. It is when the church, through prayer and wisdom and often in the teeth of opposition, acts with decisive power in the real world – to build and run a successful school, or medical clinic; to free slaves or remit debts; to establish a housing project for those who can't afford local rents, or a credit union for those ashamed to go into a bank; to enable drug users and pushers to kick the habit and the lifestyle; to see hardened and violent criminals transformed by God's love – that people will take the **message** of Jesus seriously. Of course there will then be opposition, because we shall be invading territory that is currently under alternative occupation. But God's power will be at work, and people will know it.

ACTS 5.17–26

The Words of This Life

[17]Then the high priest got up, and all who were with him, namely the group called the 'Sadducees'. They were filled with righteous indignation, [18]and seized the apostles and put them in the public jail. [19]But an angel of the Lord came in the night, opened the prison doors, and brought them out.

[20]'Go and take your stand in the Temple', he said, 'and speak all the words of this Life to the people.'

[21]When they heard this, they went in at early morning and began to teach.

When the high priest arrived with his entourage, they called the official Assembly and all the elders of the children of Israel, and they sent to the prison to have the apostles brought in. [22]But when the attendants went, they didn't find them in the prison. So they came and reported back.

[23]'We found the jail shut up with maximum security', they said, 'and the guards were standing in front of the doors. But when we opened up we found nobody inside.'

[24]When they heard these words, the commander of the Temple police and the chief priests were at a loss about them, with no idea what had happened. [25]But then someone came with a message for them.

'Look!' he said. 'The men you put in prison are standing in the Temple and teaching the people!'

[26]Then the commander went with his attendants and brought them. They didn't use force, though, because they were afraid that the people might stone them.

When our second child was born, we had decided on names. If it was a boy, it would be Oliver; if it was a girl, it would be Emily. Well, it was a girl (we got our Oliver later); but when we looked at her, we both knew she wasn't Emily. Who was she? Puzzled, we racked our brains.

'What's she called?' asked the nurse as we went back to the ward.

'We don't know!' we replied. 'We'll tell you in a while.'

We sat there with this little scrap in her cot, and went right back through our long list, alphabetically. When we arrived at the Rs, we knew who she was. It didn't feel as though we were making something up; it was more as if we were discovering something that was already true. Rosamund. A beautiful name for a beautiful young lady.

Sometimes, when people want to give a name to a new building, or a new business company, or even a new town, they have a competition. People sit round and think it out and come up with bright ideas.

One of the fascinating things about Acts is that nobody knew what to call the new movement. Even the angels seem to have had trouble with it. It wasn't called 'Christianity' for quite some time; indeed, it's only in chapter 11, when the movement has reached some non-Jews up north in Syria, that anyone calls the followers of Jesus 'Christians', that is, '**Messiah**-people'. Even so, there is still a bewildering variety of names and descriptions given not just to the **apostles** and their larger company but to the movement itself, to the fact that something new was happening. Later on we find it referred to as 'the Way'. Here, for the only time, but significantly, it is referred to as 'this **Life**'. 'Go and stand in the **Temple**,' said the angel, 'and speak to the people *all the words of this Life.*'

It's a strange way to put it but we can see what was meant. What the apostles were doing was quite simply to *live* in a wholly new way. Nobody had lived like this before; that, indeed, was one of the extraordinary challenges which impinged on people as the **gospel** set off around the wider world. This was 'a way of life', as we say, that people hadn't ever tried. In fact, nobody had ever imagined it.

But of course it wasn't just 'a way of life' in the sense of 'a way of conducting your personal day-to-day living', though it was that – a way which involved living as 'family' with all those who shared your belief in Jesus, a way which involved a radically new attitude to property and particularly to the sacred symbol of the holy land, a way which meant that, though you would still worship in the Temple, the centre of your life before God came when you broke bread in individual houses, in remembrance and invocation of Jesus. It was all of that, but it was much more. It was 'a way of Life' in the sense that Life itself had come to life in quite a new way; a force of Life had broken through the normally absolute barrier of death, and had burst into the present world of decay and corruption as a new principle, a new possibility, a new power. And it was this Life, of course, which was carrying the apostles along with it, like a strong wind driving sailing boats out across a wild sea.

And this Life had to be spoken as well as lived. 'Go and speak to all the people *the words* of this Life.' Of course the words had to be rooted in the reality of the way the apostles were living, and the work of healing they were doing. But wordless symbols, however powerful, remain open to a variety of explanation. From the very beginning, the apostolic **faith** has been something that demands to be explained, that needs to be taught. There is much to say, because people fill their heads with all kinds of half-truths or downright untruths. Things need to be spelled out carefully step by step: who Jesus was and is, what God did through him, how it all drew to its head the long scriptural story of God's people, what it all meant in terms of the long-awaited '**kingdom of God**'. As we shall see in the next chapter, it was one of the two primary tasks to which the apostles were called (the other of course being prayer). People sometimes scoff at the wordiness of Christianity, and it is of course all too possible for people to go on and on about not very much. But without the words to guide it, faith wanders in the dark and can easily fall over a cliff. The angel didn't just get the apostles out of prison; they were given specific instructions for an urgent continuing task. 'Go and speak to the people all the words of this Life.' We don't even know, yet, what to call it, but you've got to get on and speak it.

And this was of course even more 'in your face' as far as the authorities were concerned. We shouldn't be surprised, granted what had happened so far (and the provocative fact that the apostles were meeting, in increasing numbers, literally on the doorstep of the Temple), that the **high priest** and his aristocratic family and colleagues would regard the movement as a direct threat to their status, power and importance. (They would of course have said it differently; they would have said that it was a direct threat to the honour of God and the proper reverence for God's House, the Temple.) Luke uses a particular word to describe how they felt, a word which we need to unpack a bit.

They were, he says, filled with 'righteous indignation'. The word I have translated that way is often simply expressed as 'zeal'; but 'zeal' to a first-century Jew didn't just mean what it means to us. With us, it means a fervent, enthusiastic approach to whatever is going on: a base-ball coach makes a 'zealous attempt' to enthuse the team, a politician becomes 'very zealous' for a particular reform she is championing, and so on. But with first-century Jews 'zeal' had a very specific meaning. It was 'zeal for the honour of God'. When you cashed this out, it often meant 'zeal for the purity of the Temple and the land'. And, particularly in the case of the **Pharisees** (as we shall see with Saul of Tarsus), it meant 'zeal for the **law**'. In other words, they were all aware that their God was a holy God, who had called Israel to be his special people, a people gathered around the symbols of Temple, land, law and family identity. Anything that challenged those symbols was a challenge to God, and had to be resisted 'zealously'. Only if we grasp that will we understand what is going on at this moment and in several later moments.

The present challenge was all about the power of the **Sadducees** and the chief **priests**. They had this power because they were the guardians of the central shrine, the holiest spot on earth. They could not simply allow the apostles to carry on the way they were doing. God's hon-our would be compromised; Israel would be led astray; disaster might strike. These people had to be stopped. And so the authorities did their best. They had efficient police and secure jails. But one of the things we find in Acts is that there are no locked doors in the kingdom of God.

This, too, is sometimes a real puzzle. Why does Paul languish in jail for two whole years (Acts 24.27), when he ought to be on his way to Rome, and when God is capable of sending an angel and letting people free? This is the kind of mystery we have to get used to. It's no use pretending that, because that's what 'ought to have happened', maybe nothing at all happened, no angel, no release, no puzzlement of guards (another echo there, this time of Jesus' own **resurrection**). That kind of dog-in-the-manger theology won't get us anywhere, and reduces Acts and indeed the whole New Testament to a pile of irrel-evant old mumblings. The apostles were teaching 'the words of this Life'; the authorities were increasingly worried that they were under-mining the very fabric of Judaism as they had known it, and so were desperate to prevent them taking things any further. But, as the next passage reveals, they were in danger of fighting, not against a human movement, but against God himself.

ACTS 5.27–42

Human Inventions and Divine Instructions

[27]So they brought them and stood them in the Assembly. The high priest questioned them.

[28]'We gave you strict orders, didn't we?' he demanded. 'We told you not to teach in this Name, and look what you're doing! You have filled Jerusalem with your teaching, and you're trying to bring this man's blood on us!'

[29]'We must obey God, not human beings!' responded Peter and the apostles. [30]'The God of our ancestors raised Jesus, after you had laid violent hands on him and hanged him on a tree. [31]God exalted him to his right hand as Leader and Saviour, to give repentance to Israel and forgiveness of sins. [32]We are witnesses of these things, and so is the holy spirit, which God gave to those who obey him.'

[33]When they heard this, they were infuriated, and wanted to kill them. [34]But then a Pharisee by the name of Gamaliel stood up in the Assembly. He was a law-teacher, highly respected by all the people. He ordered the men to be put outside for a short while.

[35]'Men of Israel,' he said to the gathering, 'be careful what you do to these men. [36]Before these times Theudas rose up, claiming to be someone special, and about four hundred men went off to join him. But he was killed, and all the people who had trusted him were dispersed. The movement came to nothing. [37]After that, Judas the Galilean arose, in the days of the Census, and drew a crowd after himself. But he was killed, and all those who trusted him were scattered. [38]So my advice to you now is this. Leave off from these men; let them be. You see, if this plan or this work is of merely human origin, it will come to ruin. [39]But if it's from God – well, you won't be able to stop them. You might even be found to be fighting against God!'

They were persuaded by him, [40]and they called the apostles back in. They beat them and told them not to speak in the name of Jesus. Then they let them go. [41]They, however, went out from the presence of the Assembly celebrating, because they had been reckoned worthy to suffer disgrace for the Name. [42]And all day, in the Temple and from house to house, they did not stop teaching and proclaiming Jesus as the Messiah.

We stared at the parcel as it lay on the floor inside the front door. Nobody had heard the delivery man. Nobody knew why it had arrived at this time of the day. The parcel was bulky, somewhat misshapen, with various semi-legible scrawlings on various labels. It looked as if it had been wrongly delivered somewhere else and then, through different addresses crossed out and replaced, had found its way to us.

'The key thing is,' said one of the children, 'where has it come *from*?'

It was just at the time when the newspapers were full of terrorist threats, of parcel bombs being delivered to unlikely places, of warnings about suspicious packages. There was no particular reason why anyone should target *us*, of all people, but you never know, and conspiracy theories are always more attractive than boring or obvious answers.

We poked and prodded it. Eventually someone spotted a small scribble round the back. It was the name of a place we had visited some months before. At once light dawned. It wasn't a bomb, or anything else suspicious. It was the winter clothes we had had for a particular foreign visit. We hadn't needed them on the rest of the trip, so we'd left them to be parcelled up and sent back to us by slow freight.

The key thing is, where has this come *from*? That was the question which the Jerusalem leaders were faced with as they thought, angrily and resentfully, about this new call-it-what-you-will movement ('this **Life**', 'the Way', or whatever). This, interestingly, was a question Jesus himself had faced, not about his own ministry (though that was implied as well), but about **John the Baptist**: where had all that come from? Was it from God, or was it a purely human invention (Luke 20.1–7)? Had John the Baptist had a genuine call from God, or did he just wake up one day and think, of his own initiative, that it might be a good idea to splash water over people and say that God's **kingdom** was on the way? And the question, naturally, had direct practical implications. If God wasn't in the movement, then it was leading people astray and ought to be stopped. But if God was working through it, *then it meant that God's kingdom really was on the way, and in a surprising and disturbing manner.* There was no third option.

The chief **priests**, of course, were quite clear that God simply couldn't be in 'this Life', this subversive new gang who were going around talking about Jesus and getting everybody excited. For a start, they weren't operating through the proper channels. Everybody knew that God lived in the **Temple** and worked through it to bring **forgiveness** and **salvation** to his people. For another thing, the **apostles** were going on telling people that Jesus had been crucified because they, the crowds and their leaders, had sent him to his death, and were insisting that people should repent of that as a kind of basic sin; in other words, the chief priests, instead of being the people who told everyone else how to behave, were being labelled as the chief sinners! Clearly they couldn't let this sort of thing go on. So they brought the apostles back from the Temple and questioned them again.

Peter's answer only serves to enrage them even more (verse 33). He insists, as he did before (4.19), that they are faced with a challenge: shall we obey God, or shall we obey the authorities? This question stands in interesting parallel to the question of Luke 20.1–7 and then Acts 5.38–39: is the movement from God, or from human initiative? Shall we obey God, or shall we obey human authorities? It is the question which Jesus still poses, both to those outside the faith (was he from God, or was he a deluded fanatic?) and to those inside the **faith** (shall we compromise our allegiance to him by going along with human instructions that cut against the **gospel**, or shall we remain loyal even at the risk of civil disobedience?). Luke, in telling the fast-paced and dramatic story of the early days, is also putting down some markers for how Christians have to think through issues from that day to this.

Interestingly, just as nobody in the early days quite knew what to call the new movement, so nobody seems to have had a single definite idea of how to refer to Jesus himself. By the time Paul is writing his letters, about 20 or 30 years after the time we are now reading about, things have settled down: Jesus is the **Messiah** ('**Christ**'), the Lord, the Saviour. But at this stage they were still ransacking various possibilities to try to say who he was and what he'd done. Peter declares that 'the God of our ancestors' (in other words, don't imagine this is a different God we are talking about, we are not leading Israel astray after strange divinities, we are being deeply loyal to the highest Jewish traditions) has raised up Jesus and exalted him as 'Leader and Saviour'. Leader, because he has pioneered the way into God's new creation, and is drawing people into that new world where **heaven** and earth overlap – as people had thought heaven and earth overlapped in the Temple, but now in a quite new way. Saviour, because he has broken through the power of death itself and is therefore ready to rescue people not only from that ultimate enemy but from such other enemies, whether sickness, oppression, persecution or imprisonment, as they may face from time to time.

Peter rubs it in: this Jesus, the one you handed over to be killed, is now offering a new start for his people Israel. He will give them **repentance** and forgiveness of sins – the very things the Temple was supposed to provide; and now here was Peter, an upstart from Galilee, telling the Temple authorities that *they* needed it and that the Jesus he was proclaiming would give it to them! Once again, we are not surprised that the issue of the Temple, and its status in God's newly unfolding plan, would come to a head within a chapter or two. But, on the way, we must note the point that 'repentance' itself is not simply something humans do, as though to persuade God to be gracious to them. Repentance itself remains a gift from God, something the **holy spirit** brings about (see too 11.18). There is another mystery here, but it's one the early Christians lived with, and indeed lived by.

What Peter said was easily provocative enough to have the authorities kill them all on the spot, if they could have got away with it. What happens next is a surprise – though not so much as we get to know the underlying story which Luke is telling, because again and again he insists that, though various authorities want to do away with the early leaders, there is a twist which brings them out safely after all. Sometimes it's an angel letting people out of prison; sometimes it's a little boy hearing about a plot just in time to thwart it; sometimes, as here, it's a thoughtful outsider who points out the disturbing truth to the people who are about to do violence.

Gamaliel is well known from Jewish sources of this period and later. He was remembered as one of the greatest **rabbis** of all time, a man of exemplary devotion and piety, who knew the law forwards, backwards, inside out and upside down, and taught it to all who would sit at his feet – including, as we shall see, Saul of Tarsus (see 22.3). At this stage there were two great schools of interpretation of the **law**, which had been pioneered by the famous teachers of the generation before the time of Jesus, Shammai and Hillel. Shammai always tended to take the hard line, politically as well as in strict legal application: one had to be zealous for the law in all possible ways, and if that meant using violence against those who broke the law or questioned it, so be it. That's what Phinehas and Elijah had done in the ancient scriptures (Numbers 25; 1 Kings 18), and that's what had to be done today. Hillel, however, had taken a different line. What God wants is for Israel to keep his law. Since that is a matter of the heart, we don't need to fight people to establish it. We will follow God's law, but we will let other people do what they think is right. Live and let live.

Gamaliel was, clearly, a follower of Hillel – though at least one of his hot-headed **disciples** wasn't satisfied with that, as we shall see. On this occasion he spells out the principle clearly. There have been, he points out, other movements, other rebellions, other uprisings in the recent past. Gamaliel hasn't got it all quite straight: Theudas and Judas pretty certainly came in the other order and, though Judas' followers were scattered at the time, they regrouped, found new leaders from within Judas' own family, and continued as a revolutionary movement for another 40 years. But the principle is clear: if this is a human invention, it will fall by its own weight, but if it's from God, beware. And since at the moment you can't tell which it is (the chief priests probably thought they could, but Gamaliel's wise words won the day with the larger Assembly), you'd better leave it alone.

The church can never anticipate who will suddenly speak up for our right to exist, and to preach and teach about Jesus. Our job is to be faithful and, when a clash comes, to obey God rather than human authorities. We may have to suffer, whether actual violence as they did (verses 40–41), or simply sneering and mockery. Either way, we have to hold cheerfully to our course. If we really believe that God has raised Jesus, then the question Gamaliel left open, as to whether God is with us or not, has been decided once and for all.

ACTS 6.1–7

Problems of Family Living

¹Around that time, as the number of disciples increased, the 'Hellenists' raised a dispute with the 'Hebrews' because their widows were being overlooked in the daily distribution of food. ²So the Twelve called the whole crowd of disciples together.

'Listen', they said. 'It wouldn't be right for us to leave the word of God to wait on tables. ³So, brothers and sisters, choose seven men from among yourselves who are well spoken of and filled with the spirit and wisdom. We will put them in charge of what needs to be done in this matter. ⁴We will continue to pay attention to prayer and to the ministry of the word.'

⁵The whole gathering was pleased with what they said. They chose Stephen, a man full of faith and the holy spirit, and Philip, Prochorus, Nicanor, Timon, Parmenas and Nicolaus (a proselyte from Antioch). ⁶They presented them before the apostles, who prayed and laid their hands on them.

⁷The word of God increased, and the number of disciples in Jerusalem grew by leaps and bounds. This included a large crowd of priests who became obedient to the faith.

Late one night there was a knock at the door. It was a good friend of ours. His hat was on crooked and he had wild excitement in his face.

'It's twins!' he shouted as we ushered him in. 'We had no idea! Two girls! The doctors hadn't spotted it! The first one was born, just fine, and then they said there was another one in there!'

He could hardly contain his excitement. But when he calmed down he began to reflect on the new problem.

'We've only got one cot', he said. 'There's only one set of everything. Suddenly we have to go out and get a whole second kit. We never bargained for this!'

I had the joy of baptizing the twin girls some months later. And I was reminded of the story of that night by thinking of the problem the

apostles faced so early in the movement. Actually, it reminded me of another story as well.

A friend of mine, a famous publisher, once asked me to write a book called *Jesus at Sixty*. I was puzzled, so he explained what he meant. Jesus, he said, was a young visionary. He had a dream and went about sharing it. Everyone was excited. But if he'd lived another 20 or 30 years, instead of being killed so soon, his movement would have grown and he'd have had to get into administration. He'd have had to work out how to organize things, to delegate, to have rules and systems, and generally to do all the things that middle-aged people do which take the shine off their early vision and enthusiasm.

I refused to write the book (with some frustration, because we were very short of cash at the time and he was offering an advance). I did suggest that I write a different one, explaining why that wasn't the sort of task Jesus had in mind, but he wasn't interested. And of course, as this chapter demonstrates, it wouldn't have taken another 30 years, until Jesus had been 60, before serious questions of organization came up. Already, in these early days, Jesus' followers faced problems about how to run things.

What was the problem, and why had it arisen?

As we saw at the end of chapters 2 and 4, those who were following Jesus had, from the beginning, shared their resources. This wasn't just a primitive form of communism. Nor was it a sign (as some have suggested) that they thought the world was going to end very soon, so they wouldn't be needing property any more. No: it was, rather, a sign that they knew they were called to live *as a single family*. They were the nucleus of God's renewed Israel. (This, we recall, was why they had carefully chosen a replacement for Judas, so that the idea of '**the Twelve**', the foundation of this renewed people, would remain firmly in place.) Like any family in that world, and many in today's world, they would all own everything together.

But how is that going to work when the family is suddenly double the size you expected it to be – like the surprising twins? How are you going to cope? You're going to have to sort something out pretty quickly. And the pressure in the early movement came to a head, not surprisingly, along a fault-line which would continue to be a problem for many years to come: the subtle distinctions between people from different ethnic or linguistic groupings, and the question of their relative status within the new movement.

The problem came to a head over the treatment of widows. This shows that already in the early church the question of 'living as a single family' had clear negative as well as positive implications: normally, widows would be taken care of among their own blood-relations, but those family ties appear to have been cut when people joined the new movement. As in some parts of the world to this day, **baptism** meant saying goodbye to an existing family as well as being welcomed into a new one. And the new one therefore had to take on the obligations of the old. That, by the way, is why we find regulations being drawn up about such things in 1 Timothy 5.3–16. Some have speculated that the problem was exacerbated, in the case of the early church, because many Jewish couples would come from far and wide in the Jewish 'Diaspora' (the dispersion of Jews all around the known world) to live in and around Jerusalem in old age so that, eventually, they could be buried in the vicinity. The husband might then die, leaving a dispro-portionate number of widows from different geographical origins all in the neighbourhood of Jerusalem.

Whatever we think about that, the distinction in verse 1 between 'Hellenists' and 'Hebrews' is probably one of those things with a variety of elements mixed together. Nobody had planned for a complex and intricate welfare system. It had been invented on the hoof, when there were other things (such as persecution by the authorities) to think about. It would be surprising if such a system could proceed without difficulties. And in a complex society such as that in Jerusalem, which was both a deeply traditional culture, very conscious of its historic and religious significance, and a cosmopolitan mixture of Jews from all over the world, it is not surprising that people would be eyeing one another to see if this or that group appeared to be taking advantage.

So those who were native-born Palestinian Jews (i.e. from Galilee or Judaea), who spoke Aramaic as their mother tongue, might well feel they had more in common with one another, especially in a world where many women would only speak one language, than they did with the Greek-speaking folk who had come from the wider world where Greek was at least everyone's second language and often their first. Most of these women were Jews, it seems, not proselytes (a proselyte is a non-Jew who has decided to become Jewish, renounc-ing paganism and, in the case of men, becoming **circumcised**). The awkward question of bringing Jews and non-Jews together in the same family would arise soon enough; the present crisis seems to have been a small-scale anticipation of it. Whenever even a small number of peo-ple try to live together, let alone to share resources, sometimes even tiny distinctions of background and culture can loom very large and have serious consequences.

In the present case, the apostles were quite clear what they should *not* do. They shouldn't at once rush to do the work themselves. Like Moses in Exodus 18, faced with an administrative crisis – and that may, indeed, be a parallel not entirely absent from Luke's mind – they must *delegate*. Jesus, after all, had shared his ministry with them in various ways, and there was every reason to draw in a wider circle of people to active and recognized work. In particular, if there was a problem about people from different linguistic and cultural backgrounds, why then it made sense to include in the work, front and centre, people who shared the background of those who had felt they were being treated as second-class citizens. And so it came to be. Stephen, Philip and the others became the first 'deacons' in the church. (That title, originally simply a word meaning 'servants', has come to have several other meanings attached to it in various later Christian traditions.)

The heart of the apostles' reasoning in all this was *the priority of the* **word** *of God and prayer*. Only when a crisis emerges do we see what is really important. We noted earlier that 'the apostles' teaching' was top of the list of the defining marks of the church (2.42), and that the apostles, faced with persecution, were instructed by the angel to 'go and speak the words of this **Life**' (5.20). The temptation for leaders in the movement, from the earliest days until now, has always been to heave a sigh of relief at being spared the spiritually and mentally demanding task of preaching and teaching, of explaining scripture, opening up its great narrative and its tiny details, applying it this way and that, enabling people to live within its story and make its energy their own. Running committees, though tricky at times, is not nearly so demanding. Sometimes people even dismiss the ministry of biblical teaching as a kind of optional extra for those who like that kind of thing. But the early apostolic testimony stands solidly: the task of an apostle is the word of God and prayer. Interestingly, it is at the end of this passage that Luke introduces another of his regular ways of talking about how the **gospel** message spread: 'the word of God', he says, 'increased'. He says something similar in 12.24; and Paul talks like this too, in, for instance, Colossians 1.5–6 and 1 Thessalonians 2.13. In all these cases we may suspect that there are strong Old Testament roots, for instance in Isaiah 55.10–13.

This whole way of talking about God's word is a gentle reminder that however much work anyone puts into the task of expounding scripture, into teaching the **message** of Jesus which stands on the shoulders of the biblical witness, into explaining and applying the whole thing, it is still God's work, not the preacher's or teacher's. Making 'the word of God' as it were a kind of autonomous agent is, if you like, a way of keeping the apostles in their place. They are not 'growing the church'; God is growing the church, and using their ministry of teaching and preaching as the primary way of doing so.

The fact that they mention prayer in the same breath in verse 4 is highly significant. Of course, all Christians are called to pray, to make time for it, to soak everything that they do in it. But the apostles cite it as a reason why they can't get involved in the organization of daily distribution to those in need. That implies, not that those who do the distribution can do without prayer, but that the apostles must give themselves to far, far more prayer. Here, along with the challenge to a ministry of teaching and preaching, is a quiet but explosive hint to all leaders in today's and tomorrow's church.

ACTS 6.8–15

Stephen Becomes a Target (See map 5, page xvii.)

[8]Stephen was filled with grace and power, and performed great signs and wonders among the people. [9]But some from the 'Freemen's Synagogue', as it was named, and from Cyrene, Alexandria, Cilicia and Asia, stood up and disputed with Stephen. [10]They could not, however, resist the wisdom and the spirit with which he spoke.

[11]Then they put up men to say, 'We heard this man speaking blasphemous words against Moses and against God!' [12]They aroused the people, the elders and the scribes. They set upon him, seized him, and took him in front of the Assembly. [13]They set up false witnesses to say, 'This man never stops speaking words against this holy place and the law! [14]We heard him say that this Jesus the Nazorean will destroy this place, and change the customs which Moses handed down to us!'

[15]Everyone who was sitting in the Assembly looked hard at Stephen. They all saw that his face was like the face of an angel.

Without in any way wishing to complain, I do have a fellow feeling with Stephen in this passage. He has only just been appointed a 'deacon', with particular responsibility for helping organize the daily distribution of food to the community that was dependent on the 'new family' of those who believed in Jesus. Like some of the others, he has found himself caught up, not only in administration, but also now in a wider and more active ministry of healing and teaching. (You never know, once you lay hands on people and pray for God to work through them, what new things they will get up to, or rather what new things God will do through them!) But, almost at once, he is embroiled in controversy. And all kinds of accusations start being hurled at him.

That's where my fellow feeling comes in. Far be it from me to pretend that I make no mistakes, or that all my own teaching is an exact account of what scripture says and what we must understand by it today. I wish it was and am always ready to learn new things and understand the Bible better. But I have observed the way in which, in some circles, there are standard charges which are thrown around at people who dare to say things which their hearers don't expect. In my world, people of a traditional turn of mind are often on the lookout for anyone 'going soft' on the affirmation of Jesus' full divinity; on the full meaning of his death on the cross; on the promise of his **second coming**; and on some key doctrines, like 'justification by **faith**'. And, if they hear something they hadn't heard before, even if it doesn't have anything to do with any of these topics, they will readily jump to the conclusion that the speaker (for instance, myself) 'must' really be denying one of these cherished doctrines. For the record, I don't; I affirm them all. (A few days after writing this paragraph I received an email from someone I didn't know informing me that a professor in another country was going about saying that Tom Wright didn't really believe in the Trinity. That, too, is ridiculous.)

Meanwhile, people of a more radical turn of mind are often on the lookout for anyone denying some of the currently fashionable teachings about politics and ethics, or affirming anything that looks to them like old-fashioned, uncritical Bible-thumping. Offer the slightest suggestion that you really do hold to a traditional line on several key topics, and all the rhetoric comes tumbling out: you're a conservative, a fundamentalist, a reactionary, you probably hate women, you're leading us back to the Dark Ages. (For the record, I'm not.)

Now these things are unimportant in themselves, except as a sad but predictable index of the way in which, as in several previous generations, people today find real debate about actual topics difficult, and much prefer the parody of debate which consists of giving a dog a bad name and then beating him for it, and lashing out, too, at anyone who associates with the dog you happen to be beating at the time. There is far too much of that in the church, and the only answer is more listening, more actual thinking, and more careful and humble speaking. But with Stephen things became very hot very quickly; because, as any first-century Jew could have told you, there were certain key things, certain symbols of what it meant to be God's people in the midst of a wicked pagan world, and it was absolutely vital that all Jews stuck by them come what may. And anyone who started saying anything different was immediately pounced upon and accused of straightforwardly denying what all good Jews knew perfectly well they ought to be affirming.

There were (as I've said before) four key symbols of Judaism in the period. There was the **Temple** itself; the **law** ('**Torah**' in Hebrew); the holy land, focused on Jerusalem and the Temple; and the national ethnic identity, the family of all Jews (and proselytes). And, behind all this, and assumed to be involved in it all, was the question of God himself. At a time when the swirling, polyglot world of ancient paganism was all around (Judaea and Galilee were in this respect part of the general world of the ancient Near East, not a quiet haven from which pagan presence and ideas had been banished!), all loyal Jews knew they had to stick by the God of Abraham, Isaac and Jacob, and not to have any truck with compromise, with fancy new ideas which could and would only lead to following idols, blaspheming nonsenses. So, whenever Stephen spoke, out came the accusations: you're undermining the law of Moses! You're speaking against the Temple! And, behind it all, 'You're blaspheming God!'

Now of course, as we shall see in the extraordinary speech Stephen makes in his defence, there is a grain of truth in the first two at least, seen from the point of view of a hard-line first-century Jew (someone, say, like Saul of Tarsus). But the early Christian claim always was *that the God of our ancestors, in fulfilment of the purposes for which he gave the law and the Temple in the first place, is now doing a new thing.* Paul had to wrestle with this over and over again. His thinking was misunderstood in the first century, and has been on and off ever since, by people who find it easier to deal in simple, clunky affirmations and denials rather than appreciating that the **word** of God itself tells a *story* which is moving forward and, quite deliberately and necessarily, getting to new points as it does so. The story of my journey from here to London includes walking to the car, driving to the station, taking the train, and then, when I arrive in London, getting on the underground. The fact that when I get to the train I leave the car behind, or that when I get to the underground I leave the train behind, or that when I get to my destination I stop travelling altogether, doesn't mean that the car, the train or the underground were bad things, or that I wish I hadn't used them. It means that they are good things and I'm glad I did. That is the kind of point which Stephen, and later Paul, made all the time. God really did give the law and the Temple, but this was part of a great story which has now reached a new point. But this regularly fell, and falls, on deaf ears.

Stephen, it seems, was at home in the wider world of Greek-speaking Jews. Such people were by no means necessarily 'soft' on the law and the Temple when compared with their Aramaic-speaking, native-Judaean, Jewish cousins. Far from it. As Paul found on his travels, sometimes the people who live further away from the centre geographically are all the more insistent on the cultural symbols by which they mark themselves out from their pagan neighbours (like English people abroad insisting on having tea at four o'clock even though not many people in England itself do so any more). But what has happened with the preaching of Stephen represents a new and wider venture within the early movement. Up to now, it seems (though of course Luke may well have omitted all sorts of other intermediate stages; we simply don't know), the followers of Jesus were simply taking their stand day by day in the Temple porches and teaching people as and when they could. Their main catchment area, and hence their main opposition, was within the Temple itself. But Stephen was going around Greek-speaking synagogues within the Jerusalem area, and the people he was speaking to weren't trying to defend a position of power, since they didn't have any. They were defending a world-view, a way of looking at things which coloured their whole life. And they saw the proclamation of Jesus as a threat to that whole way of thinking and living.

Luke tells us two things about Stephen in the midst of all this. We already know he was a man of the **spirit**, faith and wisdom (verses 3 and 5). Now we discover that this was put to good effect in debate, even when surrounded by hostile audiences (verse 10): they were not able to controvert him, because he kept coming up with excellent arguments, with the conviction and power of the spirit, to support what he was saying. When people are faced with this kind of thing, they have a choice. Either admit he's probably right, or throw as much mud as you can at him. They chose the latter. And soon it wasn't just mud.

But the second thing was this. Stephen was hauled before the official Assembly, the top legal body known as the Sanhedrin. But he seemed to have changed. They all stared at him. His face looked like the face of an angel. Now I have no idea how you know, in advance as it were, what an angel's face looks like. I doubt if the Assembly could have told you, either. But perhaps what we are meant to understand is that there was a kind of light, illuminating Stephen from the inside. A kind of serenity, humble and unostentatious, but confident and assured. In the middle of arguments, controversies, false accusations, and now a serious charge before the highest court, he found himself standing, as the Temple claimed to stand, at the overlap of **heaven** and earth. The speech he was about to make, and the death he was about to suffer, were simply the final stages in his own travelling, his journey of witness to the risen Jesus, and to the word of God which provided the explanation of what Jesus was all about.

ACTS 7.1-16

Stephen Tells the Story

¹The high priest addressed Stephen.

'Are these things true?' he said.

²'My brothers and fathers,' replied Stephen, 'please give me a hearing.

'The God of glory appeared to our father Abraham when he was in Mesopotamia, before he moved to live in Haran. ³"Leave your land and your family," he said to him, "and go to the land which I will show you." ⁴So he left the land of the Chaldeans and went to live in Haran. Then, from there, after his father's death, God moved him on to this land in which you now live. ⁵God didn't give him an inheritance here, not even a place to stand up in. Instead, he promised (when Abraham still had no child) that he would give it as a possession to his seed after him. ⁶This is what God said to him: that his seed would be strangers in a foreign land, that they would serve there as slaves, and that they would be afflicted for four hundred years. ⁷But God said that he would judge the nation that had enslaved them, and that they would then come out and worship him "on this mountain". ⁸And he gave them the covenant of circumcision. So Abraham became the father of Isaac, and he circumcised him on the eighth day. Isaac became the father of Jacob, and Jacob the father of the twelve patriarchs.

⁹'Now the patriarchs became angry with Joseph, and were jealous of him. They sold him into Egypt. But God was with him, ¹⁰and rescued him from all his troubles and gave him grace and wisdom before Pharaoh, king of Egypt, making him ruler over Egypt and over all his household. ¹¹But then there was a famine over the whole of Egypt and Canaan, which resulted in great hardship. Our ancestors couldn't find food to eat. ¹²Jacob, however, heard that there was grain in Egypt, and sent our ancestors there on an initial visit. ¹³On their second trip, Joseph made himself known to his brothers, and revealed to Pharaoh what family he was from. ¹⁴So Joseph sent and summoned Jacob his father and all the family, seventy-five people in all. ¹⁵Jacob came to Egypt, and he and our ancestors died there. ¹⁶They were brought back to Shechem, and buried in the tomb which Abraham had bought with silver, at a named price, from the sons of Hamor in Shechem.'

One of the most obvious differences between cricket and baseball is the way the ball is projected towards the person who is trying to hit it. As most people will know, the person who 'pitches' in baseball stands on a single spot, where he (or she; but let's stick with professional male sport for the sake of argument) swings round and hurls the ball, with a jerky movement of the arm, towards the person with the bat. In cricket, that would be strictly illegal: not the standing on one spot, but the jerk of the arm. That's 'throwing'. In cricket, you have to 'bowl', with the arm coming over straight all the time, like the top part of a wheel, letting go of the ball just after the highest point so that it comes from there down towards the batsman.

It's quite hard to bowl while standing still – or at least to bowl with any skill, speed or cunning, all of which are important. So almost all bowlers, throughout the history of the game, have taken a run, in a careful build-up, to the point where they have to deliver the ball, and then, within the rhythm of the whole run (which can be 15 paces or even more), the bowling action follows, getting its energy and direction from that run-up. And therefore the run-up itself becomes enormously important. A bowler will carefully pace it out, and mark it out, before starting, because if you get the run-up wrong – like someone doing the long jump, or the triple jump, in track and field athletics – the whole thing will be inefficient, out of rhythm, jerky and useless. Often, when a bowler is having difficulties, you will see him pace out his run again, and even try it out once or twice, so that he lands at exactly the right spot, from exactly the right angle, and at exactly the right speed. If he gets any of those even slightly wrong, the ball won't do what he wants it to do.

Now that's a trivial illustration to make a very serious point, serious for us as we grapple with the nature of the Bible, extremely serious for Stephen as he stood up to defend himself against charges which, if they stuck, would likely call for the death penalty. He had been accused of speaking against the **Temple** and the **law**; of saying that Jesus would destroy the Temple and change the customs which Moses had given, heavy as those customs were with cultural and religious symbolic significance. How was he to respond?

He could simply have waved the charges away. They are obviously false. He hasn't been saying that at all. Or he could have avoided them and used the opportunity to speak about Jesus himself, about his cruel death and astonishing **resurrection**, about the future hope of the renewal of all things which was now coming true in him. Instead, he takes the bull by the horns and goes for the big picture. What you need, he says, is to rework your run-up. Tell the story again from the very beginning and get it right this time. Pace out the whole journey, from Abraham onwards, so that you arrive at the present moment at exactly the right speed and from exactly the right angle. Then, and only then, will you understand who Jesus is, and what I and my friends, who believe in him, have and haven't been saying. In delivering this speech, Stephen (and Luke, in highlighting it so prominently) is doing something which many other Jews of the time were doing, in line with a long biblical tradition (e.g. Nehemiah 9; Daniel 9; Psalms 105 and 106; and, in the first century, the major works of Josephus and sundry other Jewish writings).

This explains why much of the speech doesn't seem to be a direct answer to the charges made against Stephen. What we have to do is to listen carefully, to see the way he is telling the whole story, and to note which points, out of the thousands of different things that one could deduce as 'the moral' from different bits of the story, he wants to high-light. Instead of a head-on rebuttal of the charges, he has chosen a kind of outflanking movement. Tell the story *this* way, he is saying, and you will see what I am saying about Jesus and how it relates to everything else that matters.

He starts with Abraham; or rather, of course, he starts with God. 'The God of glory' – a title which, though it sounds obvious, only occurs elsewhere in scripture at Psalm 29.3. Just in case anyone should repeat the charge that he is speaking blasphemies against the God of their ancestors (Acts 6.11), he is going to set things straight from the start. But then we get to Abraham. The significance of Abraham for understanding both second-Temple Judaism and Christianity as its surprising but powerful offshoot can hardly be overestimated. It is with Abraham that the story of the Jewish people begins; and it is with Abraham that Genesis begins the story of *how the world is to be set right*. The story of the people of Israel, in other words, does not come as a separate, free-standing entity, but as a way of saying: this is how the creator God is acting to deal with the problem of human sin, social catastrophe and cosmic disaster as set out in Genesis 3—11. The whole history of the people of Israel is to be understood under this rubric. The call of Abraham to be different, to leave his ancestral home and go to a new land (Acts 7.2–4), is a way of marking him out, of giving him a new vocation. Stephen isn't denying that. He's insisting on it.

Stephen homes in particularly, as does Paul in Romans 4 and Gala-tians 3, on Genesis 15, the chapter in which God makes a **covenant** with Abraham and tells him, long in advance, that his descendants will be enslaved by a foreign nation but will be brought out and given the land as their inheritance – the land where at present he lives as a resident alien. The question of the holy land looms large at this point in Stephen's speech. Even though it has not been mentioned in the charges laid against him, its importance to a first-century Jew (as, in similar ways, to twenty-first-century Jews, though that raises all sorts of other questions!) was beyond question. Perhaps people were already starting to comment on the way in which the followers of Jesus were cheerfully selling up ancestral property. But, whether or not that is likely, the Temple – which becomes the eventual sharp point of Ste-phen's speech – was the theological centre, the place where all the ideo-logy about the land of promise became focused. So Stephen is happy to speak of Abraham's purchase of a burial place, and of its use by the patriarchs. Apart from anything else, it all sets the scene quite carefully for the story of the **Exodus**, which, alongside God's call of Abraham and God's covenant with him, forms an essential pillar of Jewish iden-tity, and which stands at the heart of what Stephen wishes to say.

But before he gets there, he is already building in to his selective retelling a point which he will develop further in talking about Moses. Joseph was rejected by his brothers, but God used him to become the ruler of all Pharaoh's household, and indeed of the whole land of Egypt. When his brothers needed food, the man they had to go to was the man they had been jealous of and so had rejected. Fortunately for them, he was gracious to them and gave them what they needed.

Were there already some in Stephen's audience who saw where this was going? One of the great arts of Christian theology is to know how to tell the story: the story of the Old Testament, the story of Jesus as both the climax of the Old Testament and the foundation of all that was to come (not, in other words, a random collection of useful preaching material with some extraordinary and 'saving' events tacked on the end), and the story of the church from the first days until now. Sometimes we, too, have to take a long walk back and have another run at things to make sure we get everything in the proper rhythm, and draw out the lessons we need for our own day. Sometimes a story is the only way of telling the truth.

ACTS 7.17–34

Stephen and Moses

[17]'God had sworn an oath to Abraham', Stephen continued. 'When the time drew near for this promise to be fulfilled, the people had increased and multiplied in Egypt, [18]until another king arose over Egypt, one who had not known Joseph. [19]He got the better of our people, and ill-treated our ancestors, forcing them to abandon their newborn children so that they would die.

[20]'It was at that time that Moses was born, and he was a noble-looking child. He was nursed for three months in his father's house. [21]But, when they abandoned him, Pharaoh's daughter claimed him and brought him up as her own son. [22]So Moses was educated in the full teaching of Egyptian wisdom, and he was powerful in what he said and did.

[23]'When he had grown to about forty years old, it came into his heart to see how his family, the children of Israel, were doing. [24]He saw someone being wronged, and came to the man's defence; he took revenge on behalf of the man who was being oppressed, by striking down the Egyptian. [25]He thought his kinsfolk would grasp the fact that God was sending him to their rescue, but they didn't.

[26]'The next day he showed up as two Hebrews were fighting, and he tried to bring them back together again. "Now then, you two," he said, "you are brothers! Why are you wronging each other?" [27]But the man who was wronging the other wasn't having it. "Who d'you think you

are?" he retorted, pushing him away. "Who made you a ruler or judge over us? [28]Do you want to kill me in the same way you killed the Egyptian yesterday?" [29]At that word, Moses ran away, and lived as a guest in the land of Midian, where he had two sons.

[30]"After another forty years, an angel appeared to him in the desert at Mount Sinai, in the flame of a burning bush. [31]When Moses saw it, he was amazed at the vision. But, as he came closer to see, there came the voice of the Lord: [32]"I am the God of your ancestors, the God of Abraham, of Isaac, and of Jacob." Moses was very frightened, and didn't dare to look. [33]But the Lord said to him, "Take your sandals off your feet, for the place where you are standing is holy ground. [34]I have looked long and hard at the trouble my people are having in Egypt. I have heard their groaning, and I have come down to rescue them. So, come on now: I'm going to send you to Egypt.'"

Where do you get your sense of national identity?

In America, people often look back to three great moments. First, there was the arrival in America of the first settlers from Europe, particularly from Britain. Second, there was the glorious revolution of the late eighteenth century, when George Washington led the people to get rid of the hated British, and established a constitution which has lasted, with careful amendments, from that day to this. Third, there was the Civil War in the middle of the nineteenth century, which for better and for worse established the shape and direction of American society ever afterwards. Talk of the founding fathers, or of the constitution, with even a slight reference to the cultures (and the assumed lifestyles) of North and South, and everyone not only knows what you're talking about. They are ready to take sides.

In Britain we go back a bit further, though we are often hazy about the details. Magna Carta, the 'great charter', ensured certain liberties and rights, and still remains, though it's now a somewhat battered ideal. The Reformation of the sixteenth century, and the revolution and Civil War (under Oliver Cromwell) in the seventeenth, followed by the restoration of the monarchy, all provide movements which, though different people assess them differently, have left their mark on our national sense of identity.

In Europe, there are all kinds of similar markers. For the French, of course, the revolution of the late eighteenth century, parallel to that in America, remains foundational. For Germans and Italians, what matters has often been the moments of national unification, bringing together different regions under one roof. For some countries, it is a great vic-tory, for others a great defeat (the Battle of Mohács in 1526 for the Hungarians, for example, when they were massively defeated by Suleiman the Magnificent and his Ottoman Empire). For Eastern European countries, the events of 1989, with the demise of Soviet power and the fall of the Berlin Wall, will live for many generations as the moment both of new liberty and of new perplexity. For many parts of Africa, Latin America and South-East Asia, the moment above all to which reference is made is the departure of the old colonial powers and the discovery both of freedom and of national identity – and, once more, of the perplexity of what to do with freedom now you have it.

For most of us, it takes a considerable effort of the imagination to think what it must have meant to live in a society which, despite all kinds of disasters and new starts, still looked back about 1,500 years to the great moment when God himself had given his law to his people. The figure of Moses towers over ancient Judaism even more than Abraham, David, Solomon or Elijah. It was Moses through whom God had given the **law**, with all its fascinating details, strict prohibitions and stern commands. Though there were by this time various divergent schools of thought as to how the Mosaic law should be interpreted, nobody would have challenged the statement that it was this law, rather than anything else, which should determine the shape of life for God's people. The law was God's will, fixed and unalterable.

Stephen has been accused of going soft on Moses and his law; very well, he will go back to the story of Moses and see what it says. He tells the story of Moses so as to highlight three things in particular.

First, Moses was raised up by God, and trained in such a way that, through a strange providence, he became exactly the right leader for God's people. The new king (Egyptian kings had the title 'Pharaoh') over Egypt had taken it into his head to oppress the resident Hebrew population, the descendants of Jacob. Part of the deal was that male Hebrew children were to be killed off, to stop the population getting too numerous. But, though Moses' parents had to abandon him because of this edict, he was rescued by none other than Pharaoh's daughter herself, and brought up as her son. As a result, he was educated in the wisdom of the Egyptians, which was already legendary in Old Testament times (see 1 Kings 4.30; Isaiah 19.11). God, in other words, had planned for Moses to be just the man he needed for what he had in mind.

Second, Moses became the rejected rescuer. Realizing his own ancestry, despite his upbringing in Pharaoh's court, Moses set about trying to make things better for his kinsfolk. It was a disastrous failure, but that's not what Stephen is drawing attention to. Rather, he highlights the fact that here was this man, sent by God to deliver the people (albeit not yet ready to do so properly), being rejected by the very people he was supposed to be rescuing. 'Who made you a ruler or a judge over us?' asked the Hebrew man whom Moses had been rebuking.

But, third, Moses was the one to whom, and through whom, 'the God of glory', the God of Abraham, Isaac and Jacob, revealed himself in a fresh way. We have already seen a reference to the same passage that Stephen is referring to (Exodus 3) in a speech of Peter (Acts 3.13). Part of the point here, as always in early Christian explanation before fellow Jews, is that the God they have come to know in and through Jesus is not a different God from the one made known to their ancestors, but precisely the same one doing precisely the same thing, that is, rescuing his people in fulfilment of his ancient promises. And now, at the burning bush, as Moses is serving long years as a shepherd on behalf of his father-in-law, far away from Egypt and the people he is supposed to be rescuing, God addresses him again. **Heaven** and earth come together in a moment of vision, and neither Moses, Israel nor the world are ever the same again.

Nothing Stephen has said throughout this discussion is in any way disparaging of Moses. He insists that Moses was indeed prepared by God and equipped by God, through his sense of vocation and then his moment of dramatic call at the burning bush. And in that moment of vision we see the beginnings of a new sense of 'holy ground', more ancient than the **Temple** itself. Wherever God reveals himself as the saviour of his people, bringing about plans which, though they seem new and surprising, are nevertheless the fulfilment of what he had said long ago (see verse 7), that place becomes holy. What Stephen is about to go on to say is that the holiness of what God has done and is doing in Jesus himself is now substantially upstaging the holiness of the Temple. He has chosen to plead 'not guilty' to the charge of speaking against Moses. But with the Temple it's different.

Once again, the main thing we have to watch is the question of how to tell the story – the story of the Israelites, of Jesus and the early Christians, and of ourselves. But it isn't a matter simply of careful and skilful narrative. It's a matter of watching for the places, both in the story and in our own lives, where suddenly God wants to reveal himself afresh. There are 'burning bushes' or near equivalents all over the place, if we knew where to look. What new stories will people tell, in days to come, as they look back at your church and ask what new things God was doing in your day?

ACTS 7.35–53

Handmade Shrines

[35]'So', Stephen continued, 'this same Moses – the one they rejected, saying "Who made you a ruler or judge?" – this is the man God sent as ruler and redeemer, by the hand of the angel who had appeared to him in the bush. [36]He did signs and wonders in the land of Egypt, and

led them out, through the Red Sea and for forty years in the wilderness. [37]This is the Moses who said to the children of Israel, "God will raise up a prophet like me from among your brothers." [38]And this is the one who was in the Assembly in the desert with the angel who had spoken to him on Mount Sinai, and with our ancestors; and he received living words to give to us.

[39]"This is the one whom our ancestors had not wanted to obey, but instead rejected him and turned back in their hearts to Egypt, [40]by saying to Aaron, "Make us gods who will go before us; for this Moses, who brought us out of the land of Egypt – we don't know what has become of him!" [41]They made a calf in those days, and offered sacrifice to an idol. They celebrated things their own hands had made.

[42]"Then God turned and handed them over to worship the host of heaven, as it stands written in the book of the prophets: "Did you bring sacrifices and offerings to me in those forty years in the wilderness, O house of Israel? [43]You took up the tent of Moloch, and the star of your god Rhephan, the carved images you made to worship! I will remove you beyond Babylon!"

[44]"Our ancestors had the "tent of meeting" in the desert. God had commanded Moses to make it according to the pattern which he had seen. [45]Our ancestors in their turn brought it in when, with Joshua, they dispossessed the nations whom God drove out before our ancestors, and it was there until the time of David. [46]David found favour with God, and requested permission to establish a Tabernacle for the house of Jacob. [47]But it was Solomon who built him a house.

[48]"The Most High, however, does not live in shrines made by human hands. The prophet put it like this:

[49]"Heaven is my throne, and earth my footstool!
What sort of house will you build me, says the Lord,
or what place will you give me to rest in?
[50]My own hand made all these, did it not?

[51]"You stiff-necked people! Your hearts and ears are uncircumcised! You always resist the holy spirit, just as your ancestors did before you! [52]Which of the prophets did your ancestors not persecute? And they killed those who announced in advance the coming of the Righteous One – and now you have betrayed him and murdered him. [53]You received the law at the command of angels, but you didn't keep it!'

When you go into a store in my country, and you see a sign saying 'Made by Hand', you know what it means. 'This is good quality; it wasn't just turned out by some faceless machine or computer; someone has taken personal trouble over it; you will appreciate it!' (And, of course, 'Please buy it!') This applies whether it's a sweater or a wood carving, a pair of shoes or a piece of furniture.

But in the world of the ancient Israelites, saying something was 'made by hand' had a very different meaning. It meant that God had *not* made it or commanded it, and that it was a merely human invention. And when the phrase was applied to something which someone worshipped, things were about as bad as they could get. The primal sin, in all major Jewish writing, is idolatry, worshipping something as if it was God when it wasn't. And the way idols get produced is, of course, by human hands. That's what the prophets and other biblical writers had said, time and time again (see, for example, Deuteronomy 4.28; 2 Kings 19.18; 2 Chronicles 32.19; Psalm 115.3–8; 135.15–18; Isaiah 37.19; 44.10–20; 46.6–7; Jeremiah 10.2–5). The sheer absurdity of it is rubbed in scornfully in the ancient Jewish writings: first you manufacture a god, then you worship it? What kind of nonsense is that?

And the thrust of the final section of Stephen's great speech is that this is precisely what his own people had done – with their own **Temple**! This is startling, even horrifying, and it more or less guaranteed Stephen's swift and violent death. Up to this point he has been tracking their story closely, following through from Abraham to Joseph to Moses. Some might have objected to the way he was highlighting certain strands of thought, but they could hardly object to his overall telling of the narrative. But then, building on the fact that the children of Israel had rejected Moses when God sent him as rescuer and deliverer, Stephen suddenly launches into a much more serious charge. Having rejected Moses, they then failed to worship God himself even after he had delivered them. Although God went with them in the wilderness, they didn't worship him properly even then, but worshipped idols instead even while God was providing for them the way of true worship. And as for the Temple: well, it was always at best ambiguous, since God doesn't actually live in houses made by human hands, and at its worst it, too, has become an idol.

So the glorifying of the Temple, and the way in which it is being used to bolster up the Jewish leaders' rejection of Jesus, is a sign that they are radically out of line with their own tradition. They are the children of Abraham, but they are not obeying God as Abraham did. They are the heirs of Moses, but even though the **law** was given to him at the hands of angels, they have not kept that law. They are indeed the heirs of the earlier generations of the children of Israel, but sadly they are doing what most of their ancestors had done, killing prophets and righteous men sent to them by God. The speech suddenly stops being a careful historical account of the early days of Israelite history, and draws swiftly and shockingly to its close in a burst of denunciation. Stephen must have known what the effect would be.

He tracks the beginning of the Israelite idolatry, as it was easy to do, right back to the time in the wilderness. Part of his point is not to say, 'I disagree with Moses', but 'Moses was God's chosen leader, but right from the start the Israelites preferred idolatry.' He has been challenged about his attitude to Moses, and he is showing what the 'books of Moses' actually say about Moses himself and the events that were going on around him. Here, ironically, Stephen agrees with one of the later **rabbis**, who declared that all Israel had drunk in wickedness from two calves, the golden calf that Aaron had made (as in Acts 7.41, referring to Exodus 32) and then the calves that Jeroboam, the rebel king of the northern tribes, set up as an alternative shrine to Jerusalem (1 Kings 12.25–33). What Aaron had done set a pattern. However devoutly Israel seemed to be worshipping her true God, the possibility of idolatry was never far away.

In particular – it may seem a puzzling part of the speech, but it's important – the prophets lay a charge against Israel that, even during the wilderness years, when according to the early books of the Bible God was providing the sacrificial system by which they might worship him, the people were in fact continuing to worship pagan gods, the 'host of heaven' (presumably astral deities of various kinds) and 'Moloch' and 'Rephan' (Acts 7.43). This quotation from Amos 5.25–27 is a damning indictment of a period that many Jews must have seen as in some ways the honeymoon period between God and Israel. It was in fact, says Amos (and Stephen), a time of rank rebellion, of idolatry rather than true worship.

It is that part of the story, as well as the pattern of rejecting the one who would turn out to be the chosen deliverer, that the generation of Jesus' day had chosen to follow. This is turning the tables indeed. It isn't Stephen who has been a heretic, blaspheming the true God and the Temple; it is the Jewish rulers, following their idolatrous ancestors! The defence turns into an attack. Yes, David planned the Temple, and Solomon built it (verses 45–48). But Isaiah (66.1–2) had already declared, following Solomon's own prayer of dedication (1 Kings 8.27), that since God's own hand makes all things, the idea that human beings can produce a handmade building which will somehow contain God is the actual blasphemous nonsense. At a stroke, Stephen has taken the entire Jewish Temple-theology and, using Israel's own story and her own prophets, has overturned it. The Most High doesn't live in shrines like this. **Heaven** is his throne, and earth his footstool. The entire cosmos cannot contain him, since he made it all in the first place. What God wanted instead was to come into his world as a human being, 'the Righteous One' (Acts 7.52), to rescue his people. But, like their

91

ancestors, the Jewish leaders of Jesus' day had refused their appointed deliverer and had preferred their own homemade, handmade system and building. Moses and all the prophets would unite with Stephen in condemning them.

It is an astonishing speech – unsatisfying in some ways, since we would have liked to know what Stephen would have said in more detail to the actual charges laid against him. But he does something more powerful, and more important. He takes to a new level the charge which Peter and the others have been laying, all through, against the Jewish leaders of the day. It isn't just that they rejected God's **Messiah**, the Righteous One, and handed him over to be killed by the pagans. In doing so, they were simply acting out, at long range, the pattern of rebellious behaviour set by their ancestors. Instead of the recounting of Israel's history becoming a 'story of **salvation**', as so often, it turns out to be a 'story of rebellion'. Stephen is claiming the high moral ground. He stands with Abraham, with Moses, with David and Solomon, and with the prophets, while the present Jewish leadership are standing with Joseph's brothers, with the Israelites who rejected Moses, and with those who helped Aaron build and worship the golden calf. As we consider our own traditions, and think of them lovingly since they 'prove' that we ourselves are in the right place in our worship and witness, perhaps sometimes we need to allow the story to be told differently, and to see whether we ourselves might be in the wrong place within it.

ACTS 7.54—8.3

The Stoning of Stephen

[54]What Stephen said was a blow right to the heart. When they heard it, they gnashed their teeth against him. [55]He, however, was filled with the holy spirit, and looked steadily up into heaven. There he saw the glory of God, and Jesus standing at God's right hand.

[56]'Look!' he said. 'I can see heaven opened, and the son of man standing at God's right hand!'

[57]But they yelled at him at the tops of their voices, blocked their ears and made a concerted dash at him. [58]They bundled him out of the city and stoned him. The witnesses laid down their cloaks at the feet of a young man named Saul.

[59]So they stoned Stephen.

'Lord Jesus,' he cried out, 'receive my spirit.'

[60]Then he knelt down and shouted at the top of his voice, 'Lord, don't let this sin stand against them.'

Once he had said this, he fell asleep.

^{8.1}Now Saul was giving his consent to Stephen's death.

That very day a great persecution was started against the church in Jerusalem. Everyone except the apostles was scattered through the lands of Judaea and Samaria. ²Devout men buried Stephen, and made a great lamentation over him. ³But Saul was doing great damage to the church by going from one house to another, dragging off men and women and throwing them into prison.

Francis Thompson was a strange and powerful English poet of the early twentieth century. He was a believing Christian, but his life had been sad and difficult in a number of ways. Yet in the middle of his personal suffering he discovered a strange truth, which he put into memorable verse. At the very moment when all seems most bleak, just then the presence of Jesus Christ, and of his angels, can be so real and powerful that it is as though some of the scenes from the gospels are coming true before your very eyes. Since Thompson lived in London, that is where he places his remarkable vision:

But (when so sad thou canst not sadder)
Cry; – and upon thy so sore loss
Shall shine the traffic of Jacob's ladder
Pitched betwixt Heaven and Charing Cross.

Yea, in the night, my Soul, my daughter,
Cry, – clinging Heaven by the hems;
And lo, Christ walking on the water,
Not of Gennesareth, but Thames!

This goes, in my mind, with the reflection that sometimes in the Bible when angels appear it is precisely to people who are beside themselves with grief, like Mary at the tomb of Jesus in John 20. This isn't a reason, of course, for seeking out misery. But it may help a little bit in understanding what is going on in this dramatic passage, the story of the first Christian martyrdom.

What is a 'martyr'? As is now widely known, the word technically means 'witness'. A 'martyr' is someone who gives evidence. Why then do we call people who die for their **faith** 'martyrs'? Well, at one level at least, because in being prepared to die for their faith they are showing that they, at least, reckon that this faith is not just a set of ideas, not merely a nice religious glow, but the very living truth itself, worth more than one's own life. That is no doubt true.

But in this story, and in several others like it, there are other levels of 'witness' as well, which we ought to ponder.

First, there is the extraordinary statement which Stephen makes as the members of the court are grinding their teeth in fury at the offensive things he's said. Suddenly – though we have been prepared for this, perhaps, by Luke's statement in 6.15 that his face looked like that of an angel – he seems to have a vision.

'Look!' he shouts out. They can't, of course, since nobody else can see what he has suddenly seen. 'I can see **heaven** opened!' That doesn't mean, by the way, that he could see, far off up in the sky, a small door through which a distant place called 'heaven' might just about be visible. Visions like this are more like what happens when you've been standing on a mountain in thick cloud, hardly able to see the person walking six feet ahead of you, and suddenly a great wind sweeps away the cloud and you can see not only your companions, not only the crags and peaks all around, but far away, down in the valley, the streams and trees and villages in the afternoon sun. All those things had been there all the time, but you can only see them when the mist lifts. That's what it seems to have been like for Elisha and his servant when the Lord opened their eyes and they discovered themselves surrounded by horses and chariots of fire (2 Kings 6.17). That is what it was like, I believe, with Stephen. *There was the heavenly court, suddenly superimposed upon the earthly one.* Instead of the **high priest** and his fellow judges, there was the scene such as we find in Daniel 7, with the Ancient of Days, the God of glory himself, sitting in judgment, and with the **son of man**, not (as in Daniel) 'coming' towards him to be seated, but *standing* before him to act as advocate in the court. The human judges might be condemning Stephen to death, but the heavenly court was finding in his favour. Perhaps, indeed, a long memory of that double scene, etched on an impressionable young mind, may lie behind 1 Corinthians 2.8 and Colossians 2.14–15.

The point of being a 'martyr', then, a 'witness', is not just that giving one's life to death provides striking confirmation of one's faith (when facing death, what's the point in being a hypocrite?). It may be much more: that the point at which a person stands at the very threshold of heaven and earth, still in earth but called to give up their life for the faith, is the point where they may for a moment be in a position where they can, as it were, see both dimensions of reality, and speak about the normally hidden one to the people who cannot yet see it for themselves. This, again, from Luke's point of view, is itself part of the meaning of the whole scene. The **Temple** was supposed to be the place where heaven and earth met. Stephen is demonstrating that heaven and earth in fact come together in Jesus and his followers.

Clearly not all 'martyrs' in the normal sense have given that kind of testimony. But equally clearly, not only in the case of Stephen, but

94

also in several others through the violent history that has followed the preaching of the **gospel** down the years, there have been many who seem to have been given that kind of sight of things normally unseen, and who have been allowed to speak of them in their dying moments. Archbishop Thomas Cranmer called out something similar as he was being burned at the stake outside the gate of Balliol College, Oxford.

But there is something else to which Stephen is a 'witness'. There had been many 'martyrs' during the last few centuries of Jewish history before the time of Jesus. About 200 years before Jesus' day, a pagan king from Syria took over Jerusalem, desecrated the Temple, and forced many Jews to renounce their **law**, their ancestral way of life, and even to eat pork, which was of course forbidden in the law. The aim was obvious: get them to renounce their national charter, and they will be easier to govern, less likely to rebel. But many Jews resisted, and there are vivid accounts of how they met their deaths. We are told, in particular, what they said. One after another (the most striking account is in 2 Maccabees 7) they not only bear witness to their own faith, particularly in the **resurrection** they believe they will enjoy on the last day; they also threaten their torturer with dire punishments to come. 'Do not think', says one, 'that God has forsaken our people. Keep on, and see how his mighty power will torture you and your descendants!' That is utterly typical of many Jewish stories of people being tortured and killed for their belief and way of life.

And the extraordinary thing is that, even though the earliest Christians were all first-century Jews to whom that kind of response would have been normal and expected, none of them, going to their death, say anything like that at all. Stephen has just laid a pretty ferocious charge against the Jewish leaders in his speech. But when it comes to his own death, he shouts out a prayer at the top of his voice, as rocks are flying at him and his body is being smashed and crushed, asking God not to hold this sin against them. That is every bit as remarkable as the vision of the open heaven and the son of man standing as counsel for the defence. It is the upending of a great and noble tradition. If we knew nothing about Christianity except the fact that its martyrs called down blessing and **forgiveness**, rather than cursing and judgment, on their torturers and executioners, we would have a central, though no doubt puzzling, insight into the whole business.

There is of course only one explanation. They really had learned something from Jesus, who made loving one's enemies a central, non-negotiable part of his teaching (not, as so often in would-be 'Christian' society, something one might think about from time to time but not try very hard to put into practice). On the cross Jesus himself prayed that those nailing him up might be forgiven (Luke 23.34).

There is much else worth pondering in the death of Stephen – not least the fact that, from early on in church history, the event has been commemorated on the day after Christmas Day, reminding us that Christmas is not simply about a nice little baby surrounded by friendly animals, but the sudden arrival of the new life of heaven within an inhospitable and downright dangerous world. But one thing more is worth noticing. As Jesus' followers are marked out and hunted down, scattered across the surrounding countryside, the young man called Saul, who had been a principal witness to Stephen's death, goes off to seize as many as he can. When you're doing that kind of thing, you only arrest people who are likely to be a problem, people who are full members of, and possibly also potential leaders in, the movement. It is striking, here and elsewhere, that this number regularly, from the very beginning of the movement, included not only men but also women.

ACTS 8.4–25

Samaria, the Spirit and Simon Magus (See map 6, page xviii.)

[4]Those who were scattered went all over the place announcing the word. [5]Philip went off to a town in Samaria and announced the Messiah to them. [6]The crowds, acting as one, clung to what Philip was saying, as they heard him and saw the signs he performed. [7]For unclean spirits came out of many of them, and several who were paralysed or lame were cured. [8]So there was great joy in that town.

[9]But there was a man named Simon, who had lived in the town for some while and who practised magic. He used to astonish the Samaritan people, giving out that he was some great personage. [10]Everyone, small and great alike, paid attention to him, and said, 'This man is the one called "God's Great Power"!' [11]They had been under his spell for some time, since they were amazed at the magic he could perform. [12]But when they believed Philip as he was announcing to them the message about God's kingdom and the Name of Jesus the Messiah, they were baptized, men and women alike. [13]Simon too believed and was baptized, paying close attention to Philip. When he saw signs, and great and powerful deeds, it was his turn to be astonished.

[14]When the apostles in Jerusalem heard that Samaria had received God's word, they sent Peter and John to them. [15]When they arrived, they prayed for them, asking that they would receive the holy spirit, [16]since up to that point the spirit had come upon none of them; they had simply been baptized into the name of the Lord Jesus. [17]Then they laid their hands on them, and they received the holy spirit.

[18]When Simon saw that the spirit was given through the laying on of the apostles' hands, he offered them money.

[19]'Give me this power too,' he said, 'so that anyone I lay my hands on will receive the holy spirit.'

[20]'You and your silver belong in hell!' retorted Peter. 'Did you really think that God's gift could be bought with money? [21]You have no part or share in this word! Your heart is not straight before God. [22]So repent from this wickedness, and pray to the Lord. Perhaps he will forgive the scheme you had in your heart. [23]I can see that you are still stuck in the bitter poison and chains of unrighteousness.'

[24]'Pray to the Lord for me,' said Simon in reply, 'that none of what you've said will happen to me.'

[25]After Peter and John had finished bearing witness and speaking the word of the Lord, they returned to Jerusalem, announcing the good news to many Samaritan villages.

As a bishop, one of the things I do quite a lot is to go round laying hands on people and praying for God's **holy spirit** to come upon them. It is often a very moving and exciting time, not least at the Easter Vigil when we come in darkness into the great cathedral, led by the candle symbolizing the risen Jesus, and then, with lights coming on, loud playing on the organ and other instruments, and shouts of 'Alleluia!', we celebrate the **resurrection**. We renew the vows we made at our **baptism**; and then, sometimes pausing to baptize people as well, we welcome into our **fellowship** through confirmation (the laying on of the bishop's hands, with prayer) those who had been baptized earlier, probably as infants, and who now want to make real for themselves the promises which had been made on their behalf some while before.

When people ask me, as they sometimes do, what it's all about, the present passage is one of the ones we usually go back to. I do not imagine for a moment that our modern practice, in the church to which I happen to belong, is an exact reproduction of what Luke says took place in Samaria on that occasion. I am not an **apostle** come from Jerusalem, and the people I confirm are not Samaritans, needing for the first time to know the presence and power of the **spirit**. But since there is in fact no single, identical pattern of Christian initiation running right across our earliest documents, the church has, in my view wisely, developed patterns which broadly correspond to what seems to have been done by the first apostles themselves, as much by decisions taken as they went along as by carefully thought-out regulation. I should say, by the way, that sometimes when I meet people I have confirmed a year or so before they have remarkable stories to tell of what God has been doing in their lives since then. It is by no means, as sceptics sometimes assume, an empty and irrelevant old bit of ritual.

Luke tells the story of what happened on this occasion in Samaria for several reasons, which overlap and bounce off one another and make it, at first sight, difficult to figure out what his main point actually is. Let's try to disentangle the various strands of his rather complicated story.

To begin with, we meet Philip, one of the seven deacons who were appointed in chapter 6. He seems, like Stephen, to have quickly outgrown the purely administrative job to which he had been appointed. He, like others, has had to leave Jerusalem in a hurry following the death of Stephen, but he is by no means in hiding. On the contrary, he has gone off to a town in Samaria. Later in the chapter we find him down in Gaza; and later in the book (21.8) we find him living in Caesarea, on the coast, with four daughters who all have prophetic gifts. And, significantly, at that point he is referred to as an 'evangelist'; clearly, we may suppose, the different 'offices' in the early church were not mutually exclusive, and Philip could still be a 'deacon' while engaging in other work as well.

But far more important than Philip is where he went to. Samaria, the hilly part of the country in between Judaea in the south and Galilee in the north, had for centuries been home to people whom the Jews on either side regarded with deep suspicion and hostility. They were the people who had been in the land while the Jews had been in Babylon, and when they returned from Babylon they found themselves alongside one another. The Samaritans (who are still there, by the way, in small numbers and often, alas, treated as a mere tourist attraction) kept to a form of Judaism but with significant elements changed. There was no love lost between them and the Jews, and there had been several incidents of mutual violence.

Yet it was part of the agenda which Jesus set his followers, at the start of Acts, that they should be his witnesses not only in Jerusalem and Judaea, but in Samaria – and on, to the very ends of the earth (1.8). Like many things in Acts, they don't seem to have had much of a plan for how to achieve this, and they don't seem to have thought out in advance what such a plan might look like if they did; but it began to happen anyway, as we have seen, because of the persecution in Jerusalem and the scattering of people who were eager to talk about Jesus to anyone they met, whether they were proper Jews or not. And so Philip cheerfully breaks a centuries-old taboo (as, of course, Jesus himself had done, for instance in John 4 and Luke 17.11–19), and the Samaritans, equally cheerfully, accept his news about the Jewish **Messiah** – not least, it appears, because of the remarkable healings that Philip performed at the same time.

More important still, from Luke's point of view, than the fact of Samaritans hearing about Jesus as Messiah, is what happened next.

Many of the local people believed and were baptized in the name of Jesus. News of this reached the leaders in Jerusalem, and they made an unprecedented move. It appeared that, despite the Samaritan converts coming to **faith** and being baptized, they had not experienced the **holy spirit** in the same way that Jesus' followers in Jerusalem had done on the **day of Pentecost**. This seems to have been interpreted in terms of the significant move that was taking place across the traditional boundary of culture and suspicion. It was important, they appear to have concluded, that what was happening in Samaria would not be dismissed by suspicious people in Jerusalem or elsewhere as merely some eccentric occurrence which could be waved away and discounted, leaving the new movement belonging only to bona fide Jews.

So, just as church leaders in the fifth century decided that it was important for the bishop and only the bishop to lay hands on people in what has come to be called 'confirmation', thus making it quite clear that the new believers really are being welcomed into the central life of the church and not merely into some sort of private club, the Jerusalem apostles decided to send Peter and John to Samaria to lay hands on the converts and pray for the holy spirit. This they did. We are left to conclude (though Luke doesn't say so explicitly in verse 17) that they spoke with **tongues**, as the first believers had on the day of Pentecost; not that that is the only sign of the spirit's working in the New Testament, as some have supposed, but that such an occurrence would be the visible proof of what had happened. What happened next makes it apparent that some clear outward sign of the spirit's presence had been given.

What followed was darker and, in its way, more dramatic. The story of Simon (often referred to as Simon Magus, since 'Magus' means 'magician') reminds us that wherever the **gospel** makes its way, there will be new and often unexpected challenges. To begin with, all seems to go well. Simon has been a leading figure in the local Samaritan district, and has gained a great reputation through his magic powers. People have been hailing him as a manifestation of 'the great God'. Quite what they meant by that Luke does not explain further. It is possible that Simon had been seen as, or even that he had described himself as, the incarnation or manifestation of the one true God, but we cannot be sure. In any case, he quickly seems to have recognized in what Philip was doing a power greater than the one he himself possessed. He not only believed and was baptized, but stuck close to Philip.

But all was not well. When Peter and John came down and laid hands on those who had believed – curiously, it seems as though Simon may not have been one of those who experienced this at this stage – he was enormously impressed by what he recognized as their still more powerful 'magic'. The people who had the apostles' hands laid on them were miraculously transformed! Something happened to them, a new power, new tongues . . . and Simon wanted it. He wanted, not the gift of the spirit itself, but the power to lay hands on people and have the spirit come upon them. And he thought that Peter would sell him this power for money. This is the origin of the word 'simony', which means the attempt to buy spiritual office, status or power.

Peter's reply is sharp and swift. Destruction is the only destination for such money, he says – and you along with it. We are not told, frustratingly, what happened; only that Simon received a dire warning, and begged Peter to pray that he would be spared. Luke is not interested in Simon's fate, so much as in the general point, that any attempt to bring the spirit under human control is a nonsense and to be rejected outright. The spirit is the spirit of the sovereign God, who blows where he wants and how he wants. Neither Peter, nor John, nor Philip, nor any human being then, since or now can do other than be open to what the spirit wants, ready to be blown along by the rushing mighty wind.

And that is precisely what happened to Philip next.

ACTS 8.26–40

Philip and the Ethiopian (See map 7, page xviii.)

[26]An angel of the Lord spoke to Philip.

'Get up and go south', he said. 'Go to the desert road that runs down from Jerusalem to Gaza.'

[27]So he got up and went. Lo and behold, there was an Ethiopian eunuch, a court official of the Candace (the queen of Ethiopia), who was in charge of her whole treasury. He had come to Jerusalem to worship, [28]and was on his way back home. He was sitting in his chariot and reading the prophet Isaiah.

[29]'Go up and join his chariot', said the spirit to Philip. [30]So Philip ran up, and heard him reading the prophet Isaiah.

'Do you understand what you're reading?' he asked.

[31]'How can I', he replied, 'unless someone gives me some help?'

So he invited Philip to get up and sit beside him. [32]The biblical passage he was reading was this one:

He was led like a sheep to the slaughter
and as a lamb is silent before its shearers,
so he does not open his mouth.
[33]In his humiliation, judgment was taken away from him.
Who can explain his generation?
For his life was taken away from the earth.

[34]'Tell me,' said the eunuch to Philip, 'who is the prophet talking about? Himself or someone else?'

[35]Then Philip took a deep breath and, starting from this biblical passage, told him the good news about Jesus.

[36]As they were going along the road, they came to some water.

'Look!' said the eunuch. 'Here is some water! What's to stop me being baptized?'

[38]So he gave orders for the chariot to stop, and both of them went down into the water, Philip and the eunuch together, and he baptized him. [39]When they came up out of the water, the spirit of the Lord snatched Philip away, and the eunuch didn't see him any more, but went on his way rejoicing. [40]Philip, however, turned up at Azotus. He went through all the towns, announcing the good news, until he came to Caesarea.

I was once visiting Cambridge (the English Cambridge, not the American one) to do some lectures. One afternoon I was working on the themes for the lectures still to come, when I found to my surprise an urgent thought in my head: Go to Evensong at King's College. Now I love Choral Evensong; but I was going to be attending other services, I had lots of work to do, and if I had been going to attend Evensong I might have thought of going to St John's College, whose choir was the more famous at that time. But the thought wouldn't leave me alone. Back and back it came: Go to Evensong at King's. So eventually, feeling rather foolish, and not even sure what time the service was to be, I went.

I arrived just at the last minute, as the choir was about to process in. The massive chapel seemed to be absolutely full, mostly of Japanese tourists. Glancing around I could only see one spare seat anywhere; fortunately it was on the end of a row. I hurried over and took the seat as the choir came in and the music began.

As I sat down, somewhat breathless, I felt a hand grip my arm. I looked round, and saw to my astonishment an old friend, a New Testament scholar much older than myself, Bill Farmer from Dallas in Texas.

'Tom Wright!' he said. 'What are *you* doing here?' He had no idea I was going to be in Cambridge (I lived in Lichfield at that time).

'Bill!' I replied. 'What are *you* doing here?' I had had no idea he was going to be in England, let alone in Cambridge, let alone in King's, and in that seat.

The music had begun and we couldn't continue our conversation. Instead, he pulled out a small pocket diary. In the space for that date, he had written three words, in block capitals: CALL TOM WRIGHT. We stared at it in amazement. Bill (who has now gone to his rest) was a man of **faith** and prayer. He hadn't phoned. But the call had got through anyway.

I am not suggesting that Bill and I were somehow like Philip and the Ethiopian; merely that, like many people, I very occasionally have a sense of something strange going on, and I find myself somewhere I hadn't expected and know that whatever is going on I'd better go with it. And in this case the parallel is somewhat closer than it might be; because the reason Bill wanted to call me was because he was organizing a conference, and he wanted me to be one of the speakers. The conference was to be on the interpretation of Isaiah 53 in the New Testament. I went. It was a deeply formative experience for me and helped me enormously with the work I was doing at the time.

And of course the interpretation of Isaiah 53 – the Old Testament passage the Ethiopian was reading, which Philip interpreted to him – is what our present passage is all about. At least, that is at the heart of it. Surrounding that question is another, intriguing one: who was this Ethiopian? What was his relation to Judaism? What happened to him next?

Luke describes him as a eunuch (a castrated man; it was common in the ancient Near East for men who had been castrated to serve in positions of state) who held office in the Ethiopian court under the queen, Candace. He was her chief finance minister. It is very unlikely, virtually impossible, that he would himself have been Jewish; and, being a eunuch, he could not have been a proselyte to Judaism. He was thus an outsider, forever to remain so within the Jewish system. But there was something about the Jewish God and the Jewish way of life which had attracted him, as it did with many in the ancient world (if you think of the kind of gods that were worshipped by other nations, and of the kind of practices that were often associated with them, you might well see Judaism as a wonderful oasis of clean, calm wisdom). So he had made the long journey to Jerusalem to worship, perhaps at one of the festivals; and he had procured, or perhaps he already possessed, a copy of some or all of the Jewish scriptures. And while from one point of view this story rounds off Luke's chapter about the remarkable doings of Philip, the deacon-turned-evangelist, from another point of view it continues the theme of the opening up of the **gospel** to the non-Jewish world, anticipating both the **conversion** of Paul (who was to become the missionary, par excellence, to non-Jews) and the story of Peter at the house of Cornelius (chapters 10 and 11).

Like many then and now, the Ethiopian was benefiting from a simple truth. When you find yourself attracted towards the faith, the scriptures provide, marvellously, something you can have and hold and take away and which, however far you are geographically from a place of worship, can become the source of living water from which you can drink at your own pace and in your own way. But of course, sooner or later, you find yourself faced with a passage which sounds powerful and important – but you don't know what it means. And then you need help. Fortunately, help is often available, as it was in this case.

The question the Ethiopian had run into is one which many have discussed in our own day (including at the conference Bill Farmer organized). Who was the prophet writing about when he described the one 'led like a lamb to the slaughter', killed as an innocent victim?

Now at this point it is important to stress how the early church read the prophets. It wasn't just a matter of discovering strange passages here and there and lining them up with Jesus in some arbitrary fashion. As we saw in Stephen's speech, and will see again in Paul's great address in chapter 13 (and as we can see in Paul's letters, too), they were aware of the Hebrew scriptures primarily as a great *narrative*. This story stretched forward from Abraham – and, behind him, the creation of the world and of humans, and the disaster of human rebellion – through Moses, David and the prophets, and on towards the present day. And the question was not only whether there are passages here which give us a foretaste of what is to come, but more particularly, how does this story reach its climax? And how do the hints and guesses along the way contribute to that climax?

Isaiah, you see (we'll call the writer that, though most people think the book was compiled over several generations), wasn't simply looking through a long-range prophetic telescope, seeing Jesus a few hundred years away, and describing him in cryptic poetry. Rather, he was meditating deeply on the fate of Israel in exile, and on the promises and purposes of God which remained constant despite Israel's failure to be the light to the nations, or even to walk in the light herself. Gradually a picture took shape in his praying, meditating mind: the figure of a Servant, one who would complete Israel's task, who would come to where Israel was, to do for Israel and for the whole world what neither could do for themselves, to bear in his own body the shame and reproach of the nations and of God's people, and to die under the weight of the world's wickedness. Only so, he perceived, could the promises be fulfilled. Isaiah was writing a kind of job description: This is what we want! A Servant who will accomplish God's will, and rescue Israel and the world! He had, no doubt, many partial images in mind, of prophets who had suffered for what they had spoken, of the righteous sufferers in some of the Psalms. But what he was talking about was the way in which, and the one through whom, the long night of Israel's exile would arrive at its new dawn, and with it the promise of blessing for the world, of a new **covenant** (Isaiah 54) and a new creation (Isaiah 55) – and, with that, a blessing even for outsiders and foreigners, and, yes, even for eunuchs (Isaiah 56).

That hadn't happened yet, but now it was beginning to, declares Philip; because the job description had found the right candidate at last. Jesus was the one through whom the slow and winding story of God's people had reached its destination, and with it the moment of **redemption** for the whole world. No wonder the Ethiopian was excited. When you tell the story of Israel like that, with Jesus at its climax, it opens up to include everybody, including people like him, doubly excluded and now wonderfully welcomed. No wonder he wanted to share in the death and **resurrection** of this Jesus by being baptized, by having the whole story become his personal story. No wonder he went on his way celebrating – to become, if later tradition is to be believed, the first evangelist in his own native country. We today should ponder, too, the fact that the first non-Jew to come to faith and **baptism** in Luke's great story is a black man from Africa.

No wonder, too, when the church reads Isaiah 53 today, we find ourselves in awe once more at the story of the one who was 'wounded for our transgressions, bruised for our iniquities'. Luke has many more things to tell us about how the early church developed and grew, not least how it read the scriptures. But he plants this story at the heart of the moment when the gospel is starting to go out into the wider world, to make it abundantly clear that wherever you go, whatever culture you come to, whatever situation of human need, sin, exclusion or oppression you may find, the **message** of Jesus as the one in whom all the promises of God find their 'Yes!' (2 Corinthians 1.20) is there to meet that need. And, among all the promises, the promise of the Servant, through whose death the power of evil has been broken and its punishment exhausted, stands supreme, whether you are on a lonely road through the Gaza desert, in a great medieval chapel in Cambridge, or on your knees in the privacy of your room.

ACTS 9.1–9

The Conversion of Saul (See map 8, page xix.)

[1]Meanwhile, Saul was still breathing out threats and murder on the Lord's disciples. He went to the high priest [2]and requested from him official letters to the synagogues in Damascus, so that he could find people who belonged to the Way, men and women alike, tie them up and bring them back to Jerusalem.

[3]While he was on the journey, and was getting near to Damascus, suddenly a light from heaven shone around him. [4]He fell to the ground and heard a voice speaking to him.

'Saul, Saul!' said the voice. 'Why are you persecuting me?'

[5]'Who are you, Lord?' he asked.

'I am Jesus,' he said, 'and you are persecuting me. ⁶But get up and go into the city, and you will be told what you must do.'

⁷The men who were travelling with Saul stood speechless. They heard the voice but couldn't see anybody. ⁸Saul got up from the ground, but when he opened his eyes he couldn't see anything. So they led him by the hand and brought him to Damascus. ⁹He went for three days, still unable to see, and he neither ate nor drank.

When I was young, nobody much in the culture I knew practised yoga. It was regarded as peculiar, a bit too exotic, and probably likely to lead to dislocation of your joints. There was a suspicion, as well, that you might find yourself getting into various kinds of Eastern religions; and we modern Westerners didn't like the sound of that. You might end up mumbling meaningless syllables all morning in the hope of attaining some kind of inner enlightenment. All very irrational and quite unlike the cool, sensible religion that was on offer in carefully controlled ecclesiastical contexts.

The trouble is, of course, that if there is a God, if there is a spiritual dimension to life, if there are indeed many dimensions to our world, then you are unlikely to get in touch with them, or only at a great distance, by holding off from anything which might open you to the enormous and powerful world which throbs with life and possibility never suspected by the average Western churchgoer in the days of my youth. I'm not knocking faithful, quiet, persistent prayer and worship of the kind I grew up in. It formed me, and I am deeply and daily grateful for it. But for many of my contemporaries it simply didn't do the trick. And now, with Eastern religions, yoga, gurus of every kind, every religion under the sun being splashed around the average bookstall, it's obvious that the things we kept at arm's length 50 years ago have come back with a bang into the mainstream of popular culture.

In fact, of course, techniques of prayer and meditation have been known in all religions, not least in Judaism and Christianity themselves. Jews who repeated the 'Shema' prayer over and over ('Hear, O Israel, YHWH our God, YHWH is one!'), and Christians who repeated their variation on it ('One God the Father, and one Lord Jesus Christ', as in 1 Corinthians 8.6), already knew the power of invoking the Name – a theme, as we have seen, to which Luke draws attention. But there were and are other techniques as well. Many Christians today use the Ignatian method, taking a scriptural story and trying to 'get inside' it, living imaginatively within one of the parts in the drama and seeing what happens, hearing what God, or Jesus, says to you as a character in the story.

There was one type of Jewish meditation, not unrelated to that idea, which became famous. It involved sustained contemplation of the great vision of the first chapter of the book of the prophet Ezekiel, the vision in which Ezekiel sees something like a great chariot, with whirling wheels and flashing lights. He describes, first, the four-faced angels who are carrying the chariot: they move this way and that, sparkling and glowing. Then he describes the wheels of the chariot, whirling and flashing, their rims full of eyes. Finally he describes the larger scene, with a dome above, a rainbow all around, and a throne, like a great jewel. And the point of meditating on this throne-chariot, for some Jews of Jesus' day who used this technique, was to see if, by devout prayer and fasting, holiness, devotion and contemplation, one might come even in this life to share in the climax of the vision:

> Seated above what looked like a throne was something that seemed like a human form. Upwards from what appeared to be the waist I saw something like gleaming amber, something that looked like fire enclosed all round; downwards from what appeared to be the waist I saw something that looked like fire. There was wonderful light all around. Like the bow in a cloud on a rainy day, such was the appearance of the wonderful light all around. This was the appearance of the likeness of the glory of YHWH. (Ezekiel 1.26–28)

Notice how cautious Ezekiel is. He doesn't say he saw God himself, merely that he saw 'the appearance of the likeness of the glory' of YHWH, Israel's God. But it isn't surprising, with such an astonishing passage, that people who studied the scriptures deeply, and longed to share the vision of the God they loved and trusted, would come to use the first chapter of Ezekiel in prayer, hoping that somehow they might be allowed to glimpse the same glory, to see God face to face on his throne, even if the sight of such glory would hurl them flat on their own faces on the ground.

What I'm going to suggest now is only a guess. But it's one which several serious scholars have proposed; and, whether or not it's exactly right, it introduces us to the world of thought and experience which we need to understand if we are to grasp the full impact of a story which was so important to Luke that he tells it no fewer than three times – here in Acts 9, and then again, from Paul's own lips, in chapters 22 and 26. We know from Paul's writings that he was, from his earliest days, a deeply devout Jew, for whom prayer and meditation would have been a daily reality, and the study of the scriptures a lifelong passion. What's more, he came from that part of Judaism – the deep, out-and-out devotion to God and his **law** that characterized the strictest of the **Pharisees** – where meditation of the kind I have been describing was taught, at least in some circles. So it is quite possible that he knew, and sometimes tried to practise, the throne-chariot meditation.

Allow yourself to imagine that that is what Saul of Tarsus – not yet called Paul – was doing, on the long, slow road from Jerusalem to Damascus. (A journey might be an ideal time for such a thing, with the steady plod of the horse, and the quiet countryside around.) You might then be able to grasp the impact of what happened to him. He was on his way to act for the glory of God, the glory which he believed was being besmirched by these crazy followers of Jesus. He needed to keep that glory firmly before his eyes, to make sure his zeal was properly fired up and rightly directed. To that end, shall we suppose, he had been in prayer and meditation, trying to envisage the divine throne-chariot. He had gazed with the eyes of his heart on the angels. He had stared at the wheels as they flashed to and fro. He had longed to be able to raise his eyes from the angels and the wheels to the chariot itself, and then (would it be possible? he must have wondered; would he be allowed?) to the figure which sat on the chariot, flaming with fire, surrounded by brilliant light. Imagine his excitement as, in the depth of devout meditation, he saw with the eyes of his heart, so real that it seemed as though he was seeing it with his ordinary physical eyes, and then so real that he realized he *was* seeing it with his physical eyes, the form, the fire, the blazing light, and – the face!

And the face was the face of Jesus of Nazareth.

Suddenly Saul's world turned upside down and inside out. Terror, ruin, shame, awe, horror, glory and terror again swept over him. Years later he would write of seeing 'the glory of God in the face of Jesus the **Messiah**' (2 Corinthians 4.6), and though, to show that this was something he shared with all Christians, he described it as God shining 'in our hearts', elsewhere he makes it clear that his own 'seeing' was unique, a seeing, like Stephen in his death, which involved the coming together of **heaven** and earth, earthly eyes seeing heavenly reality. 'Am I not an **apostle**?' he wrote to the Corinthians (1 Corinthians 9.1). 'Have I not seen Jesus our Lord?'

But this 'seeing' went far, far beyond a mere qualification for office, ticking one of the boxes under the category 'apostle'. It confirmed everything Saul had been taught; it overturned everything he had been taught. The law and the prophets had come true; the law and the prophets had been torn to pieces and put back together in a totally new way. It was a new world; it was the old world made explicit. It showed him that the God he had loved from childhood, the God for whose glory he had been so righteously indignant, the God in whose name and for whose honour he was busy rounding up those who were declaring that Jesus of Nazareth was Israel's Messiah, that he was risen from the dead, that he was the Lord of the world (this Jesus who had led Israel astray with his magic tricks and false prophecy about the **Temple**, this Jesus who the Romans had, thankfully, crucified, to make it clear that whoever was God's Messiah it certainly couldn't be him!) – it showed him that the God he had been right to serve, right to study, right to seek in prayer, the God of Abraham, Isaac and Jacob, had done what he always said he would, but done it in a shocking, scandalous, horrifying way. The God who had always promised to come and rescue his people had done so in person. *In the person of Jesus.*

Everything that Saul of Tarsus said and did from that moment on, and particularly everything that he wrote, flowed from that sudden, shocking seeing of Jesus. He was a highly intelligent, superbly educated, supremely biblically literate young man. We can imagine, not just Ezekiel's chariot wheels whirling and flashing this way and that, but the well-stocked recesses of his mind and imagination darting and glancing to and fro, from passage to passage of scripture, from the recent memory of Stephen, dying under a hail of rocks and with a prayer to Jesus on his lips (so unlike other martyrs Saul had heard of), to his parents, his teachers, his fellow students, his family, his fiancée (that's a guess, of course; we don't know if he was married, as almost all young Jewish men would be, or if he was expecting to be), and back again to the stories of Abraham and Isaac, of Moses and the burning bush, to the prophecies of Isaiah and Daniel, to the Psalms, to the great royal promises, 'I will *raise up your seed after you*, and I will be to him a father, and he will be to me a son'; 'the Lord said to my Lord, Sit at my right hand, until I make your enemies your footstool.' Surely it couldn't mean – surely it didn't mean – supposing it really did mean . . .

And Saul sank to the ground, blinded by the light, with the words ringing in his head. 'I am Jesus, and you are persecuting me.' *Me?* Somehow, these men and women Saul was dragging off to prison were Jesus' people; his family; his own extended self. It was all too much. They led him by the hand and brought him to Damascus. It was three days before he could do anything except, simultaneously, recoil from the horror of what had happened and gasp at its glory. We call this event a '**conversion**', but it was more like a volcanic eruption, thunderstorm and tidal wave all coming together. If the death and **resurrection** of Jesus is the hinge on which the great door of history swung open at last, the conversion of Saul of Tarsus was the moment when all the ancient promises of God gathered themselves up, rolled themselves into a ball, and came hurtling through that open door and out into the wide world beyond.

ACTS 9.10–19a

Ananias and Saul

¹⁰In Damascus there was a disciple named Ananias. The Lord spoke to him in a vision.

'Ananias!' he said.

'Here I am, Lord', he replied.

¹¹'Get up', said the Lord to him, 'and go to the street called Straight. Enquire at the house of Judas for a man from Tarsus named Saul. Look – he's praying! ¹²And he has seen, in a vision, a man named Ananias coming and laying his hands on him so that he can see again.'

¹³'Well, Lord', replied Ananias, 'I've heard about this man from several people . . . all about how he's done wicked things to your holy people in Jerusalem . . . ¹⁴and now he's come here with authority from the chief priests to tie up everybody who calls on your Name!'

¹⁵'Just go', replied the Lord. 'He is a chosen vessel for me, to carry my Name before nations and kings – and the children of Israel, too. ¹⁶I am going to show him how many things he is going to have to suffer for the sake of my Name.'

¹⁷So Ananias set off, went into the house, and laid his hands on him.

'Brother Saul', he said, 'the Lord has sent me – yes, Jesus, who appeared to you on the road as you were coming here – so that you may be able to see again, and receive the holy spirit.'

¹⁸At once something like scales fell off his eyes, and he was able to see. He got up and was baptized. ¹⁹ᵃHe had something to eat, and regained his strength.

As the concert progressed, I watched the different players in the orchestra. There at the back sat a man who looked very, very bored. In fact, he disappeared for about half an hour at one point. (There are stories of musicians turning up in bars near the concert hall and ordering a drink while still counting the bars in the music out loud: 'Ninety-three, two, three, four, Ninety-four, two, three, four, dry white wine please, two, three, four, Ninety-six, two, three, four . . .') When he came back he still looked bored. The music was great, but he seemed to have nothing to do with it. At last we approached the great climax of the symphony. We were nearly at the very end. He got up, took a deep breath, and picked up his pair of cymbals. Nearly there now. Was he going to miss it? Here . . . it . . . comes – and then, in a single great swoop, he gave the one almighty *crash* that topped off the decisive chord, that lifted it beyond anything that had come before it. The symphony ended; the applause went on and on. The conductor, pointing to different players who had made special contributions, came at last to him. The audience laughed and applauded some more. He had had his moment of glory.

I thought of him getting on the bus and going back to a small house in the suburbs. For that one moment, he had been king of the world.

Something like that is how Ananias must have felt, being sent by the Lord to greet Saul and enable him to receive his sight. We never hear of Ananias again. We don't know how he became a follower of Jesus. We know nothing about him except this passage, and it's enough: that he was a believer, that he knew how to listen for the voice of Jesus, that he was prepared to obey it even though it seemed ridiculously dangerous, that he went where he was sent and did what he was told. And he did it with love and grace and wisdom. You can't ask for more.

Actually, it's quite surprising that there were any followers of Jesus left in Damascus by the time Saul of Tarsus arrived. Word had clearly got round that he was on the way. After all, it wasn't every day that the **high priest** himself gave authority to a young hothead to go and carry out a particular task, in this case raiding the synagogues of a far-off town, in another country, to sniff out people who were following this pestilent new heresy. (We note that, as a **Pharisee**, Saul had no authority of his own. As we have said before, the Pharisees were a populist pressure group, not an official body with any official power. Saul, zealous for God and the **law**, was prepared to do more than the high priest had yet envisaged. No doubt, like many rulers, the high priest was only too glad to have someone else willing to do the dirty work.) So Ananias, and the other followers of Jesus in Damascus, must have been shivering in their shoes. Little did he know that he was about to have his moment of glory. Like many such moments, it was frightening when it came.

The way the Lord made it clear to Ananias that it would be all right is very telling.

'He is praying'; yes, but all Pharisees prayed, all devout Jews prayed. That by itself didn't tell Ananias anything except that Saul might well be stoking up his religious fervour in preparation for the assault on Jesus' followers. Ah, but – 'He has seen a vision; and it's a vision about you! He doesn't know you, Ananias, but in his vision someone with your name is coming to lay hands on him so that he can see again.' A vision about a vision; this is getting complicated, but Ananias takes the point. He is still worried, though: we all know why Saul has come here, we all know what he's already done in Jerusalem, and you're asking me to go and see him?

But at this point Ananias discovers something which the rest of us had not yet been told – though Paul, telling the story later in Acts, includes it as part of the initial vision on the road. The Lord is calling Saul for a particular task. The time has come for the message about the one true God, the Jewish **good news** of the God of Abraham, Isaac and Jacob, to be told to the wider world, the world of pagans, **Gentiles**, people who know nothing and care less about this God. And the person to do this task, to spearhead the work of getting the **message** out to those outside the law, must be the one who most clearly, of all others of his generation, had been the most keen to stamp the message out. Nobody must ever be able to say that people took the message to the Gentiles because they weren't bothered about Israel and its traditions, or because they didn't understand how important the law itself really was. No: when you want to reach the pagan world, the person to do it will be a hard-line, fanatical, ultra-nationalist, super-orthodox Pharisaic Jew. And then they say that God doesn't have a sense of humour.

Jewish humour, of course. And, like much Jewish humour, it makes a lot of sense, too. Ananias saw that sense, knew he had to obey, and went and did so. 'Just go', said the Lord, and he did. In addition, significantly, the Lord informs Ananias that he himself will show Saul what he will have to face. He, too, will have to suffer, indeed will face constant suffering, for the sake of the Name. Nobody will be able to say that he, or the other **apostles**, was in this business for the sake of a comfortable life, or for human glory, power or wealth. When God calls someone, said Dietrich Bonhoeffer, he bids them come and die. So it was with Saul; so it was with Ananias; so it is with us.

The gentle wisdom of Ananias has become legendary. This was his moment, and he didn't get it wrong.

'Brother Saul,' he begins. Brother! Part of the family! Bound, already, by ties of a new sort of kinship – the kinship indicated on the road when Jesus told Saul that he was persecuting, not just his followers, but him. And if Saul could see that, he could see anything and everything. Hands were laid on him; scales fell from his eyes; he saw, was baptized, and ate. Was it of this passage, perhaps, that George Herbert was thinking?

> I, the unkind, ungrateful? Ah, my dear,
>   I cannot look on thee.
> Love took my hand, and smiling did reply,
>   Who made the eyes but I?
> Truth, Lord, but I have marred them; let my shame
>   Go where it doth deserve.
> And know you not, says Love, who bore the blame?
>   My dear; then I will serve.
> You must sit down, says Love, and taste my meat.
> So I did sit and eat.

ACTS 9.19b–31

'He Is God's Son' (See map 9, page xix.)

> ^{19b}Saul stayed with the disciples in Damascus for a few days. ²⁰At once he proclaimed Jesus in the synagogues, saying, 'This really is the son of God!' ²¹Everyone was astonished, and said, 'Isn't this the man who caused havoc to those in Jerusalem who call on this Name? And here he is, coming to tie them up and take them off to the high priests!' ²²But Saul grew all the stronger, and threw the Jews in Damascus into confusion by demonstrating that Jesus is indeed the Messiah.
>
> ²³After some days, the Jews made a plot to kill him, ²⁴but Saul got wind of their plan. They were watching the city gates day and night so that they could do away with him. ²⁵But the disciples took him by night and let him down through the wall, lowering him in a basket.
>
> ²⁶When he got back to Jerusalem he tried to join the disciples, but they were all afraid of him, not believing that he really was a disciple. ²⁷But Barnabas took him, brought him to the apostles, and explained to them how he had seen the Lord on the road, and that he had spoken to him, and how in Damascus he had spoken boldly in the name of Jesus.
>
> ²⁸He was with them in Jerusalem, coming and going and speaking boldly in the name of the Lord. ²⁹He spoke, as well, to the Hellenists, who tried to kill him. ³⁰But the family heard of it and took him down to Caesarea. There they sent him off to Tarsus.
>
> ³¹So the church in all Judaea, Galilee and Samaria found itself at peace. It was built up and gained in numbers, living in the fear of the Lord and the comfort of the holy spirit.

'How did you start your great missionary career, Paul?'

'I was let down through the wall in a basket and ran away!'

Actually, that is more or less what Paul himself wrote, at the end of 2 Corinthians 11, quite deliberately showing the proud Corinthians that the God he was proclaiming is the one who takes delight in standing everything on its head. All human boasting, all human pride, has to be upended, so that God's glory can shine through. So we shouldn't be surprised that the first chapters in what was, indeed, a great missionary career are full of plots and runnings away. You can almost feel the sigh of relief in verse 30, as the Jerusalem **apostles** and the rest finally pack Saul off by boat from Caesarea to Tarsus. Phew! That's one bit of trouble out of the way. Perhaps there is a shade of irony, then, in verse 31: once he was gone, Jesus' followers could have a bit of peace.

Actually, of course, Luke means a lot more than that. There was a new energy about the place, a new spring in the step. The fact that someone like Saul of Tarsus, with the reputation he had had, had been confronted by Jesus himself, stopped in his tracks and turned around, and was now using his very considerable biblical skill and way with words to demonstrate to all and sundry that Jesus really was the **Messiah** – well, this was bound to encourage all the Jesus-followers who heard about it.

And not just encourage them: inform them, show them more clearly how to read the scriptures, how to understand the vast sweep of God's promises on the one hand and the fascinating but telling details on the other. And, in particular, this is the first time in Acts that we find Jesus being referred to with the title which became standard right across early Christianity: he is the **son of God** (verse 20).

But what did that mean? Two verses later we find Paul insisting that Jesus really was 'the Messiah' – or, perhaps we should translate it, 'that "the Messiah" really was this man, Jesus'. It wasn't simply that Jewish people in the synagogues had heard about Jesus and were trying to figure out who he was; they had, much more thoroughly, heard in scripture and sermon and song for many generations that there might be a new 'anointed king', a 'Messiah', on the way. But who would it be? To that question, Paul was answering simply: it's Jesus, despite what you might think at first glance.

But what is the relationship between 'son of God' and 'Messiah'? Luke doesn't explain, but his strong emphasis on the Old Testament context of everything that is said about Jesus, coupled with Paul's later writings in which both ideas occur frequently, helps us to see how it works out. The phrase 'son of God' isn't used very much in the Old Testament, but when it is it refers to two things, or people, in particular: the people of Israel ('Israel is my son, my firstborn,' said God to Pharaoh, 'so let my people go!') and the **son of David**, the Messiah himself. God had promised David that he would have a son who would build the **Temple**. God would 'raise him up' and he would sit on David's throne; 'I will be a father to him,' declared God, 'and he will be my son' (2 Samuel 7.12–14). This point is rammed home in Psalm 2, which as we have seen was invoked by the early church when they prayed about the onset of persecution (4.25–26). Confronting the malevolent rulers of the world, God declares that he has established his King in Zion, the one before whom the nations must tremble, the one to whom God has said in a firm decree, 'You are my son, this day I have begotten you' (Psalm 2.7). The whole point is that, through Israel's Messiah, God will reach out to the **Gentiles**, giving this King the nations of the world (not just the holy land, we note) as his 'inheritance'. These lands will no doubt need to be brought firmly into line with the will of the creator God, but they will then be ready to be ruled over in wisdom and justice

(Psalm 2.8–12). In other words, invoking Psalm 2 doesn't just give you a sense of the Messiah, the true anointed king, as God's 'son'. It fits in perfectly with the typically Jewish notion, which was the foundation of Paul's missionary vocation, that when God does for Israel what he's going to do for Israel then the nations will come under his judging and saving rule.

The same point is made in Psalm 72, and again in Psalm 89, where, in verses 26 and 27, there is an echo of the passage quoted above from 2 Samuel 7. And, significantly, there are signs that passages like these were being used in the **Dead Sea Scrolls**, not so long before the time of Jesus, as people tried to puzzle out who the Messiah would be and what he would do. In other words, this way of reading these ancient texts was not unknown already in Paul's world, though of course nobody had dreamed of applying them to someone like Jesus of Nazareth. Because, after all, he had been crucified, which nobody ever supposed would happen to the Messiah of all people. According to Psalm 2, he was meant to defeat the pagan enemies, smashing them to pieces like a potter's vessel, not being himself smashed to pieces at their hands.

And yet. In the very Psalms which Paul must have meditated on many times, and in the prophecies which went alongside them, there was another, darker strand. Psalm 89 itself, after celebrating the great promises of God to the king and through the king, ends with a lament: why has it all gone so horribly wrong? Why has the nation, and the king, apparently been rejected? And this ties in with other Psalms of lament, of the righteous sufferer who commits his cause to God and is eventually vindicated; and with prophecies, not least as we have seen the central prophecies of the book of Isaiah, which speak of the suffering Servant of the Lord who will 'bear the sin of many' and thereby establish God's new **covenant** and new creation. In and through all of this, the *messianic* meaning of 'son of God' was steadily being fused with the *Israel* meaning: the king represents his people, so that he can and must stand in for them. What happens to him, happens to them, and vice versa.

And, of course, with the suffering and vindication there came into view the central feature of the new movement, to which Paul would later refer back as the main point of his preaching and life: the **resurrection** (see 23.6–10; 24.15, 21; 25.19; 26.8, 23). It was the resurrection of Jesus through which the God he called 'Father' had declared, 'See! He really was my son all along!' That is the point Paul makes at the beginning, and as the foundation, of the greatest letter he ever wrote (Romans 1.3–4). And, if that is so, then all sorts of things follow: the death of Jesus is to be understood not as a messy or tragic accident, but precisely as the death of the one who was the living expression of the Father's love. 'He who did not spare his own Son,' wrote Paul in a passage of great and powerful pathos, 'but gave him up for us all – how shall he not, with him, freely give us all things?' (Romans 8.32).

But wait a minute. Has not the phrase 'son of God' subtly changed in the process? Yes, it has. It has gone from meaning simply 'Messiah', or simply 'Israel', to something else, something which the Old Testament had not envisaged, or not in that way, but which looms up behind as a great unspoken possibility. Sometimes, when Paul speaks of God 'sending his son' (Romans 8.3; Galatians 4.4), the language reminds us of the strange Jewish writings in which God 'sends' the figure of 'wisdom' into the world, 'wisdom' who is God's second self, the 'wisdom' through which God made the world in the first place. Somehow, it seems, the early Christians, and perhaps pre-eminently Paul, are discovering that *within* the expectation of a Messiah who would be, in some sense, 'God's son', there was a deeper truth: that the Messiah, when he came, would be God's own second self, God in human form, wisdom incarnate. The phrase 'son of God' came, very early in the Christian movement, to carry all of that meaning, without leaving behind (indeed, depending for its full sense upon) the 'messianic' sense. And all of it made shocking but very clear sense of what Saul had seen in his vision on the road: 'the glory of God in the face of Jesus the Messiah'.

All this would of course appear blasphemous nonsense to Jews who took the view that Saul of Tarsus had himself taken a matter of days before. And to have him of all people announcing it, demonstrating it, arguing it from scripture – it was intolerable. And so there began the sequence of plots and persecutions from which Saul was never again to be free. He runs away from Damascus. In Jerusalem he begins under heavy suspicion from the Christians, and ends with a Jewish plot against his life. (Barnabas appears on the scene, bless him, as the 'son of encouragement', explaining to the suspicious believers what had happened to Saul on the road to Damascus.) What is one to do with someone like that?

The answer is significant. He must go back home. He must go to his own people. He needs to start where they know him. There will be pain there – pain which may be reflected in the tears at the start of Romans 9. But there will be missionary opportunities of the sort he must grasp. So, not for the last time, Saul takes a ship to go preaching. The pattern of the rest of his life has been established.

ACTS 9.32–42

Back to Peter (See map 10, page xx.)

³²As Peter was going through various places among all the believers, he went down to God's people who lived in Lydda. ³³There he found a paralysed man named Aeneas who had been confined to bed for eight years.

³⁴'Aeneas,' Peter said to him, 'Jesus the Messiah heals you! Stand up and fold up your bed!'

And at once he stood up. ³⁵Everyone who lived at Lydda and Sharon saw it, and they turned to the Lord.

³⁶In Joppa there was a disciple named Tabitha, whose name translates as 'Dorcas'. She was full of good works and generous deeds. ³⁷Around that time she fell ill and died. They washed her and laid her in an upper room. ³⁸Lydda is near Joppa, and the disciples, hearing that Peter was there, sent two men to him with the urgent request that he shouldn't delay, but come to them at once. ³⁹So Peter got up and went with them. When he arrived, they took him to the upper room, where all the widows were weeping. They showed him the tunics and the other clothes that Dorcas had made while she was with them.

⁴⁰Peter sent them all out. Then he knelt down and prayed, and turned to the body.

'Tabitha,' he said, 'get up!'

She opened her eyes, and when she saw Peter she sat up. ⁴¹He gave her his hand and lifted her up. Then he called God's people, including the widows, and presented her alive.

⁴²This became known throughout the whole of Joppa, and many believed in the Lord. ⁴³Peter stayed on in Joppa for some days, at the house of Simon the tanner.

When I look out of the window from where I am sitting, I have two quite different types of view. If I stretch my eyes and look through the trees (it is still spring, and the leaves have not yet blocked the view) I can see the ruined castle, standing on the headland two or three miles away, looking out to sea. If I look near at hand, I can see, a mere eight feet or so from the window, a riot of small birds playing among my neighbour's roses and shrubs. Sometimes a robin comes and sits on the fence, staring in at me, as though she's trying to discover what I'm writing about.

One of the glories of Luke's writing is that he can take us, in a couple of strides, from the enormous, earth-shattering, history-changing moments like the **conversion** of Saul to a small, intimate scene: an upstairs room in a poor home, filled with the knitting and sewing that had occupied the good lady who has just died. This too, of course, plays its part in the larger whole, since what Luke is doing here is to bring us back into Peter's story, having inserted Saul with appropriate and violent suddenness into the narrative of the Jerusalem **apostles**. And he is getting us ready, in particular, for another long view, as Peter, having found his way down to Joppa, will be called from there on another and more widely significant errand. (Joppa, by the way, is on the coast north-west of Jerusalem, near today's Tel Aviv. Lydda is about ten miles inland. The area known as Sharon is the coastal plain north from there, on the way to the port of Caesarea.)

But there is no such thing as a small errand in the **kingdom of God**. If all we knew about Peter was that he had healed the disabled Aeneas, and had raised Dorcas from the dead, that would be enough to know that the power of God was working through him; and perhaps these apparently smaller stories were told here by Luke to remind anyone who might be disposed to think otherwise that Peter was where he was on proper business from the Lord, the **gospel** business of healing and encouraging and building up God's people. (Note, incidentally, how Luke here and elsewhere, still not often using the word 'church' to describe Jesus' followers, has taken to describing them as 'God's people', which is how I've translated a word which literally means 'the holy ones' or 'the saints'. The force of the word is that these are the people whom God is setting apart as belonging specially to himself, called for his particular purposes.)

These two healings, unlike the one which occurred in chapter 3, seem to have provoked no controversy. Nobody started an inquisition against Peter because he had used the name of Jesus and had once again discovered its great power. But then, he wasn't standing beside the **Temple**. Things had moved on. These healings are signs of hope, bringing people to **faith**.

There remain mysteries attached to them, though, as perhaps there are to all healings. Why is Peter called to this person who has just died, and not to any one of the others (Dorcas cannot have been the only follower of Jesus to have died in the first years of the movement)? Why does Aeneas get healed, rather than all the other disabled people in the area? Why do some people get called to new work by an inner prompting, others by an angelic visitor, and others again by an ordinary messenger coming from a neighbouring town? If Luke had wanted to tell us that God keeps people guessing, he couldn't have done it much better.

Two other things stand out from this small pastoral interlude. First, there is Dorcas herself, who stands as it were for all those unsung heroines who have got on with what they can do best and have done it to the glory of God. Had it not been for Peter, she might never have made it into the pages of the New Testament, and we have to assume that

117

there were dozens in the early years, and thousands in later years, who, like her, lived their lives in faith and hope, bearing the sorrows of life no doubt as well as celebrating its joys, and finding in the small acts of service to others a fulfilment of the gospel within their own sphere, using traditional skills to the glory of God. Luke is right to draw our eyes down to the small-scale and immediate, in case we should ever forget that these are the people who form the heart of the church, while the apostles and evangelists go about making important decisions, getting locked up, stoned or shipwrecked, preaching great sermons, writing great letters, and generally being great and good all over the place. I am privileged to know plenty of Dorcases. The day before I wrote this I met one whose speciality is chocolate truffles. When I meet such people I greet them as what they are, the beating heart of the people of God.

Second, the group Peter visited in Joppa was basically a group of widows (verses 39, 41). As we saw in chapter 6, the widows were beginning to form an important group within the life of the church. There is something poignant about this group, who by definition were all carrying one of life's largest forms of grief, becoming recognized and acknowledged as having, not merely a claim on the general resources, but a significant contribution to make. Do not belittle the ministry of stitching, sewing, knitting and generally providing for the needs of the larger community – especially at a time before anyone dreamed of mass-produced clothes. And do not forget to celebrate, as Luke does here, the fact that the apparently ordinary people are not ordinary to God, and that when we tell the story of the great sweep of God's purposes in history there are, at every point, the Aeneases and the Dorcases who smile out of the page at us, like the robin in the garden, and remind us what it's really all about.

ACTS 10.1–16

Peter's Vision (See map 11, page xx.)

¹In Caesarea there was a man named Cornelius, a centurion with the cohort called 'the Italian'. ²He was devout, and he and all his household revered God. He gave alms generously to the people, and constantly prayed to God.

³He had a vision. Around three o'clock in the afternoon he saw, quite clearly, one of God's angels coming to him.

'Cornelius!' said the angel.

⁴He looked hard at him, terrified.

'What is it, Sir?' he said.

'Your prayers and your alms have come to God's notice', said the angel. ⁵'What you must do is this. Send men to Joppa, and ask for someone called Simon, surnamed Peter. [6]He is staying with a man called Simon, a tanner, whose house is beside the sea.'

[7]When the angel who had spoken with him went away, he called two of his household and a devout soldier from among his retinue. [8]He explained everything to them, and sent them off to Joppa.

[9]The next day, as they were on their journey and getting near the town, Peter went up onto the roof of the house to pray. It was around midday; [10]he was hungry, and asked for something to eat. While they were preparing it, he fell into a trance. [11]He saw heaven opened, and a vessel like a great sail coming down towards the earth, suspended by its four corners. [12]In the sail there was every kind of four-footed creature, reptiles of the earth and birds of the air. [13]Then he heard a voice: 'Get up, Peter!' said the voice. 'Kill and eat!'

[14]'Certainly not, Master!' said Peter. 'I've never eaten anything common or unclean!'

[15]'What God has made clean,' said the voice, coming now for a second time, 'you must not regard as common.'

[16]This all happened three times, and then suddenly the sail was whisked back up to heaven.

When I went off to university it was much more of an awesome experience than it is for many today. I had scraped into Oxford by the skin of my teeth, having spent too much of my teenage years doing everything else, particularly sport and music, rather than studying. And, in any case, I was from the north of England. I had only spent occasional holidays in the south. Coming as I did from a small town, I had never lived in a city, still less an ancient and stunningly beautiful one like Oxford. There was a mystique about the whole thing which, even in the ultra-cynical 1960s, you couldn't ignore.

And of course there were the dons – professors, the Americans would call them: world authorities in their various fields, writing books, giving lectures, debating high-flown points in abstract concepts and several languages at once, arguing with one another over old oak dining tables, taking time out here and there to advise governments, make television programmes, or lead expeditions to remote and dangerous corners of the world. Of course, once you attended the first lectures and tutorials most of them quickly came down to the size of ordinary mortals. But when you first arrived, you saw those gowned figures (as they often were in those days) and regarded them as demigods. They were the people. They were what the place was all about.

That is a pale reflection of how, in the first century, the rest of the world regarded Rome. Rome had become mistress of the world in the first century BC, based on a centuries-long history of solid democratic republicanism (they could teach today's Western world a thing or two about all that) and an even more solid tradition of military power. Actually, make that relentless brutality. Rome carried all before it, most of the time at least (we draw a veil, as they did, over those three legions that went missing in Germany, and one or two other embarrassing disasters). And if you lived in one of the far-flung corners of the Roman Empire, such as Britain in the far north-east or Judaea in the far south-west, you would hear of Rome, as a country boy from the north of England hears of Oxford, spoken of in glowing tones. And, in a city and empire built on military success, the demi-gods who strode around and made things happen were of course the military officers. They could make or break an emperor. They could snap their fingers and have you flogged or killed, or your house demolished. When you got near Rome, or a Roman military base anywhere in the world, you would see one or two of them walking around, and you would think: there they are. Those are the people. They are what it's all about.

Gradually, very, very slowly, Luke is going to take us to Rome itself. He wants us to be getting ready.

But, astonishingly, the first Roman we meet in this book completely overturns the stereotype. Yes, he's a real, solid, no-nonsense Roman. He's a military officer in the army which the whole world feared. Caesarea was an important garrison town, the port which Herod the Great had built up to force all traders to come through it and pay a handy tax as they did so. It was where the governor normally resided, down in the warm weather by the sea, only going up to chilly Jerusalem for festivals and other special occasions. (All right, Jerusalem is often as hot as anywhere else in the Middle East, but it's about a mile above sea level, high up in the hills, and for several months in the year it can be bitterly cold. Down by the sea is a more natural place for an Italian.) There were plenty of backwaters in the Roman Empire where a soldier who wasn't really worth his salt could be sent, but Caesarea wasn't one of them. It was a key port in a key strategic zone. Rome was desperate to keep the Middle East as peaceful as possible, because Rome depended utterly on the grain that was shipped, throughout the sailing season, from Egypt. Any centurion (a middle-ranking officer, with 100 men under him) posted to Caesarea must have been a good and trusted soldier.

And Cornelius was devout. He was a man of prayer. He had great respect for the Jewish people and their traditions. He was a seeker after God. He was generous with his money. He had won the respect not only of his peers in the Roman army but of the Jewish community in the neighbourhood. What is Luke trying to tell us? Or what (since we haven't yet discussed the question of who he was really writing for) might this tell us about his intended audience?

There is more going on, then, in this story than simply the remarkable moment (repeated twice in case we were asleep the first time, a technique Luke uses more than once in this book) when a whole group of **Gentiles** hear the **gospel** of Jesus, believe it, and receive the **spirit**. This was so shocking, so startling, to the Jewish believers who up to then had made up more or less the entire community (apart from those converts in Samaria, and apart from the Ethiopian eunuch we met in chapter 8), that it needed, as we shall see, to be stressed for this reason alone. But we shouldn't allow this great theme, the **conversion** of the Gentiles, to make us ignore the other theme which, small at the moment, will become more and more important as the book moves on: the gospel and the Romans.

For the moment, though, let's stick with the conversion of the Gentiles. Luke makes it clear that God was preparing the way most carefully, step by step. It's a case of double vision: Cornelius sees an angel telling him to send for Peter; Peter sees a sail full of unclean animals and is told to eat. Cornelius' vision makes, at first sight, more immediate sense than Peter's, but Peter's is hugely important at the level of symbol as well as content.

Peter has found his way to Joppa, about 30 miles down the coast from Caesarea. He is staying by the sea, and has leisure to pause at midday to pray. Then comes his vision, the sort of thing at one level a hungry man might fantasize about – a large vessel, like a sail or sheet, full of every sort of creature you might want to eat and a large number you decidedly wouldn't. Especially if you were a devout Jew.

At this point we must remind ourselves of one of the basic points about the Jewish food laws. It wasn't just that the Jews weren't allowed to eat pork. There was a whole range of meat which they were forbidden; they are listed (for example) in Leviticus 11, and were much discussed by later generations. And these food laws, whatever their origin, served to mark out the Jewish people from their non-Jewish neighbours, a rule reinforced by the prohibition on Jews eating with non-Jews, sharing table **fellowship**. The reasoning was clear: the people you sit down and eat with are 'family', but the Jewish 'family' has been called by God to be separate, to bear witness to his special love and grace to the world, and must not therefore compromise with the world. Of course, there were less complimentary ways of putting that as well, and the food taboos were regularly used as a weapon in a larger war of words, with Jews accusing Gentiles of all kinds of wickedness and uncleanness, and Gentiles responding with sneers. All of this we must keep in mind as we join Peter on the roof and watch this great sail descending from **heaven** – with unclean food in it.

'Get up, Peter!' says a voice. 'Kill and eat!'

121

Peter is horrified. 'Certainly not! I've never done that before and I'm not going to start now! It's unclean!'

Then comes the response which echoes through the centuries, and still challenges all kinds of prejudice.

'What God has made clean, you must not regard as common.'

Peter didn't know, of course, what was about to happen, and hence what this vision was supposed to mean. We know, because Luke has told us at the start of this passage. But, as the story progresses – and there are some surprises to come – we must make sure we are standing in the shoes of a first-century Jewish fisherman, feeling his way towards some astonishing and revolutionary understandings. And, also, of a first-century Roman centurion, accepting the fact that he is at the moment outside the people of the God he was coming to worship and respect, and waiting humbly – just what *is* Luke saying to his Roman audience? – to hear a fresh and startling **message**.

ACTS 10.17–33

Peter Goes to Cornelius

[17]When Peter came to himself, he was puzzled as to what the vision he had seen was all about. Then, suddenly, the men sent by Cornelius appeared, standing by the gate. They had been asking for Simon's house, [18]enquiring if someone by the name of Simon called Peter was staying there. [19]Peter was still pondering the vision, when the spirit spoke to him.

'Look', said the spirit. 'There are three men searching for you. [20]It's all right; get up, go down and go with them. Don't be prejudiced; I have sent them.'

[21]So Peter went down to the men.

'Here I am', he said. 'I'm the one you're looking for. Why have you come?'

[22]'There is a man called Cornelius', they replied. 'He is a centurion, and he is a righteous and God-fearing man. The whole people of the Jews will testify to him. A holy angel told him in a vision to send for you to come to his house, so that he can hear any words you may have to say.'

[23]So he invited them in and put them up for the night.

In the morning he got up and went with them. Some of the believers from Joppa went with him. [24]They reached Caesarea the following day. Cornelius had summoned his relatives and close friends and was waiting for him.

[25]When Peter came in, Cornelius went to meet him. He fell down at his feet and worshipped him.

[26]'Get up!' said Peter, lifting him up. 'I'm just a man, too.'

²⁷So they talked together, and Peter came in and found lots of people assembled.

²⁸'You must know', he said to them, 'that it is forbidden for a Jewish man to mix with or visit a Gentile. But God showed me that I should call nobody "common" or "unclean". ²⁹So I came when I was asked, and raised no objections. Do tell me, then, the reason why you sent for me.'

³⁰'Four days ago', answered Cornelius, 'I was praying in my house at around this time, about three o'clock, and suddenly a man stood beside me in shining clothes. ³¹"Cornelius," he said, "your prayer has been heard, and your almsgiving has been remembered by God. ³²So send someone to Joppa and call Simon, who is named Peter; he is staying in the house of Simon the tanner, beside the sea." ³³So I sent for you at once, and you have been kind enough to come. So now we are all here, in God's presence, to listen to everything which the Lord has told you to say.'

There is a story told of C. S. Lewis, as a small boy – about six or seven, I think. One day he announced to his father,

'Daddy, I have a prejudice against the French.'

'Why?' asked his father, not unreasonably.

'If I knew that,' replied the precocious youngster triumphantly, 'it wouldn't be a prejudice.'

He was quite right, of course. The point about a prejudice is that it's what you have when you are 'pre-judging' a case: making your mind up before you know the facts.

Now of course there are many halfway stages between naked prejudice and completely well-informed opinion. Frequently we back up our prejudices by finding out just enough facts that support our case, and conveniently ignoring the rest. Bad historians, clever politicians and lazy theologians do that all the time. And in the case of the ancient world people did it a lot, too. Many Jews could tell stories about the wicked things that **Gentiles** got up to. One of the reasons some Jews gave for not going into Gentile houses and eating with them was that the houses were polluted because Gentiles forced their womenfolk to have abortions and then put the dead foetuses down the drains or under the floorboards. In the same sort of way, some Gentiles were taught that Jews were stuck-up, unsociable people, because they wouldn't eat pork (which was the cheapest meat available in most places), because they insisted on having a day off work each week, and because they wouldn't join in with normal social activities, like the parties which went on around pagan temples and the great games which celebrated the gods, or sometimes the emperors. A particularly interesting slur was that Jewish people robbed pagan temples, presumably because,

123

since they didn't regard the pagan divinities as real, nobody actually owned what was in their shrines so they might as well help themselves. But so far as we can tell there were large numbers of Gentiles and Jews who lived quite happily alongside one another and gave the lie to the prejudices.

The prejudices remained, however, not least because of the biblical calling of the Jewish people to be separate, to be holy, to stand apart from the rest of humanity so that through them God's light might shine. In other words, when the Jewish people sometimes told stories to explain why one should not visit Gentiles and eat with them, this was not a way of backing up a mere irrational, knee-jerk fear of foreigners. In fact, to suggest that that's what was going on might be just another example of Gentile prejudice against Jewish scruples! The New Testament writers, including Paul, are quite clear that the Mosaic **law**, which contains the basic prohibitions, was God's **word** to Israel and should be respected as such.

But Paul and the others are equally clear that, in the light of Jesus Christ, it was to be seen as God's word *for a particular period and for a particular purpose.* Imagine a mother seeing her child at the other side of the street, about to cross a busy road. 'Stand still!' she shouts urgently. Then, a minute later, seeing that the traffic has come to a stop at the light, she shouts again, 'Walk across!' She hasn't contradicted herself. The initial command was the right one for the time. Indeed, it is because she wanted the child to walk across in the end that she told him to stand still for the moment. If he hadn't, he wouldn't have made it across at all.

That is the kind of shift in thinking which was going on as Peter went to Cornelius' house. He knew, of course, the scriptural promises that Israel would be the light of the world. He knew that Jesus had spoken of a time when people would come from east and west (this, significantly, was following Jesus' own meeting with a devout centurion, in Matthew 8) into God's new world. But it seems that he, like the others, had assumed that non-Jews who wanted to share in the life of God's new world, the **messianic** world that had been opened up through Jesus, would have to do what Gentiles had always had to do: to become proselytes, to take upon themselves Jewish identity, to renounce their own ethnic past and embrace Judaism lock, stock and barrel.

And there is still a sense in which that is true. Paul, remarkably, addresses the ex-pagan Gentiles precisely as that, *ex*-pagans: 'When you were pagans,' he says, 'you were led astray to dumb idols' (1 Corinthians 12.2). So what are they now? Well, they seem to have been incorporated into the Jewish story and family. 'Our fathers', he says to the same ex-pagan Corinthians, referring to Moses and the patriarchs, and assuming that the ex-pagans are now part of the family (1 Corinthians 10.1). Being Jewish, in some sense or other, still matters. It's just that the category has become, to say the least, somewhat more confusing than it used to be.

This is the point at which we have to be extremely careful. It would be all too easy, following precisely our own late-Western, postmodern prejudices, to imagine that the whole episode to do with Cornelius was simply about getting rid of all distinctions and being 'tolerant' of everyone. That would be a bad mistake. If what Peter had discovered was that God simply accepts everyone the way they are, what was the fuss for Cornelius to be devout and god-fearing? Why bother sending for Peter to come and tell him about Jesus? Why not just stay as he was? People today sometimes refer to this present story as a sign that, within the New Testament, there is a recognition that 'all religions lead to God', or even that all religions are basically the same. That is certainly not what Luke intends, and both Cornelius himself and Peter himself would have been shocked at any such suggestion. The reason Cornelius was a devout worshipper of Israel's God was precisely that he was fed up with the normal Roman gods and eager to follow what seemed to him the real one. It is not the case, then, that God simply 'accepts us as we are'. He *invites* us as we are; but responding to that invitation always involves the complete transformation which is acted out in **repentance**, **forgiveness**, **baptism** and receiving the **spirit**.

No: what is at stake here is not the eighteenth-century principle of 'tolerance', but the glorious first-century truth that, in Jesus the **Messiah** of Israel, God has broken down the barrier between Jews and Gentiles, humiliating both categories (Jews, because they apparently lose their privileged position; Gentiles, because they have to acknowledge the Jewish Messiah) in order to reveal God's mercy to both. This is, of course, what Paul says in Romans 9—11, and Luke is not taking us that far into theology just now; but we do well to note what is going on. Peter knew that Jews who wanted to belong to the new movement had had to repent of sin (Acts 2.38). Up to now, he would have said that Gentiles, if they wanted to belong, would have had to become Jews as well. But the point which is being made in this graphic and deeply human story (complete with Cornelius' understandable and over-enthusiastic *faux pas* of falling down and worshipping Peter, and Peter telling him quickly to get up) is that, though Gentiles too had to repent and believe in Jesus just as Jews did, they did not have to become Jews before or after that process.

Look at it like this. We saw in chapter 7, in the speech of Stephen, building on earlier hints, that the **Temple** was being made redundant by the fact of Jesus. Jesus had become the place where, and the means by which, the God of Israel was now meeting with his people in grace and mercy. In the same way, the taboos of food and family had been set up by God in the first place to do a proper and important job of keeping Israel for himself, separate from the rest of the world, against the day when he would finally act to do through Israel what he had always planned. Now, in Jesus and by the spirit, God had carried out that plan. The time had therefore come when all alike, Gentile as well as Jew, could be welcomed into God's family on exactly the same terms. That, incidentally, is near the heart of what Paul means when he talks about 'justification by **faith**'; but that is a topic for another occasion.

ACTS 10.34–48

Telling the Gentiles about Jesus

[34]Peter took a deep breath and began.

'It's become clear to me', he said, 'that God really does show no favouritism. [35]No: in every race, people who fear him and do what is right are acceptable to him. [36]He sent his word to the children of Israel, announcing peace through Jesus Christ – he is Lord of all! [37]You know all about this, and how the word spread through all Judaea, beginning from Galilee after the baptism which John proclaimed.

[38]'God anointed this man, Jesus of Nazareth, with the holy spirit and with power. He went about doing good and healing all who were overpowered by the devil, since God was with him. [39]We are witnesses of everything he did in the land of Judaea and in Jerusalem. They killed him by hanging him on a tree; [40]but God raised him on the third day, and allowed him to be seen, [41]not indeed by all the people, but by those of us whom God had appointed beforehand. We ate and drank with him after he had been raised from the dead. [42]And he commanded us to announce to the people, and to bear testimony, that he is the one appointed by God to be judge of the living and the dead. [43]All the prophets give their witness: he is the one! Everyone who believes in him receives forgiveness of sins through his Name.'

[44]While Peter was still saying all this, the holy spirit fell on everyone who was listening to the word. [45]The circumcised believers who had accompanied Peter were astonished, because the gift of the holy spirit had been poured out on the Gentiles too. [46]They heard them speaking with tongues and praising God.

Then Peter spoke up.

[47]'Nobody can deny these people water to be baptized, can they?' he said. 'They have received the holy spirit, just like we did!' [48]So he ordered them to be baptized in the name of Jesus the Messiah.

Then they asked him to stay for a few days.

When the children were younger, we used to play story tapes in the car on long journeys. They sat very, very still right through entire books like *The Railway Children* or the *Narnia* cycle. They didn't want to miss a thing. Right through, nobody asked how far we still had to go, or whether they could have a sandwich now, or could we stop for a bathroom break. Something about the story drew them into a whole new world. As long as they were living in that world, it had them in its power. Even the simplest of stories can do this.

Jesus himself, of course, told stories a good deal. The parables were designed to woo people in to a different world, a different way of looking at things. When the story finished, they were left somewhere quite different from where they had begun. They had changed, because their way of looking at the world had changed.

The first **apostles** themselves went on telling and retelling the stories which Jesus himself had told, but they quickly found that they had another story to tell which was even better: the story about Jesus himself. You could tell it this way, you could tell it that way, you could make it longer or shorter (though always with the same decisive ending, of course), but whichever way you did it this story carried power of a new kind. It had all the power of the good story, the novel, the parable, the story-tape in the car, but it had two extra things as well. First, it was the focal point of the true story of the creator God and his world, of the **covenant** God and Israel: at this point, the greatest narratives of all time come rushing together. Second, it was the story in which the name of Jesus himself was front and centre. We have learnt quite a lot, reading Acts, about the power which the name carried in itself, let alone in a narrative framework acting as a kind of showcase.

So we shouldn't be as surprised as Peter was when, with the story only told in barest outline, the **holy spirit** fell on all those who are listening. This is, though, a moment we have been waiting for since the first two chapters. Jesus told his followers that they would be his witnesses in Jerusalem, Judaea, Samaria and to the ends of the earth, and the holy spirit had fallen on the believers in Jerusalem (Acts 2) and in Samaria (Acts 8). Now at last, the spirit comes on **Gentiles** as well. Granted, Caesarea is hardly 'the ends of the earth', but the **message** has now reached out to embrace not only Gentiles but Romans. From here, it may be a long step geographically but it's only a short step culturally to everywhere else in the then known world, from Britain and Spain in the west to Parthia, India and Egypt in the east.

So what is this message about Jesus? How did they tell the story in those early days? Well, as I said, they told it in a wide variety of ways. But Peter's short address here follows a fairly standard pattern, the pattern which was, more or less, worked up by Luke and the other gospel writers into their much longer writings.

It begins with Jesus' preaching to Israel. This wasn't a generalized message which just happened to be sent to the Jews because Jesus just happened to be Jewish. Israel was the nation entrusted with God's promise for the whole of creation; it is noticeable that when addressing the Gentiles Peter doesn't omit or tone down this particularity, even when he's just said that God shows no favouritism. This tension must not be dissolved, as so many theological schemes have done; it is of the essence of the message. Indeed, what Peter says throughout might be thought to be so Israel-specific as to be quite irrelevant to the Gentiles he's talking to. **John the Baptist** announced his message to Israel, Jesus went around Judaea and Galilee, the events came to their climax in Jerusalem, and now we, a group of Jewish people, are witnesses to Jesus' **resurrection**. The only mention, throughout all of this, of anything that looks wider than the story of Israel, with Jesus in the middle of it, is Peter's declaration near the beginning that 'He (Jesus) is Lord – of all!' (verse 36). Oh, and the final line: *everyone* who believes in him receives **forgiveness** of sins through his name (verse 43).

So why did this message, about the mission of Jesus to Israel, have the effect it did on Cornelius and his family and friends? At one level, of course, because this message is itself powerful. When Paul talks in his letters about 'the **gospel**', he doesn't primarily mean 'the way you too can get saved'. He means 'the message that says that Jesus, the crucified and risen one, is the Lord of the whole world'. And, he says, that message itself carries its own power. It acts as a summons to all who hear it. Some mock, of course; but others find themselves gripped, changed from the inside out, aware of a new presence and power inside them. So it was that day.

But there is something else going on here as well. Here we see a message that stands, as it were, at the threshold. Peter's words to the Jews in Jerusalem on the **day of Pentecost** started where they started, with the recent events concerning Jesus, and the meaning those events had for all who heard of them. Paul's messages in Acts 14 and Acts 17 are given to Gentile audiences who have no thought that they might have anything to learn from Jews or Judaism, let alone from such an odd mutation within Judaism as Christian **faith** appeared to be. But what we have here is a message to someone who had been on the outside of Judaism but pressing his nose hard against the window to look in; one who respected and valued the Jewish traditions, and was doing his best to honour the God of Israel as far as the normal limits permitted. Peter is saying, in effect, 'Well, you have been standing in the doorway looking in with admiration at Israel and its traditions; now see how God has fulfilled Israel's dreams in sending Jesus.'

The key things to be highlighted, within that framework, are the things that God did. The gospel is after all a message about God, a message whose subject matter is Jesus. We already know, and Peter already knew, that Cornelius had showed boundless reverence for Israel's God. So he tells the story of Jesus as the story of God's actions.

To begin with, *God sent the message of peace* through Jesus (verse 36). When Jesus announced God's **kingdom**, he did so in the teeth of nationalist expectation of imminent armed revolt against Rome. No, declared Jesus: it was a message of peace (Luke 10.5–6; 19.42). But, to underwrite the message, *God anointed Jesus* with the spirit and power: in other words, he really was 'the **Messiah**', the anointed one, even though his form of kingship didn't look like what people had expected. Third, *God was with him*, a phrase which those who carry the Bible in their heads will recognize as a promise going way back into Israel's traditions of leadership and monarchy (Exodus 3.12; Joshua 1.9; Judges 6.12, 16; 1 Samuel 10.7, and many other passages), and coming forward into Jesus' own sense of vocation and the divine presence (John 10.38, etc.). Fourth, *God raised him from the dead*, the central affirmation of the story; fifth, *God chose us as witnesses*, which is why we're here in the first place; sixth, *God told us to preach* and spread the **word**; and, finally, overlapping with the punchline at the end of Paul's speech in Athens, and vital for the overall truth of the gospel, *God ordained Jesus as judge* of the living and the dead. In other words, Peter is saying: 'Cornelius: the God whom you have worshipped from afar has done all this, as part of his global plan to set everything right at last; and, at every stage, Jesus is in the middle of it all! God has thus fulfilled the purposes for which he called Israel in the first place; and you, Cornelius, and everyone everywhere who believes this message, will receive a welcome at once, without more ado, into the family whose home has, written in shining letters above the door, the wonderful word "forgiven".'

Cornelius and his household don't even have a chance to say, 'We believe.' The spirit comes upon them and they **speak with tongues**, just as the apostles did on the day of Pentecost. There are many signs of new **life** recorded in Acts, of which 'tongues' is only one, and it is by no means always present; but sometimes, when it happens, it happens for a purpose. Here the purpose is clear: Peter and those with him (**circumcised**, that is, Jewish, men) need to know that these *uncir*cumcised people have been regarded by the holy spirit as fit vessels to be filled with his presence and voice. And if that is so, there can be no barriers to **baptism**. All this is what is meant by the opening line of Peter's speech, 'God has no favourites.' This doesn't mean that God runs the world as a democracy, or that he simply validates and accepts everyone's opinion about everything, or everyone's chosen lifestyle. It means that there are no ethnic, geographical, cultural or moral barriers any longer in the way of anyone and everyone being offered forgiveness and new life. That is a message far more powerful than the easy-going laissez-faire tolerance which contemporary Western society so easily embraces. Cornelius didn't want God (or Peter) to *tolerate* him. He wanted to be welcomed, forgiven, healed, transformed. And he was.

ACTS 11.1–18

Controversy and Vindication

¹The apostles, and the brothers and sisters with them in Judaea, heard that the Gentiles had received the word of God. ²So when Peter went up to Jerusalem, those who wanted to emphasize circumcision took issue with him.

³'Why did you do it?' they asked. 'Why did you go in to visit uncircumcised men and eat with them?'

⁴So Peter began to explain it all, step by step.

⁵'I was in the town of Joppa', he said, 'and I was praying. I was in a trance, and I saw a vision: something like a great sail suspended by its four corners was let down from heaven, and came towards me. ⁶I stared at it, then I began to look in, and I saw four-footed land animals, wild beasts, reptiles and birds of the air. ⁷I heard a voice, saying to me, "Get up, Peter! Kill and eat!" ⁸"Certainly not, Lord," I replied. "Nothing common or unclean has ever entered my mouth!" ⁹Then the voice came from heaven a second time: "What God made clean, you must not regard as common." ¹⁰All this happened three times, and then the whole lot was drawn back up into heaven.

¹¹'Just then, suddenly, three men appeared at the house where I was, sent to me from Caesarea. ¹²The spirit told me to go with them, without raising scrupulous objections. These six brothers also came with me, and we went into the man's house. ¹³He told us that he had seen an angel standing in his house and saying, "Send to Joppa and fetch Simon called Peter, ¹⁴who will speak to you words by which you and all your house will be saved." ¹⁵As I began to speak, the holy spirit fell on them, just as the spirit did on us at the beginning. ¹⁶And I remembered the word which the Lord had spoken: "John baptized with water, but you will be baptized with the holy spirit."

¹⁷'So, then', Peter concluded, 'if God gave them the same gift as he gave to us when we believed in the Lord Jesus the Messiah, who was I to stand in the way of God?'

¹⁸When they heard this, they had nothing more to say. They praised God.

'Well, then', they declared, 'God has given the Gentiles, too, the repentance that leads to life!'

By common consent (even among those who disagreed with him), John Henry Newman was one of the finest minds of the nineteenth century. Having spent his young adult years as an Anglican priest, he famously converted to Roman Catholicism, and spent the rest of his life working as a theologian and pastor, ending up being honoured as a cardinal.

Newman was attacked from many sides, as people are who take an unexpected and unpopular stand. Many of these attacks he could shrug off or dismiss. But one persistent controversialist, the Reverend Charles Kingsley, eventually got under Newman's skin. It was one thing for people to disagree; but when Kingsley suggested that Newman had been insincere, had embraced a system which involved systematic and knowing untruth, Newman could abide it no longer. Writing at an extraordinary pace (and without the benefit of a word-processor!) he produced in 1864 one of the most remarkable autobiographies of all time: *Apologia Pro Vita Sua*, 'An Explanation for His Own Life'. Nothing was left out that needed to be made clear. From then on a new benchmark had been set. People might still disagree, but they could not charge him with insincerity or some kind of theological fraud.

The charges against Peter, when he got back to Jerusalem, were every bit as serious. And his defence – though a lot briefer than Newman's! – was every bit as vital for clearing the air and establishing a new position from which to go forward. For the first time we encounter a group in Jerusalem who will become more and more significant as the story goes on, and who crop up for good measure in the writings of Paul: a group of Jewish believers who were insisting on the importance of **circumcision**.

This is clearly a hard-line group *within* the Jerusalem believers, not a group of unbelieving Jewish rigorists. The phrase in verse 2 literally means 'those who are of the circumcision', which could simply mean 'all Jewish men', and that could refer to the entire company of Jewish males living in Jerusalem, which seems obviously unlikely, or the entire family of Jesus-followers in Jerusalem, which would be more likely but for the fact that verse 2 seems clearly to be talking about a smaller pressure group *within* the larger, but still Jewish, group of believers. This group seems to be the same, or similar, to the group mentioned in 15.6, and also to those about whom Paul writes in Galatians 2.12. Clearly, just as there were anxieties and divisions already within the Jerusalem

131

community at the start of Acts 6, so now a further, and potentially more divisive, split is starting to open up, which will turn within a few years into a major problem.

But for the moment Peter replies to them, as Newman replied to his critics, by telling the story from the top once more and showing, at every step, how the **holy spirit** had left him with no alternative but to do what he did, both going to Cornelius' house, accepting his hospitality, and in particular baptizing him and his household. It was the hospitality which had initially worried the 'circumcision group', since it broke the taboos we mentioned earlier. But clearly the major concern, which if allowed to stand would blow a hole right through the worldview of the 'circumcision group', was that these **Gentiles** had been admitted as full members of the new and rapidly developing Jesus-family *without having had to become Jews in the process*.

Peter's telling of the story follows so closely the account given in the previous chapter that we are forced to ask why Luke has run the risk of such major repetition within his normally fast-paced narrative. (The other obvious example is the triple repetition of the story of Paul's **conversion**. Significantly, both cases have to do with remarkable acts of God in doing new and unexpected things in people's lives, especially in extending the **gospel** to the Gentiles. Significantly, too, in both cases a story is repeated because it is needed in defence of the person concerned.) We can only conclude that for Luke the admission of Gentiles into God's people, reformed around Jesus, without needing to take on the marks of Jewish identity, i.e. circumcision and the food taboos, was one of the central and most important things he wanted to convey. Was this, we wonder, because he in his day was faced with similar controversies, and wanted to put down firm markers against any reawakening of a new 'circumcision party'? Or was it, perhaps, because he expected quite a few Roman Gentiles to be reading his book, and wanted to make it clear to them that when the first of 'their' people heard the gospel, and received the **spirit** and **baptism**, this was fully explained and fully validated against all cavil?

The other thing that stands out because of the repetition of the story is the fact that on a couple of points Luke has added small but significant details. First, Peter's report of what Cornelius had said to him now includes a new element: that the angel had said to Cornelius that Peter's message would result in him and his household 'being saved' (verse 14). Luke clearly does not suppose that Cornelius was 'saved' already and needed merely to be informed of the **message** about Jesus as an interesting addendum to a '**salvation**' he already possessed. Second, Peter tells the Jerusalem critics that the holy spirit fell on the assembled company 'as I began to speak'. It is true that what he had said in

Acts 10.34–43 was quite brief, and he may well have been intending to go on a lot longer, though at first glance we might have thought that those verses were already a summary of the whole message, since they cover so much in a short space. But Peter is clearly wanting to emphasize the sovereignty, and the surprising activity, of the holy spirit. Third, Peter now tells them, which we hadn't heard in chapter 10, that he had remembered the words of Jesus, back in the last moments before the **ascension** (1.5), telling them that the baptism in the spirit would shortly come upon them, in parallel with the baptism of **John** at the beginning.

All these are important as we ponder the ways God works and the ways in which God's people sometimes need to explain themselves to one another – an important task in all generations, since God is always doing new things, but there is equally a danger in mere human innovation. (Not all bright ideas are good ideas; not all good ideas are from God.) Part of the difficulty, of course, is identifying the work of the holy spirit. There have been, in the last century or so, many movements which have claimed to be spirit-driven, but which have resulted in all kinds of shameful behaviour. There is a constant need, particularly among Christian leaders, to be anchored in prayer, humility and deep attention to the **word** of God and particularly (as here) the words of Jesus.

Even when agreement seems to be reached, we cannot rest on our laurels. The victory which was won in verse 18, when Peter's inquisitors were reduced first to silence and then to recognizing that God had indeed been at work, seems to have been reversed again in 15.5. And the further victory of chapter 15 as a whole does not seem to have extended towards the glad recognition of non-Jewish believers as equal partners when Paul finally returns to Jerusalem in 21.20–21. What is the explanation for this?

Surely the obvious one: that things were not static in the social and political world of Jerusalem through the 40s and 50s of the first century. Far from it. The pace was hotting up. Pressure was mounting that would eventually lead to a massive revolt and the bloodiest and most disastrous war in Jewish history, ending with Jerusalem being destroyed by the Romans in AD 70. People were not, in other words, sitting around in Jerusalem discussing, as an abstract issue, the question of the value of circumcision and the food laws. These were the equivalents of the national flag at a time when the whole nation felt under intense and increasing pressure. To welcome Gentiles as equal brothers and sisters must have looked like fraternizing with the enemy. To be 'zealous for the **law**', including circumcision and the food laws, must have looked like the only way that would fit in with the will of

God for his people. If we want to understand, and learn from, the complex debates faced by the early church, we would do well to ponder their entire situation, and contemplate the ways in which our own theological debates are more conditioned than we sometimes realize by the swirling currents of political, social and cultural pressure.

ACTS 11.19–30

Taking Root – and a Name! – in Antioch (See map 12, page xxi.)

[19]The people who had been scattered because of the persecution that came about over Stephen went as far afield as Phoenicia, Cyprus and Antioch, speaking the word only to Jewish people. [20]But some from among them, who were from Cyprus and Cyrene in the first place, arrived in Antioch and spoke to the Hellenists as well, announcing the good news of the Lord Jesus. [21]The Lord's hand was with them, and a large number of people believed and turned to the Lord.

[22]News of all this reached the ears of the church in Jerusalem, and they sent Barnabas to Antioch. [23]When he arrived and saw the grace of God he was glad, and he urged them all to stay firmly loyal to the Lord from the bottom of their hearts. [24]He was a good man, full of the holy spirit and faith. And a substantial crowd was added to the Lord.

[25]Then Barnabas went to Tarsus to look for Saul [26]and, when he had found him, he brought him to Antioch. They were there a whole year, and were received hospitably in the church, and taught a substantial crowd. And it was in Antioch that the disciples were first called 'Christians'.

[27]Around that time, prophets came from Jerusalem to Antioch. [28]One of them, Agabus by name, stood up and gave an indication through the spirit that there would be a great famine over the whole world. (This took place in the reign of Claudius.) [29]Each of the disciples determined, according to their ability, to send what they could to help the brothers and sisters living in Judaea. [30]They carried out this plan, sending their gift to the elders by the hand of Barnabas and Saul.

The other day I had to go to Cambridge once more, just for a few hours. Looking for a particular shop, I walked up King's Parade, and was reminded of someone once saying that if there's anybody in the world you want to meet, you should stroll up and down King's Parade and eventually they will come by. It's ridiculous, of course, but there is a point to it. Not long after I'd turned the corner, a man I hadn't recognized hailed me and introduced himself: it was a long-retired bishop who had acted briefly as a counsellor and friend to me 30 years before. Some places in the world are indeed like that. I have always imagined that Grand Central Station in New York might function the same way, though I've never been there myself and so haven't tested the theory.

There were various places in the ancient world which functioned as the great crossroads of culture and trade, and one of them was Antioch. (This, by the way, is Antioch in Syria, not to be confused with the Antioch in Pisidia, where we shall find Paul and his friends in chapter 13; that Antioch is just south of where you'd be if you landed by air right in the middle of Turkey.) Antioch in Syria is about 15 miles inland from the sea, on the river Orontes, about as far north again from Sidon or Damascus as they are north of Jerusalem. Or, if you prefer, it's where you'd land up if you treated the long north-east spur of Cyprus as a pointing finger, followed its line by sailing to the Levantine shore, and then went a few miles up the river. And, as any map with ancient roads and regular shipping lanes will tell you, once you were in Antioch you could guarantee that half the people who travelled anywhere (a much smaller percentage of the population than now, of course) would sooner or later come by. It was a great, thriving, crowded, cosmopolitan city. And it was there that the word 'Christian' first came into use (verse 26).

It was a nickname, of course, just as 'Methodist' was originally a word used by the opponents of Wesley and his friends to sneer at their 'Methodical' ways of organizing their groups for Bible study and prayer. But, like many nicknames, it tells us a lot about the popular perception of what was going on. You would hear every language under the sun in Antioch, if you went from one part of town to another; but the one you could guarantee to be understood in was of course Greek. And '**Christ**', as we have seen many times already, was the Greek word for '**Messiah**', 'the anointed one', 'God's anointed king'. The followers of Jesus were thinking and speaking in such a way that they were thought of as 'the king's people', 'Messianists', *Christians*. True, the word 'Christ' did quite quickly become, in circles where people didn't recognize the Jewish royal overtones it carried, a kind of proper name. Since many people in the Roman world had two or three names, it might be assumed that the phrase 'Jesus Christ' was simply a double name. But that's not how it was at the beginning. Several of the things Paul writes, on into the 50s of the first century, only make sense if we assume that, for him, 'Christ' still carries its full meaning of 'Israel's anointed king, the one in whom God's purposes are summed up and brought to fulfilment'. And Paul was one of the main teachers and preachers in the lively and growing body of believers at Antioch.

He was there, as we discover in this passage, because Barnabas brought him there. We don't know why it was that Barnabas, twice now, took it upon himself to act on Paul's behalf. He seems to have spotted that Paul – or Saul, as he was still known – was a teacher and preacher

135

of exceptional gifts, and wanted to see these used to the full. So, here as in 9.27, Barnabas acts as Saul's friend at court. What Saul had done at Tarsus we have no idea, but we can only assume he had been teaching in the synagogues, trying to persuade his family and friends in the region that Jesus really was the Messiah spoken of in the scriptures. (Tarsus, by the way, was just round the north-east corner of the Mediterranean Sea from Antioch, a tricky journey overland but a short distance by boat.)

And the reason Barnabas brought Saul to Antioch was that a great number of non-Jews were becoming believers. Unlike the '**circumcision** party' we noted in 11.2, Barnabas seems to have taken what had happened in Caesarea as a firm sign that there was now an open door for non-Jews to be welcomed in to full **fellowship** alongside Jewish believers. He had been sent from Jerusalem to check out what was going on in Antioch, since word had got back that not just a single household, as in the case of Cornelius, but a large crowd of **Gentiles**, was delightedly turning in **faith** to Jesus as Lord, largely due to unnamed evangelists who had apparently seen no reason to hold back from speaking to non-Jews and had been rewarded with large numbers of converts. Luke's commendation of Barnabas is moving, and theologically pregnant: he came *and saw the grace of God*, and was glad, for he was a good man, full of the **holy spirit** and of faith. In other words, what Barnabas saw was not just a large and motley crowd of unlikely-looking people crowding into someone's house, praising God, and being taught about Jesus and the scriptures. What he saw was God's grace at work. It took humility and faith to see that; Barnabas had both in spades, thanks to the work of the holy spirit in him.

It was at that point that he thought to himself: We need someone who can teach these people, who can take this work forwards and give it the deep roots and the mental fibre it needs. And I know who can do that: Saul. Again and again the church needs not only the people who really can take the work forwards but the people who, in prayer and humility, can spot the very person that God is calling. It isn't always easy. And for Barnabas to bring Saul into an already flourishing group of **disciples**, which he had not founded, must have been potentially difficult as well. There might have been resentments, personality clashes, and the like. We shall see some of them later on; and, tragically, the close bond between Paul and Barnabas was itself fractured, as not only Acts 15.39 but also Galatians 2.13 make clear.

But for the moment there was a kind of honeymoon period, the sort of thing that sometimes happens when a work of God is being established. Testing will come later; get the roots deep while you can! And, out of that (again, as often happens when God's work is going forwards), there emerged a mood of glad generosity. Agabus (whom we shall meet again in Acts 21.10, once more with a gloomy but accurate prophecy) arrives from Jerusalem and prophesies that there will be a great famine, right across the world – a famine which has left echoes in other parts of early Christian writing, not least when Paul is talking about 'the present distress' in 1 Corinthians 7.26. At once, the Christians in Antioch do not say to themselves, 'How shall we survive?', but 'How can we help those who will be in a worse position than ourselves?' And so they resolve to send help to Jerusalem; and it is Barnabas and Saul who are chosen to take the money they collect. Collecting money was going to become a habit for Saul/Paul, and it was going to get him into trouble.

This mention of a visit to Jerusalem to bring money for the relief of the poor believers in Judaea ties in nicely with Galatians 2.1–2, where Paul speaks of going there 'according to revelation', which is best taken to refer to Agabus' prophecy. At the end of his description of the visit, in which he took the opportunity to talk to Peter and others about the nature and scope of their respective missions, he says that the Jerusalem **apostles** asked him 'to go on remembering the poor', which makes excellent sense if the visit of Galatians 2 is the same one as here. This way of reading the two texts has been very controversial as people have discussed how, if at all, the chronology we can work out from Paul's letters ties in with what we can work out from Acts and, if not, who has got what wrong. This isn't something we can go into here, nor does it hugely affect our reading of Acts itself; but I merely give my judgment, in company with many readers ancient and modern, that if we take the visit of Acts 11.29–30 to correspond to that of Galatians 2.1–10 we shall not go far wrong.

What matters far more is, of course, that the church should always be open to the cry of the poor, from whatever quarter it comes, and should always be ready to respond by sending its best help and its best people. The first 'Christians' were not just known as 'the king's people'. They were known as people who, precisely because that 'king' was Jesus himself, were committed at the deepest level to giving themselves in love to one another and to all in need.

ACTS 12.1–5

Herod Kills James

[1]Around that time, King Herod began to use violence towards some members of the church. [2]He killed James the brother of John with the sword. [3]When he saw that it pleased the Judaeans, he proceeded to

arrest Peter, too. (This was around the time of the Festival of Unleavened Bread.) [4]So, when he had seized him, he put him in prison, and gave four squads of soldiers the job of guarding him, with the intention of bringing him out to the people after Passover. [5]So Peter was kept in prison. But the church prayed earnestly to God on his behalf.

What makes a monarch act violently towards his subjects?

That question presses upon us at this point in Acts, because up to now we have heard nothing of Herod in this book. Parallels from other places, and other periods of history, may or may not be instructive. Everybody knows (in England, at least) about Henry VIII and his attack on the monasteries; most people think he was using public discontent at the increasing arrogance of the church as an excuse to get his hands on a large amount of valuable land. But he wanted stability in his realm, and he saw the early English Reformers as undermining it; so he went after them as well. English church history has tended to look back to Mary's reign, later in the sixteenth century, as the time when so many reforming church leaders were burnt at the stake. But it was Henry, ten or more years before, who had begun the process. Coming nearer to our own day, the threat from Scotland of a Jacobite rebellion in the late seventeenth and early eighteenth century was enough to provoke massive and brutal reprisals from the kings of the time. There are, sadly, plenty of more modern examples of the same phenomena around the world.

In general – is it ever possible to make such sweeping statements without challenge? – monarchs, even paranoid ones, do not often attack their subjects without at least some appearance of provocation. Of course, if we were looking for historical examples of paranoid brutality among monarchs, we might naturally turn to the grandfather of the King Herod in this story. This present Herod, whose full name was Herod Julius Agrippa, was the son of Aristobulus, one of the many sons of Herod the Great, a half-brother of Herod Antipas, the brooding and malevolent figure of the **gospels**. Our present Herod is sometimes referred to as Agrippa I, in contrast to his son, Herod Agrippa II, whom we shall meet in chapters 25 and 26. The Herod family had, shall we say, something of a reputation when it came to gratuitous violence, though none attained the standing of the patriarch Herod the Great himself in this respect. But then, by the time Antipas and the two Agrippas were reigning, Rome had taken a firmer control of the whole region, so that the client kingdom was under less pressure.

This latter feature of the period – Rome relying on the local aristocracy (such as it was: nobody actually thought Herod the Great was anything but a jumped-up half-breed warlord) to keep the peace – may explain a bit further why sudden or sporadic violence might be expected. Agrippa I was thought of by the Jewish population as 'their man', trusted (more or less) by the Romans but also popular with his people. It was strongly in his interests both to show his Roman overlords that he would not tolerate dangerous movements developing under his nose and to show his own people that he was standing up, as they would have seen it, for their ancestral traditions. To kill someone with the sword, as opposed to having them stoned as Stephen had been, strongly indicates that Herod either saw, or wanted people to think he saw, the Christian movement as a political threat. Certainly a movement whose very name, by this stage, stakes out a claim for Jesus as the true, anointed 'king of the Jews' cannot have been anything other than threatening to the person who bore that title as the gift of the Roman superpower. We recall how, in Matthew 11 and elsewhere, we see a kind of shadow-boxing between Jesus and Herod Antipas, with Jesus only claiming cryptically to be the true king, but at the same time offering an equally cryptic but devastating critique of Antipas. However much the Christian movement had developed by this stage, there is no sign that it was fomenting anything that could actually be classified as rebellion. But someone with the name of Herod was unlikely to tolerate for long a movement whose name had royal connotations.

Luke notes, tellingly, that Herod had James killed first, and then, seeing that this was a popular move with the people, made for Peter. Get one of the minor leaders first, since if people don't like it you haven't gone too far; but if they do like it, why then be bold and strike for the top. The James in question is 'the brother of John', that is, one of the two sons of Zebedee, as opposed to 'James son of Alpheus' on the one hand and 'James the brother of the Lord' on the other. They were, as we have often remarked in other contexts, short on boys' names in the Jewish world of the first century.

Thus it was that, after initial opposition from the chief **priests**, and then persecution initiated by a zealous young **Pharisee**, the followers of Jesus now at last came in for royal attention; and this enables Luke to draw the first half of his book towards its conclusion. This chapter sees virtually the last mention of **the Twelve**, apart from chapter 15; and from this chapter on it is not so much Peter (who may by this stage have been a marked man with a price on his head) but another James, the brother of the Lord, who emerges as the central leader in the Jerusalem church and, in a measure, in the worldwide movement. But that is not all. As we shall see at the close of the chapter, Luke has told the story in such a way as to leave this first half with a direct showdown between the official, reigning 'king of the Jews' and the unofficial king, Jesus the **Messiah**. The **good news** of his kingly rule has been announced in Jerusalem, Judaea and Samaria; the local king who would be most threatened by this has done his worst, and it hasn't worked. Now, Luke is suggesting, it's time to see what will happen when Jesus is announced as Lord of the world.

Luke takes care to tell us, twice, that all this was happening around Passover time. How many years have elapsed since the Passover at which Jesus himself was crucified we do not know. All Jewish traditions make it clear that Passover time was thought of as the time when God delivered his people from slavery. On this Passover it appeared that one leader was delivered and another was not. Luke is perhaps not as unconcerned about this imbalance as some have imagined. He merely puts the matter before his readers, and expects them to lay it in turn before the God whose providence remains both remarkable and inscrutable.

ACTS 12.6–19

Peter's Rescue and Rhoda's Mistake

⁶On the night when Herod was intending to bring Peter out, Peter was sleeping between two soldiers, bound with two chains. There were guards on the doors, watching the prison. ⁷Suddenly an angel of the Lord stood there, and a light shone in the cell.

The angel hit Peter on the side and woke him up.

'Get up quickly!' he said.

The chains fell off his hands. ⁸Then the angel spoke again.

'Get dressed and put on your sandals', he said. So Peter did.

'Put on your cloak and follow me', said the angel.

⁹So he went out, following the angel. He didn't think all this business with the angel was really happening. He thought he was seeing a vision. ¹⁰They went through the first set of guards; then the second; and then they came to the iron gate that led into the city. It opened all by itself. They went out and walked along a street. Suddenly the angel left him.

¹¹Then Peter came to his senses.

'Now I know it's true!' he said. 'The Lord sent his angel and snatched me out of Herod's hands. He rescued me from all the things the Judaeans were intending to do.'

¹²Once he had realized this, he went to the house of Mary, John Mark's mother. Lots of people were gathered there, praying. ¹³Peter knocked at the door in the outer gate, and a maid called Rhoda came to answer it. ¹⁴When she heard Peter's voice, she was so excited that she didn't open the gate. Instead, she ran back in and told them that Peter was standing outside the gate.

¹⁵'You're mad!' they said to her. But she insisted that it really was true.

'It must be his angel!' they said.

¹⁶Meanwhile Peter carried on knocking. They opened the door and saw him, and were astonished. ¹⁷He made a sign with his hand for them to be quiet. Then he told them how the Lord had led him out of the prison.

'Tell this to James, and to the other brothers and sisters', he said.

Then he left, and went somewhere else.

¹⁸When morning came, there was quite a commotion among the guards as to what had become of Peter. ¹⁹Herod looked for him but couldn't find him. He interrogated the guards and ordered them to be put to death. Then he left Judaea and went down to Caesarea, and stayed there.

One of the sure touches of a master writer is knowing how to create a seriously funny scene in the middle of an extremely serious one. Think of Shakespeare's subplots, with the gravedigger scene in *Hamlet* providing dark humour when all around is going wrong. Somehow the reader needs to be able to smile a little, to shift perspective and see things from a different point of view. Because many Christians assume that the Bible could never, or should never, be funny, they often ignore the humour, even when, as here, it jumps up, wagging its tail, demanding attention.

Rhoda takes the prize for being, unwittingly, the comic star turn; but it is the church at prayer that ought to raise a smile at the same time. Here is the church praying fervently for Peter. This is the church, remember, that has seen God at work in remarkable ways and that, after all, is celebrating at Passover time the **resurrection** of Jesus himself. They are people of great **faith**. They tell the story of how all of them were let out of prison, back in chapter 5. And yet. Here is Peter, released astonishingly in direct answer to their prayers. Here is Rhoda, so excited at hearing his voice that she forgets to open the door, and skitters in to say, 'It's Peter! It's Peter!' And here they are, so full of faith, so trusting in God, that they tell her she's mad. And then, when she insists, they tell her she's misinterpreted the voice, and that if it is Peter he must be already dead and addressing them from beyond the grave.

I find all this strangely comforting: partly because Luke is allowing us to see the early church for a moment not as a bunch of great heroes and heroines of the faith, but as the same kind of muddled, half-believing, faith-one-minute-and-doubt-the-next sort of people as most Christians we all know. And partly I find it comforting, because it would be easy for sceptical thinkers to dismiss the story of Peter's release from jail as a pious legend – except for the fact that nobody, constructing a pious legend out of thin air, would have made up this ridiculous little story of Rhoda and the praying-but-hopeless church. It has the ring of truth: ordinary truth, down-to-earth truth, at the very moment that it is telling us something truly extraordinary and **heaven**-on-earthish.

But of course the main point of the story, which Luke gets across nicely not least by means of this splendid little comic scene, is the vindication of Peter, as the chief representative (for the moment) of the family of the true King, and the frustration and disappointment of the official king. The end of the passage conveys a sense of the sulky grumpiness of a ruler who hasn't got his way, rather like A. A. Milne's poem about King John: Herod looked for Peter, condemned the guards, then flounced off and left Judaea, went down to Caesarea and didn't come back. That's got rid of him, then, the young church might think; and they would be right, more than they knew, as the next passage shows. In other words, as the first half of the book comes to its close, the believers in Jerusalem have been announcing Jesus as the rightful **Messiah**, King of the Jews; the present king of the Jews takes umbrage, and tries to stop it; but the grace of God and the prayers of the church (Luke is just beginning to refer to them as 'the church', this being the first such reference apart from 5.11 and 8.3) have prevailed, and we can take it that the true King is vindicated against the sham.

Not that Peter, or the church, is out of trouble or danger. Peter knows perfectly well that there will be a price on his head by morning, and the last thing he will do is to stay where all the others are, even for a short while, risking being caught himself and risking getting them all into a mess into the bargain. He also knows that he must lie low for a while at least, which is perhaps why he tells them to tell James (the brother of the Lord, presumably) what has happened. Peter can see that someone else is going to have to take over the leadership role he had had, and though nothing has been said about this it appears that James has been emerging as the obvious candidate. And Peter goes off 'somewhere else' – one of the most cryptic lines anywhere in the book. Either Luke didn't know where Peter went, or he doesn't want to tell us. (This has made some people think that Peter now went to Rome for the first time, and Luke didn't want to draw this to the attention of Roman authorities; most people seem to think this is far-fetched, but you never know.) Or Luke regarded it as unimportant.

Far more important for us at least, as an indication of how people in those days thought about things that matter quite a lot, are two almost incidental references in this story. The first is Luke's report of Peter's attitude to the extraordinary visitation of the angel. 'He didn't think it was really happening; he thought he was seeing a vision.' People sometimes write about the early Christians as though they, living in supposedly primitive times, didn't know the difference between a vision (or, as it may be called, a hallucination) and the realities of space, time and matter. This naturally affects the way some people have tried to 'explain' the stories of people meeting the risen Jesus. The answer is that they knew this distinction perfectly well; that they could draw attention to it when required; and that in some cases, as in this one, they can report when there has been genuine doubt in the mind and how that doubt has been cleared up. (This is somewhat, but only somewhat, like what happens when we have such a vivid dream that we are convinced it's true, and only several minutes of walking up and down in the bedroom will convince us that it's not; or, conversely, when something so bizarre or unpleasant happens that we think, or even hope, that it's a dream, but are forced to conclude that it isn't.) Ancient people were just as well aware as we are of the difference between visions or dreams on the one hand and concrete reality on the other.

The second important feature is the reaction of the praying group to Rhoda's insistence that it really is Peter standing outside and knocking. 'It must be his angel', they say. What do they think has happened? Some people think they are referring to Peter's guardian angel, a not uncommon idea; but there is no evidence that people in those days thought guardian angels would imitate the voices of their clients. Rather, I suggest that the gathered church suppose that Peter has been killed in the prison, and that his 'angel' is visiting them. People in the first century knew just as well as we do that sometimes, after someone we know and love dearly has died (and whether or not we know that their life was even in danger, let alone that they have in fact died), we can experience a vivid sense of them being briefly with us, speaking to us, cheering us up, smiling at us – and then they are gone. Those who believe, as the **Pharisees** believed, and as the early church believed, in the ultimate resurrection of the dead, must also believe that the dead person is still 'alive' in some sense, though not now bodily, between bodily death and bodily resurrection. As we shall see at 23.8, two of the regular available ways of describing this intermediate state were 'angel' and '**spirit**'; and the group in Mary's house opted for the former.

The point, again, is this. People have often, in recent and not so recent writing, speculated that the 'resurrection appearances' of Jesus were of this type: of the late lamented, but still thoroughly dead, friend making an 'angelic' or 'spiritual' visit, which seems very 'real' at the time but which is fully compatible with a body still being in a tomb. But what this theory fails to see is that first-century people were as aware of this phenomenon as we are. They even had language to cope with it. And they knew perfectly well that it was a completely different thing to 'resurrection'. Sometimes these little, incidental remarks, in a story basically about something else, shed floods of light on areas of discussion which, though not raised in the present passage, are nevertheless extremely important for the overall understanding of early Christianity.

ACTS 12.20–25

Herod's Vanity and Death (See map 13, page xxi.)

[20]Now Herod was angry with the people of Tyre and Sidon. They all came together to meet him, and they persuaded Blastus, who was in charge of the king's bedchamber, to seek a reconciliation. (They were, you see, dependent on the king's country for their food.) [21]So a day was set, and Herod dressed himself in his royal robes and took his seat on the official platform to make a public address to them.

[22]The people began to shout,

'The voice of a god, not of a mortal!'

[23]Immediately an angel of the Lord struck him, because he didn't give God the glory. He was eaten by worms and expired.

[24]But God's word grew and multiplied. [25]Barnabas and Saul had by now accomplished their ministry in Jerusalem, and they came back to Antioch, bringing John Mark with them.

Whether or not Luke was aware of the comic value of the previous interlude, he was certainly aware of the powerful impact of the story with which he now closes the first half of his book. The official king of the Jews plays at being a pagan princeling, and comes to a bad end; meanwhile, the **word** of God grows and multiplies. You couldn't say it much clearer than that. Herod Agrippa I died in AD 44, as we know from various sources; so Luke's story so far has covered about a dozen years (depending on when precisely we date the crucifixion of Jesus), and the second half will cover a slightly longer period.

But there is more than chronology going on in Luke's mind as he brings his book to its midpoint with the death of Herod. As we have already seen, the first half of the book is predominantly concerned with the mission of the young church to Jerusalem and Judaea, with forays into Samaria and to various **Gentiles** but nothing too ambitious as yet. In other words, Jesus has been announced as the true **Messiah**, the God-given and God-anointed King of Israel, the one who would bring **redemption** to Israel and to the world. The official Jewish leaders, starting with the **high priests**, continuing with the hard-line **Pharisees**, and now including the reigning king of the Jews himself, have all tried to squash this ridiculous nonsense and prevent it spreading; but they have failed. The chief **priests** have been left spluttering angrily into their beards in Jerusalem; Saul of Tarsus, the most prominent and violent of the Pharisaic persecutors, has been converted; and now Herod Agrippa, having had an unsuccessful attempt at killing off the church's main leadership, is himself suddenly cut down with a swift and fatal disease.

All this is of course part of the theme which Luke never tires of telling from one angle or another. Things appear to go badly for the church, this way or that. There may be real reverses, tragedies and disasters. And yet the God who has revealed himself in and through Jesus remains sovereign, and his purpose is going ahead whatever the authorities from without, or various controversies from within, may do to try to stop it.

In particular, Luke increasingly structures his material into a series of confrontations. As we shall see in the second half, Paul is regularly opposed, put on trial, hauled in front of magistrates, and so on; and equally regularly he is acquitted, the case is dropped, and people say he's innocent. On one occasion he even asks for, and receives, a public apology. All this is easily explained if, as many people have supposed, Luke was writing Acts as a document for use in the final trial which Paul would face in Rome. But though, as we shall see, there is a lot to be said for that theory, the evidence fits quite well onto a larger canvas.

Luke was aware, and reminds us from time to time, that there is coming a day on which God will judge the world, restoring all things, putting all wrongs to right (3.21; 10.42; 17.31; 24.25). At that time it will be seen who has been serving God and who has been serving their own selves, who has been worshipping the true God and who has been going after idols. For Luke, as for many Jews, the ultimate judgment of God would remain partially inscrutable in the present time, but also partially visible. But for Luke, as for the early Christians in general, the fact that God had already announced the verdict of the **last day** by raising Jesus the Messiah from the dead meant that the sequence of events between Easter and the final judgment could properly be seen in terms of various *implementations of that initial verdict* and hence *anticipations of the final one*. In other words, one can tell the story of events in the life of the church and the world in terms of a kind of continuous trial narrative with particular focal points. At these moments, the 'prosecution' seems to have made a strong point, and looks as if it's about to win the case, but then the 'defence' comes to the rescue and the church is vindicated, sometimes against all the odds. The background for this includes the dramatic scenarios in books like Daniel, where the plucky and loyal Jews find the pagan kings ranting and raging against them, but are then vindicated while the kings are proved

145

wrong. A similar story dominates the whole book of Esther. Now, as one sharp-edged outworking of this whole theme within Luke's framework, Peter has been rescued from the death that Herod had planned for him, and it is Herod instead who comes to a bad end.

This is one of the points in Luke's story where we have apparently independent coverage of the same event. The historian Josephus, never one to pass up a good, gory account, gives a vivid description of Herod Agrippa putting on gorgeous silver robes designed to catch the light of the rising sun and make it look as though he was himself shining, was himself perhaps some kind of supernatural being. Luke doesn't go that far, but instead describes how the crowd, listening to Herod's speech, shouted out that he was divine – just what many monarchs and princelings in the ancient world liked people to think about them. Luke doesn't actually say that Herod went out of his way to create this impression, but nor does he suggest that it was something Herod regretted or did anything to avoid.

The people in question came from the two famous old cities up the coast, Tyre and Sidon. The idea that they depended on Herod's territory for food is not unrealistic; Herod by this stage ruled over a large area, almost as much as his grandfather had done, and much of it was splendidly fertile. (The famine spoken of at the end of the previous chapter had clearly not happened yet; Claudius, in whose reign it took place, remained emperor for a full ten years after Herod Agrippa's death, and the evidence suggests that the famine took place in the early 50s AD.) Why Herod had been angry with Tyre and Sidon we are not told, but it seems that having people shout out that he was divine may well have been a calculated ploy to pacify him. Instead, according to both Josephus and Luke, he was struck down with a swift and serious illness which finished him off more or less on the spot.

Luke's comment says it all: 'but the word of God grew and multiplied'. Like the commands and promises in Genesis 1.26–28 (be fruitful and multiply), like the word in Isaiah 55.10–13, which comes down like rain and snow and accomplishes God's new creation, and like the seed sown in the parable (Luke 8.8), so the word is doing its own work, sometimes quietly, sometimes dramatically, always effectively. The present passage might almost be seen as a commentary on Isaiah 40.7–8:

The grass withers, the flower fades,
   When the breath of **YHWH** blows upon it;
   Surely the people are grass.
The grass withers, the flower fades;
but the word of our God will stand for ever.

And with that we may couple the rest of Isaiah 40. That splendid chapter speaks of the nations and rulers of the world like a drop in a bucket before the sovereign God, the creator; and, over against all of them, it calls out to God's herald to go and tell Zion the glad tidings that her God is coming, coming to reveal his glory, coming with might to rule the world, coming with gentleness to the lambs and the mother sheep. Luke has described the way in which the glory of the Lord has been revealed to Zion, the way in which the word is doing its work even though the surrounding human glory proves to be like grass. It is now time to show how this same word will go out and confront the nations and their rulers with the news that the God who made them, too, is revealing his glory in Jesus the Messiah, so that all flesh may see it together.

GLOSSARY

age to come, *see* present age

apostle, disciple, the Twelve
'Apostle' means 'one who is sent'. It could be used of an ambassador or official delegate. In the New Testament it is sometimes used specifically of Jesus' inner circle of twelve; but Paul sees not only himself but several others outside the Twelve as 'apostles', the criterion being whether the person had personally seen the risen Jesus. Jesus' own choice of twelve close associates symbolized his plan to renew God's people, Israel (who traditionally thought of themselves as having twelve tribes); after the death of Judas Iscariot (Matthew 27.5; Acts 1.18), Matthias was chosen by lot to take his place, preserving the symbolic meaning. During Jesus' lifetime they, and many other followers, were seen as his 'disciples', which means 'pupils' or 'apprentices'.

ascension
At the end of Luke's **gospel** and the start of Acts, Luke describes Jesus 'going up' from earth into **heaven**. To understand this, we have to remember that 'heaven' isn't a 'place' within our own world of space, time and matter, but a different *dimension* of reality – God's dimension, which intersects and interacts with our own (which we call 'earth', meaning both the planet where we live and the entire space-time universe). For Jesus to 'ascend', therefore, doesn't mean that he's a long way away, but rather that he can be, and is, intimately present to all his people all the time. What's more, because in the Bible 'heaven' is (as it were) the control room for 'earth', it means that Jesus is actually in charge of what goes on here and now. The way his sovereign rule works out is of course very different from the way earthly rulers get their way: as in his own life, he accomplishes his saving purposes through faithful obedience, including suffering. The life and witness of the early church, therefore, resulting in the spread of the gospel around the world, shows what it means to say that Jesus has ascended and that he is the world's rightful Lord.

baptism
Literally, 'plunging' people into water. From within a wider Jewish tradition of ritual washings and bathings, **John the Baptist** undertook a vocation of baptizing people in the Jordan, not as one ritual among others but as a unique moment of **repentance**, preparing them for the coming of the **kingdom of God**. Jesus himself was baptized by John, identifying himself with this renewal movement

and developing it in his own way. His followers in turn baptized others. After his **resurrection**, and the sending of the **holy spirit**, baptism became the normal sign and means of entry into the community of Jesus' people. As early as Paul it was aligned both with the **Exodus** from Egypt (1 Corinthians 10.2) and with Jesus' death and resurrection (Romans 6.2–11).

Christ, *see* **Messiah**

circumcised circumcision

The cutting off of the foreskin. Male circumcision was a major mark of identity for Jews, following its initial commandment to Abraham (Genesis 17) reinforced by Joshua (Joshua 5.2–9). Other peoples, e.g. the Egyptians, also circumcised male children. A line of thought from Deuteronomy (e.g. 30.6), through Jeremiah (e.g. 31.33), to the **Dead Sea Scrolls** and the New Testament (e.g. Romans 2.29) speaks of 'circumcision of the heart' as God's real desire, by which one may become inwardly what the male Jew is outwardly, that is, marked out as part of God's people. At periods of Jewish assimilation into the surrounding culture, some Jews tried to remove the marks of circumcision (e.g. 1 Maccabees 1.11–15).

conversion

Conversion means 'turning round', so that you are now going in the opposite direction. In Christian terms, it refers to someone who was going their own way in life (even if they thought it was God's way) being turned round by God, and beginning to follow God's way instead. Theologians have analysed what precisely happens in 'conversion', and how it relates to 'regeneration' (the 'new birth' as in John 3) and 'justification' (God's declaration that this person is 'in the right' with him). The main thing to stress is that conversion is God's work in someone's life, and that it involves a complete personal transformation by God's spirit. Sometimes conversion happens suddenly and dramatically, as with Saul of Tarsus (i.e. St Paul); sometimes it is gentle and quiet, though equally effective, as with Lydia in Acts 16.

covenant

At the heart of Jewish belief is the conviction that the one God, **YHWH**, who had made the whole world, had called Abraham and his family to belong to him in a special way. The promises God made to Abraham and his family, and the requirements that were laid on them as a result, came to be seen in terms either of the agreement that a king would make with a subject people, or of the marriage bond between husband and wife. One regular way of describing this relationship was 'covenant', which can thus include both promise and **law**. The covenant was renewed at Mount Sinai with the giving of the **Torah**; in Deuteronomy before the entry to the promised land; and, in a more focused way, with David (e.g. Psalm 89). Jeremiah 31 promised that after the punishment of **exile** God would make a 'new covenant' with his people, forgiving them and binding them to him more intimately. Jesus believed that this was coming true through his **kingdom** proclamation and his death and **resurrection**. The early Christians developed these ideas in various ways, believing that in Jesus the promises had at last been fulfilled.

day of Pentecost

A major Jewish festival, 50 days after Passover and the feast of Unleavened Bread (Leviticus 23.9–14). By the first century this had become associated with the time, 50 days after the Israelites left Egypt, when Moses went up Mount Sinai and came down with the **law**. It was on the day of Pentecost that the **holy spirit** came powerfully upon the early **disciples**, 50 days after the Passover at which Jesus had died and been raised (Acts 2). Whether or not we say that this was 'the birthday of the church' (some would use that description for the call of Abraham in Genesis 12, or at least the call of the first disciples in Mark 1), it was certainly the time when Jesus' followers discovered the power to tell people about his **resurrection** and lordship and to order their common life to reflect his saving **kingdom**.

Dead Sea Scrolls

A collection of texts, some in remarkably good repair, some extremely fragmentary, found in the late 1940s around Qumran (near the north-west corner of the Dead Sea), and virtually all now edited, translated and in the public domain. They formed all or part of the library of a strict monastic group, most likely Essenes, founded in the mid-second century BC and lasting until the Jewish–Roman war of AD 66–70. The scrolls include the earliest existing manuscripts of the Hebrew and Aramaic scriptures, and several other important documents of community regulations, scriptural exegesis, hymns, wisdom writings, and other literature. They shed a flood of light on one small segment within the Judaism of Jesus' day, helping us to understand how some Jews at least were thinking, praying and reading scripture. Despite attempts to prove the contrary, they make no reference to **John the Baptist**, Jesus, Paul, James or early Christianity in general.

demons, *see* **the satan**

disciple, *see* **apostle**

Essenes, *see* **Dead Sea Scrolls**

exile

Deuteronomy (29—30) warned that if Israel disobeyed **YHWH**, he would send his people into exile, but that if they then repented he would bring them back. When the Babylonians sacked Jerusalem and took the people into exile, prophets such as Jeremiah interpreted this as the fulfilment of this prophecy, and made further promises about how long exile would last (70 years, according to Jeremiah 25.12; 29.10). Sure enough, exiles began to return in the late sixth century BC (Ezra 1.1). However, the post-exilic period was largely a disappointment, since the people were still enslaved to foreigners (Nehemiah 9.36); and at the height of persecution by the Syrians Daniel 9.2, 24 spoke of the 'real' exile lasting not for 70 years but for 70 *weeks* of years, i.e. 490 years. Longing for the real 'return from exile', when the prophecies of Isaiah, Jeremiah, etc. would be fulfilled, and redemption from pagan oppression accomplished, continued to characterize many Jewish movements, and was a major theme in Jesus' proclamation and his summons to **repentance**.

Exodus

The Exodus from Egypt took place, according to the book of that name, under the leadership of Moses, after long years in which the Israelites had been enslaved there. (According to Genesis 15.13f., this was itself part of God's covenanted promise to Abraham.) It demonstrated, to them and to Pharaoh, King of Egypt, that Israel was God's special child (Exodus 4.22). They then wandered through the Sinai wilderness for 40 years, led by God in a pillar of cloud and fire; early on in this time they were given the **Torah** on Mount Sinai itself. Finally, after the death of Moses and under the leadership of Joshua, they crossed the Jordan and entered, and eventually conquered, the promised land of Canaan. This event, commemorated annually in the Passover and other Jewish festivals, gave the Israelites not only a powerful memory of what had made them a people, but also a particular shape and content to their **faith** in **YHWH** as not only creator but also redeemer; and in subsequent enslavements, particularly the exile, they looked for a further **redemption** which would be, in effect, a new Exodus. Probably no other past event so dominated the imagination of first-century Jews; among them the early Christians, following the lead of Jesus himself, continually referred back to the Exodus to give meaning and shape to their own critical events, most particularly Jesus' death and **resurrection**.

faith

Faith in the New Testament covers a wide area of human trust and trustworthiness, merging into love at one end of the scale and loyalty at the other. Within Jewish and Christian thinking faith in God also includes *belief*, accepting certain things as true about God, and what he has done in the world (e.g. bringing Israel out of Egypt; raising Jesus from the dead). For Jesus, 'faith' often seems to mean 'recognizing that God is decisively at work to bring the **kingdom** through Jesus'. For Paul, 'faith' is both the specific belief that Jesus is Lord and that God raised him from the dead (Romans 10.9) and the response of grateful human love to sovereign divine love (Galatians 2.20). This faith is, for Paul, the solitary badge of membership in God's people in **Christ**, marking them out in a way that **Torah**, and the works it prescribes, can never do.

fellowship

The word we often translate 'fellowship' can mean a business partnership (in the ancient world, businesses were often run by families, so there's a sense of family loyalty as well), or it can mean a sense of mutual belonging and sharing in some other corporate enterprise. Within early Christianity, 'fellowship' acquired the sense not just of belonging to one another as Christians, but of a shared belonging to Jesus Christ, and a participation in his life through the **spirit**, expressed in such actions as the 'breaking of bread' and the sharing of property with those in need.

forgiveness

Jesus made forgiveness central to his **message** and ministry, not least because he was claiming to be launching God's long-awaited 'new **covenant**' (Jeremiah 31.31–34) in which sins would at last be forgiven (Matthew 26.28). Forgiveness doesn't mean God, or someone else, saying, of some particular fault or sin, 'it didn't really matter' or 'I didn't really mind'. The point of forgiveness is that it *did* matter, God (and/or other people) really *did* mind, but they are not going to hold it against the offender. It isn't, in other words, the same thing as 'tolerance': to forgive is not to tolerate sin, but to see clearly that it was wrong and then to treat the offender as though it hadn't happened. The early Christian answer to the obvious question, 'How could a holy and righteous God do that?' is 'through the death of Jesus'. What's more, Jesus commanded his followers to extend the same forgiveness to one another (Matthew 6.12). Not to do so is to shut up the same door through which forgiveness is received for oneself (Matthew 18.21–35).

Gentiles

The Jews divided the world into Jews and non-Jews. The Hebrew word for non-Jews, *goyim*, carries overtones both of family identity (i.e. not of Jewish ancestry) and of worship (i.e. of idols, not of the one true god **YHWH**). Though many Jews established good relations with Gentiles, not least in the Jewish Diaspora (the dispersion of Jews away from Palestine), officially there were taboos against the contact such as intermarriage. In the New Testament the Greek word *ethne*, 'nations', carries the same meanings as *goyim*. Part of Paul's overmastering agenda was to insist that Gentiles who believed in Jesus had full rights in the Christian community alongside believing Jews, without having to become **circumcised**.

good news, gospel, message, word

The idea of 'good news', for which an older English word is 'gospel', had two principal meanings for first-century Jews. First, with roots in Isaiah, it meant the news of **YHWH**'s long-awaited victory over evil and rescue of his people. Second, it was used in the Roman world for the accession, or birthday, of the emperor. Since for Jesus and Paul the announcement of God's inbreaking **kingdom** was both the fulfilment of prophecy and a challenge to the world's present rules, 'gospel' became an important shorthand for both the message of Jesus himself and the apostolic message about him. Paul saw this message as itself the vehicle of God's saving power (Romans 1.16; 1 Thessalonians 2.13).

gospel, *see* **good news**

heaven

Heaven is God's dimension of the created order (Genesis 1.1; Psalm 115.16; Matthew 6.9), whereas 'earth' is the world of space, time and matter that we know. 'Heaven' thus sometimes stands, reverentially, for 'God' (as in Matthew's regular **'kingdom of heaven'**). Normally hidden from human sight, heaven is occasionally revealed or unveiled so that people can see God's dimension of ordinary life (e.g. 2 Kings 6.17; Revelation 1, 4—5). Heaven in the New Testament is thus not usually seen as the place where God's people go after death; at the end, the New Jerusalem descends *from* heaven *to* earth, joining the two dimensions for ever. 'Entering the kingdom of heaven' does not mean 'going to heaven after death', but belonging in the present to the people who steer their earthly course by the standards and purposes of heaven (cf. the Lord's Prayer; 'on earth as in heaven', Matthew 6.10), and who are assured of membership in **the age to come**.

high priest, *see* **priests**

holy spirit

In Genesis 1.2, the spirit is God's presence and power *within* creation, without God being identified with creation. The same spirit entered people, notably the prophets, enabling them to speak and act for God. At his **baptism** by **John the Baptist**, Jesus was specially equipped with the spirit, resulting in his remarkable public career (Acts 10.38). After his **resurrection**, his followers were themselves filled (Acts 2) by the same spirit, now identified as Jesus' own spirit; the creator God was acting afresh, remaking the world and them too. The spirit enabled them to live out a holiness which the **Torah** could not, producing 'fruit' in their lives, giving them 'gifts' with which to serve God, the world and the church, and assuring them of future **resurrection** (Romans 8; Galatians 4—5; 1 Corinthians 12—14). From very early in Christianity (e.g. Galatians 4.1–7), the spirit became part of the new revolutionary definition of God himself: 'the one who sends the son and the spirit of the son'.

John (the Baptist)

Jesus' cousin on his mother's side, born a few months before Jesus; his father was a **priest**. He acted as a prophet, baptizing in the Jordan – dramatically re-enacting the **Exodus** from Egypt – to prepare people, by **repentance**, for God's coming judgment. He may have had some contact with the **Essenes**, though his eventual public message was different from theirs. Jesus' own vocation was decisively confirmed at his **baptism** by John. As part of John's message of the **kingdom**, he outspokenly criticized Herod Antipas for marrying his brother's wife. Herod had him imprisoned, and then beheaded him at his wife's request (Mark 6.14–29). Groups of John's disciples continued a separate existence, without merging into Christianity, for some time afterwards (e.g. Acts 19.1–7).

jubilee

The ancient Israelites were commanded to keep a 'jubilee' every fiftieth year (i.e. following the sequence of seven 'sabbatical' years). Leviticus 25 provides the basic rules, which were expanded by later teachers: land was to be restored to its original owners or their heirs, and any fellow Jews who had been enslaved because of debt were to be set free. It was also to be a year without sowing, reaping or harvesting. The point was that **YHWH** owned the land, and that the Israelites were to see it not as a private possession but as something held in trust. People debate whether the jubilee principle was ever put into practice as thoroughly as Leviticus demands, but the underlying promise of a great remission of debts was repeated by Isaiah (61.1–2) and then decisively by Jesus (Luke 4.16–21). It is likely that this underlies the action of the first Christians in sharing property and giving to those in need (Acts 4.32–35, etc.).

kingdom of God, kingdom of heaven

Best understood as the king*ship*, or sovereign and saving rule, of Israel's God **YHWH**, as celebrated in several Psalms (e.g. 99.1) and prophecies (e.g. Daniel 6.26–27). Because YHWH was the creator God, when he finally became king in the way he intended this would involve setting the world to rights, and particularly rescuing Israel from its enemies. 'Kingdom of God' and various equivalents (e.g. 'No king but God!') became revolutionary slogans around the time of Jesus. Jesus' own announcement of God's kingdom redefined these expectations around his own very different plan and vocation. His invitation to people to 'enter' the kingdom was a way of summoning them to allegiance to himself and his programme, seen as the start of God's long-awaited saving reign. For Jesus, the kingdom was coming not in a single move, but in stages, of which his own public career was one, his death and **resurrection** another, and a still future consummation another. Note that 'kingdom of **heaven**' is Matthew's preferred form for the same phrase, following a regular Jewish practice of saying 'heaven' rather than 'God'. It does not refer to a place ('heaven'), but to the fact of God's becoming king in and through Jesus and his achievement. Paul speaks of Jesus as **Messiah**, already in possession of his kingdom, waiting to hand it over finally to the father (1 Corinthians 15.23–28; cf. Ephesians 5.5).

last days

Ancient Jews thought of world history as divided into two periods: **'the present age'** and **'the age to come'**. The present age was a time when evil was still at large in its many forms; the age to come would usher in God's final reign of justice, peace, joy and love. Ancient prophets had spoken of the transition from the one age to the other in terms of the 'last days', meaning either the final moments of the 'present age' or the eventual dawning of the 'age to come'. When Peter quotes Joel in Acts 2.17, he perhaps means both: the two ages have overlapped, so that Christians live in the 'last days', the time between God's **kingdom** being launched in and through Jesus and it being completed at Jesus' return. The New

Testament gives no encouragement to the idea that we can calculate a precise timetable for the latter event, or that the period of history immediately before Jesus' return will be significantly different (e.g. more violent) than any other (see Matthew 24.36–39).

law, *see* **Torah**

life, soul, spirit

Ancient people held many different views about what made human beings the special creatures they are. Some, including many Jews, believed that to be complete, humans needed bodies as well as inner selves. Others, including many influenced by the philosophy of Plato (fourth century BC), believed that the important part of a human was the 'soul' (Gk: *psyche*), which at death would be happily freed from its bodily prison. Confusingly for us, the same word *psyche* is often used in the New Testament within a Jewish framework where it clearly means 'life' or 'true self', without implying a body/soul dualism that devalues the body. Human inwardness of experience and understanding can also be referred to as 'spirit'. *See also* **holy spirit; resurrection.**

the life of God's coming age, *see* **present age**

message, *see* **good news**

Messiah, messianic, Christ

The Hebrew word means literally 'anointed one', hence in theory a prophet, **priest** or king. In Greek this translates as *Christos*; 'Christ' in early Christianity was a title, and only gradually became an alternative proper name for Jesus. In practice 'Messiah' is mostly restricted to the notion, which took various forms in ancient Judaism, of the coming king who would be David's true heir, through whom **YHWH** would rescue Israel from pagan enemies. There was no single template of expectations. Scriptural stories and promises contributed to different ideals and movements, often focused on (a) decisive military defeat of Israel's enemies and (b) rebuilding or cleansing the **Temple.** The **Dead Sea Scrolls** speak of two 'Messiahs', one a priest and the other a king. The universal early Christian belief that Jesus was Messiah is only explicable, granted his crucifixion by the Romans (which would have been seen as a clear sign that he was not the Messiah), by their belief that God had raised him from the dead, so vindicating the implicit messianic claims of his earlier ministry.

miracles

Like some of the old prophets, notably Elijah and Elisha, Jesus performed many deeds of remarkable power, particularly healings. The **gospels** refer to these as 'deeds of power', 'signs', 'marvels', or 'paradoxes'. Our world 'miracle' tends to imply that God, normally 'outside' the closed system of the world, sometimes 'intervenes'; miracles have then frequently been denied by sceptics as a matter of principle. However, in the Bible God is always present, however strangely, and 'deeds of power' are seen as *special* acts of a *present* God rather than *intrusive* acts of an *absent* one. Jesus' own 'mighty works' are seen particularly, following prophecy, as evidence of his messiahship (e.g. Matthew 11.2–6).

Mishnah

The main codification of Jewish law (**Torah**) by the **rabbis**, produced in about AD 200, reducing to writing the 'oral Torah' which in Jesus' day ran parallel to the 'written Torah'. The Mishnah is itself the basis of the much larger collection of tradition in the two Talmuds (roughly AD 400).

parables

From the Old Testament onwards, prophets and other teachers used various storytelling devices as vehicles for their challenge to Israel (e.g. 2 Samuel 12.1–7). Sometimes they appeared as visions with interpretations (e.g. Daniel 7). Similar techniques were used by the **rabbis**. Jesus made his own creative adaptation of these traditions, in order to break open the world-view of his contemporaries and to invite them to share his vision of God's **kingdom** instead. His stories portrayed this as something that was *happening*, not just a timeless truth, and enabled his hearers to step inside the story and make it their own. As with some Old Testament visions, some of Jesus' parables have their own interpretations (e.g. the sower, Mark 4); others are thinly disguised retellings of the prophetic story of Israel (e.g. the wicked tenants, Mark 12).

Pharisees, rabbis

The Pharisees were an unofficial but powerful Jewish pressure group through most of the first centuries BC and AD. Largely lay-led, though including some of the **priests**, their aim was to purify Israel through intensified observance of the Jewish law (**Torah**), developing their own traditions about the precise meaning and application of scripture, their own patterns of prayer and other devotion, and their own calculations of the national hope. Though not all legal experts were Pharisees, most Pharisees were legal experts.

They effected a democratization of Israel's life, since for them the study and practice of Torah was equivalent to worshipping in the **Temple** – though they were adamant in pressing their own rules for the Temple liturgy on an unwilling (and often **Sadducean**) priesthood. This enabled them to survive AD 70 and, merging in to the early rabbinic movement, to develop new ways forward. Politically they stood up for ancestral traditions, and were at the forefront of various movements of revolt against both pagan overlordship and compromised Jewish leaders. By Jesus' day there were two distinct schools, the stricter one of Shammai, more inclined towards armed revolt, and the more lenient one of Hillel, ready to live and let live.

Jesus' debates with the Pharisees are at least as much a matter of agenda and policy (Jesus strongly opposed their separatist nationalism) as about details of theology and piety. Saul of Tarsus was a fervent right-wing Pharisee, presumably a Shammaite, until his **conversion**.

After the disastrous war of AD 66–70, these schools of Hillel and Shammai continued bitter debate on appropriate policy. Following the further disaster of AD 135 (the failed Bar-Kochba revolt against Rome) their traditions were carried on by the rabbis who, though looking to the earlier Pharisees for inspiration, developed a Torah-piety in which personal holiness and purity took the place of political agendas.

present age, age to come, the life of God's coming age

By the time of Jesus many Jewish thinkers divided history into two periods: 'the present age' and 'the age to come' – the latter being the time when **YHWH** would at last act decisively to judge evil, to rescue Israel, and to create a new world of justice and peace. The early Christians believed that, though the full blessings of the coming age lay still in the future, it had already begun with Jesus, particularly with his death and **resurrection**, and that by **faith** and **baptism** they were able to enter it already. For this reason, the customary translation 'eternal life' is rendered here as 'the life of God's coming age'.

priests, high priest

Aaron, the older brother of Moses, was appointed Israel's first high priest (Exodus 28—29), and in theory his descendants were Israel's priests thereafter. Other members of his tribe (Levi) were 'Levites', performing other liturgical duties but not sacrificing. Priests lived among the people all around the country, having a local teaching role (Leviticus 10.11; Malachi 2.7), and going to Jerusalem by rotation to perform the **Temple** liturgy (e.g. Luke 2.8).

David appointed Zadok (whose Aaronic ancestry is sometimes questioned) as high priest, and his family remained thereafter the senior priests in Jerusalem, probably the ancestors of the **Sadducees**. One explanation of the origin of the Qumran **Essenes** is that they were a dissident group who believed themselves to be the rightful chief priests.

rabbis, *see* **Pharisees**

redemption

Literally, 'redemption' means 'buying-back', and was often used in the ancient world of slaves buying their freedom, or having it bought for them. The great 'redemption' in the Bible, which coloured the way the word was heard ever afterwards, was when God 'bought' his people Israel from slavery in Egypt to give them freedom in the promised land. When, later, the Jews were exiled in Babylon (and even after they returned to their land), they described themselves as undergoing a new slavery and hence being in need of a new redemption. Jesus, and the early Christians, interpreted this continuing slavery in its most radical terms, as slavery to sin and death, and understood 'redemption' likewise in terms of the rescue from this multiple and tyrannous slavery which God provided through the death of Jesus (Romans 3.24).

repentance

Literally, this means 'turning back'. It is widely used in Old Testament and subsequent Jewish literature to indicate both a personal turning away from sin and Israel's corporate turning away from idolatry and back to **YHWH**. Through both meanings, it is linked to the idea of 'return from **exile**'; if Israel is to 'return' in all senses, it must 'return' to YHWH. This is at the heart of the summons of both **John the Baptist** and Jesus. In Paul's writings it is mostly used for **Gentiles** turning away from idols to serve the true God; also for sinning Christians who need to return to Jesus.

resurrection

In most biblical thought, human bodies matter and are not merely disposable prisons for the **soul**. When ancient Israelites wrestled with the goodness and justice of **YHWH**, the creator, they ultimately came to insist he must raise the dead (Isaiah 26.19; Daniel 12.2–3) – a suggestion firmly resisted by classical pagan thought. The longed-for return from **exile** was also spoken of in terms of YHWH raising dry bones to new **life** (Ezekiel 37.1–14). These ideas were developed in the second-**Temple** period, not least at times of martyrdom (e.g. 2 Maccabees 7). Resurrection was not just 'life after death', but a newly embodied life *after* 'life after death'; those at present dead were either 'asleep' or seen as 'souls', 'angels' or 'spirits', awaiting new embodiment.

The early Christian belief that Jesus had been raised from the dead was not that he had 'gone to **heaven**', or that he had been 'exalted', or was 'divine'; they believed all those as well, but each could have been expressed without mention of resurrection. Only the bodily resurrection of Jesus explains the rise of the early church, particularly its belief in Jesus' messiahship (which his crucifixion would have called into question). The early Christians believed that they themselves would be raised to a new, transformed bodily life at the time of the Lord's return or parousia (e.g. Philippians 3.20f.).

sabbath

The Jewish sabbath, the seventh day of the week, was a regular reminder both of creation (Genesis 2.3; Exodus 20.8–11) and of the **Exodus** (Deuteronomy 5.15). Along with **circumcision** and the food laws, it was one of the badges of Jewish identity within the pagan world of late antiquity, and a considerable body of Jewish **law** and custom grew up around its observance.

sacrifice

Like all ancient people, the Israelites offered animal and vegetable sacrifices to their God. Unlike others, they possessed a highly detailed written code (mostly in Leviticus) for what to offer and how to offer it; this in turn was developed in the **Mishnah** (*c.* AD 200). The Old Testament specifies that sacrifices can only be offered in the Jerusalem **Temple**; after this was destroyed in AD 70, sacrifices ceased, and Judaism developed further the idea, already present in some teachings, of prayer, fasting and almsgiving as alternative forms of sacrifice. The early Christians used the language of sacrifice in connection with such things as holiness, evangelism and the eucharist.

Sadducees

By Jesus' day, the Sadducees were the aristocracy of Judaism, possibly tracing their origins to the family of Zadok, David's **high priest**. Based in Jerusalem, and including most of the leading priestly families, they had their own traditions and attempted to resist the pressure of the **Pharisees** to conform to theirs. They claimed to rely only on the Pentateuch (the first five books of the Old Testament), and denied any doctrine of a future life, particularly of the **resurrection** and other ideas associated with it, presumably because of the encouragement such beliefs gave to revolutionary movements. No writings from the Sadducees have survived, unless the apocryphal book of Ben-Sirach (Ecclesiasticus) comes from them. The Sadducees themselves did not survive the destruction of Jerusalem and the **Temple** in AD 70.

salvation

Salvation means 'rescue', and the meanings of the word have depended on what people thought needed rescuing, and from what. Thus, where people have imagined that the human plight was best seen in terms of an immortal **soul** being trapped in a mortal and corrupt body, 'salvation' was seen in terms of the rescue of this soul from such a prison. But for most Jews, and all early Christians, it was death itself, the ending of God-given bodily life, that was the real enemy, so that 'salvation' was bound to mean being rescued from death itself – in other words, the resurrection of the body for those who had died, and the transformation of the body for those still alive at the Lord's return (e.g. 1 Corinthians 15.50–57). For Paul and others, this 'salvation' was extended to the whole of creation (Romans 8.18–26). But if 'salvation' refers to this ultimate rescue of God's created order, and our created bodies, from all that distorts, defaces and destroys them (i.e. sin, sickness, corruption and death itself), we should expect to find, and do in fact find, that often in the New Testament 'salvation' (and phrases like 'being saved') refer, not simply to people coming to **faith** and so being assured of **the life of God's coming age** but to bodily healing and to rescue from awful plights (e.g. Acts 16.30–31; 27.44). Jesus' **resurrection** remains the foundation for a biblical view of salvation for the whole person and the whole creation, a salvation which, though to be completed in the future, has already begun with the mission and achievement of Jesus.

the satan, 'the accuser', demons

The Bible is never very precise about the identity of the figure known as 'the satan'. The Hebrew word means 'the accuser', and at times the satan seems to be a member of YHWH's heavenly council, with special responsibility as director of prosecutions (1 Chronicles 21.1; Job 1—2; Zechariah 3.1f.). However, it becomes identified variously with the serpent of the garden of Eden (Genesis 3.1–15) and with the rebellious daystar cast out of **heaven** (Isaiah 14.12–15), and was seen by many Jews as the quasi-personal source of evil standing behind both human wickedness and large-scale injustice, sometimes operating through semi-independent 'demons'. By Jesus' time various words were used to denote this figure, including Beelzebul/b (lit. 'Lord of the flies') and simply 'the evil one'; Jesus warned his followers against the deceits this figure could perpetrate. His opponents accused him of being in league with the satan, but the early Christians believed that Jesus in fact defeated it both in his own struggles with temptation (Matthew 4; Luke 4), his exorcisms of demons, and his death (1 Corinthians 2.8; Colossians 2.15). Final victory over this ultimate enemy is thus assured (Revelation 20), though the struggle can still be fierce for Christians (Ephesians 6.10–20).

scribes

In a world where many could not write, or not very well, a trained class of writers ('scribes') performed the important function of drawing up contracts for business, marriage, etc. Many scribes would thus be legal experts, and quite possibly **Pharisees**, though being a scribe was compatible with various political and religious standpoints. The work of Christian scribes was of initial importance in copying early Christian writings, particularly the stories about Jesus.

second coming

When God renews the whole creation, as he has promised, bringing together **heaven** and earth, Jesus himself will be the centre of it all, personally present to and with his people and ruling his world fully and finally at last. This Christian hope picks up, and gives more explicit focus to, the ancient Jewish hope that YHWH would in the end return to his people to judge and to save. Since the **ascension** is often thought of in terms of Jesus 'going away', this final moment is often thought of in terms of his 'coming back again', hence the shorthand 'second coming'. However, since the ascension in fact means that Jesus, though now invisible, is not far away but rather closely present with us, it isn't surprising that some of the key New Testament passages speak, not of his 'return' as though from a great distance, but of his 'appearing' (e.g. Colossians 3.4; 1 John 3.2). The early Christians expected this 'appearing' to take place, not necessarily within a generation as is often thought (because of a misreading of Mark 13 and similar passages) but at *any* time – which could be immediate, or delayed. This caused a problem for some early Christians (2 Peter 3.3–10), but not for many. For the early Christians, the really important event – the **resurrection** of Jesus – had already taken place, and his final 'appearing' would simply complete what had then been decisively begun.

son of David

An alternative, and infrequently used, title for **Messiah.** The messianic promises of the Old Testament often focus specifically on David's son, for example 2 Samuel 7.12–16; Psalm 89.19–37. Joseph, Mary's husband, is called 'son of David' by the angel in Matthew 1.20.

son of God

Originally a title for Israel (Exodus 4.22) and the Davidic king (Psalm 2.7); also used of ancient angelic figures (Genesis 6.2). By the New Testament period it was already used as a **messianic** title, for example, in the **Dead Sea Scrolls**. There, and when used of Jesus in the **gospels** (e.g. Matthew 16.16), it means, or reinforces, 'Messiah', without the later significance of 'divine'. However, already in Paul the transition to the fuller meaning (one who was already equal with God and was sent by him to become human and to become Messiah), is apparent, without loss of the meaning 'Messiah' itself (e.g. Galatians 4.4).

son of man

In Hebrew or Aramaic, this simply means 'mortal', or 'human being'; in later Judaism, it is sometimes used to mean 'I' or 'someone like me'. In the New Testament the phrase is frequently linked to Daniel 7.13, where 'one like a son of man' is brought on the clouds of **heaven** to 'the Ancient of Days', being vindicated after a period of suffering, and is given kingly power. Though Daniel 7 itself interprets this as code for 'the people of the saints of the Most High', by the first century some Jews understood it as a **messianic** promise. Jesus developed this in his own way in certain key sayings which are best understood as promises that God would vindicate him, and judge those who had opposed him, after his own suffering (e.g. Mark 14.62). Jesus was thus able to use the phrase as a cryptic self-designation, hinting at his coming suffering, his vindication and his God-given authority.

soul, *see* life

speaking in tongues

In many religious traditions, people who experience certain types of ecstasy have sometimes found themselves speaking, praying or even singing in what seem to them to be languages which they do not themselves understand. Sometimes these turn out to be actual languages which are understood by one or more listeners: this is what is described in Acts 2, and there are many examples from subsequent periods including our own. Sometimes they appear to be a kind of babbling semi-language corresponding to no known human tongue. Sometimes the speaker may be unable to decide which it is. Paul was well aware (1 Corinthians 12.1–3) that phenomena like this could occur in non-Christian contexts, but for him, and for millions since (not least in today's pentecostal and charismatic movements, though much more widely as well), such prayer was and is powerful in evoking the presence of Jesus, celebrating the energy of the **spirit**, and interceding for people and situations, particularly when it isn't clear what exactly to pray for (see, perhaps, Romans 8.26–27). There is however no good reason, within early Christian teaching, to suppose that 'speaking in tongues' is either a necessary or a sufficient sign that the **holy spirit** is at work in and through someone's life, still less that they have attained, as has sometimes been claimed, a new and more elevated level of spirituality than those who have not received this gift. To be sure, in Acts 2, and also in Acts 8.17 (by implication at least), 10.46 and 19.6, 'tongues' is a sign that the spirit has been poured out on people who weren't expected to be included in God's people. But there are plenty of other times when the spirit is powerfully at work without any mention of 'tongues', and equally every indication (e.g. 1 Corinthians 12 and 14) that praying in tongues is, for some, a regular practice and not merely an initiatory sign.

spirit, *see* **life, holy spirit**

Temple

The Temple in Jerusalem was planned by David (*c.* 1000 BC) and built by his son Solomon as the central sanctuary for all Israel. After reforms under Hezekiah and Josiah in the seventh century BC, it was destroyed by Babylon in 587 BC. Rebuilding by the returned **exiles** began in 538 BC, and was completed in 516, initiating the 'second Temple period'. Judas Maccabaeus cleansed it in 164 BC after its desecration by Antiochus Epiphanes (167). Herod the Great began to rebuild and beautify it in 19 BC; the work was completed in AD 63. The Temple was destroyed by the Romans in AD 70. Many Jews believed it should and would be rebuilt; some still do. The Temple was not only the place of **sacrifice**; it was believed to be the unique dwelling of **YHWH** on earth, the place where **heaven** and earth met.

Torah, Jewish law

'Torah', narrowly conceived, consists of the first five books of the Old Testament, the 'five books of Moses' or 'Pentateuch'. (These contain much law, but also much narrative.) It can also be used for the whole Old Testament scriptures, though strictly these are the 'law, prophets and writings'. In a broader sense, it refers to the whole developing corpus of Jewish legal tradition, written and oral; the oral Torah was initially codified in the **Mishnah** around AD 200, with wider developments found in the two Talmuds, of Babylon and Jerusalem, codified around AD 400. Many Jews in the time of Jesus and Paul regarded the Torah as being so strongly God-given as to be almost itself, in some sense, divine; some (e.g. Ben-Sirach 24) identified it with the figure of 'Wisdom'. Doing what Torah said was not seen as a means of earning God's favour, but rather of expressing gratitude, and as a key badge of Jewish identity.

tongues, *see* **speaking in tongues**

the Twelve, *see* **apostle**

word, *see* **good news**

YHWH

The ancient Israelite name for God, from at least the time of the **Exodus** (Exodus 6.2f.). It may originally have been pronounced 'Yahweh', but by the time of Jesus it was considered too holy to speak out loud, except for the **high priest** once a year in the Holy of Holies in the **Temple**. Instead, when reading scripture, pious Jews would say *Adonai*, 'Lord', marking this usage by adding the vowels of *Adonai* to the consonants of YHWH, eventually producing the hybrid 'Jehovah'. The word YHWH is formed from the verb 'to be', combining 'I am who I am', 'I will be who I will be', and perhaps 'I am because I am', emphasizing YHWH's sovereign creative power.

STUDY GUIDE

Introducing the Study

Acts for Everyone, Part 1 is one of a series of commentaries written with the general reader in mind by noted New Testament scholar N. T. Wright. Wright has written these commentaries to facilitate daily devotions, personal study or group discussion. They each include Wright's own translation of the biblical text divided into short segments followed by an accompanying section of background information and contextual explanation about each scripture segment.

In Wright's words: 'There isn't a dull page in Acts. . . . The book of Acts is full of the energy and excitement of the early Christians as they found God doing new things all over the place and learned to take the good news of Jesus around the world. It's also full of the puzzles and problems that churches faced then and face today – crises over leadership, money, ethnic divisions, theology and ethics, not to mention serious clashes with political and religious authorities. It's comforting to know that "normal church life", even in the time of the first apostles, was neither trouble-free nor plain sailing, just as it's encouraging to know that even in the midst of all their difficulties the early church was able to take the gospel forward in such dynamic ways.' The 'energy and excitement' of this first part of the book of Acts, on its own, should help encourage sufficient preparation (i.e., reading and reflecting) by members of the group and thereby facilitate thoughtful discussion.

To the Leader

'On the very first occasion when someone stood up in public to tell people about Jesus, he made it very clear: this message is for *everyone*.'

N.T. Wright makes it clear that he intends his series of commentary guides – like the message of Jesus – to be for *everyone*: to that end, he has written these guides to make the texts of the Bible (in this case, Acts 1—12) accessible to any reader. Similarly, the task of the leader is to encourage and facilitate participation by *everyone*. Consider taking time at the start of the study to set the expectation that participants read in advance the selected sections from Wright's book (including the Scripture passages) to be discussed in each session. Even minimal preparation will enhance the overall experience of the study. An easy way to do this is to send a weekly email to the group members with the selected passages or pages from *Acts for Everyone, Part 1* (see session guides) for them to read before each session.

Essentials for Participation

- Welcome the Bible as a dialogue partner and be open to the possibility of being challenged or changed by it.
- Welcome each other as dialogue partners who will bring unique insights to the group's experience, including different understandings of the Bible.

Essentials for Guiding Discussion

- Test each question provided in the session guides before using them. Make notes of your thoughts. This will enable you to see the extent to which the questions may need additional clarification to the group during their conversations with each other.
- Be open to silence during discussions; some people need more time than others to think before responding.
- Listen carefully to the group's conversation. Attentive listening is key to keeping the discussion moving along, encouraging individual contributions to the discussion, making connections among the various comments made, and determining what follow-up questions might be needed.

The Session Readings

Session 1—The Spirit Arrives

Readings: Acts 1.1—2.47 (pages 1–36)

Acts 1.1–5	Here Comes the Sequel!
Acts 1.6–8	*When, What and How?*
Acts 1.9–14	Ascension!
Acts 1.15–26	Restoring the Twelve
Acts 2.1–4	Here Comes the Power
Acts 2.5–13	*New Words for New News*
Acts 2.14–21	It's All Coming True at Last!
Acts 2.22–36	David Speaks of Jesus' Resurrection
Acts 2.37–41	God's Rescue Plan
Acts 2.42–47	*The New Family*

Session 2—The Spirit Animates

Readings: Acts 3.1—5.11 (pages 36–63)

Acts 3.1–10   *More than He Bargained For*
Acts 3.11–16 An Explanation Is Called For
Acts 3.17–26 Restoration and Refreshment
Acts 4.1–12   *Resurrection Plus the Name of Jesus Equals Trouble*
Acts 4.13–22 The Clash of Loyalties
Acts 4.23–31 Look upon Their Threats
Acts 4.32–37 Signs of the New Covenant
Acts 5.1–11   *Disaster*

Session 3—The Spirit Disturbs

Readings: Acts 5.12—8.3 (pages 63–96)

Acts 5.12–16 Healed by Peter's Shadow
Acts 5.17–26 The Words of This Life
Acts 5.27–42 *Human Inventions and Divine Instructions*
Acts 6.1–7   Problems of Family Living
Acts 6.8–15 Stephen Becomes a Target
Acts 7.1–16 *Stephen Tells the Story*
Acts 7.17–34 Stephen and Moses
Acts 7.35–53 *Handmade Shrines*
Acts 7.54—8.3 The Stoning of Stephen

Session 4—The Spirit Sends

Readings: Acts 8.4—9.31 (pages 96–115)

Acts 8.4–25   Samaria, the Spirit and Simon Magus
Acts 8.26–40 *Philip and the Ethiopian*
Acts 9.1–9   The Conversion of Saul
Acts 9.10–19a *Ananias and Saul*
Acts 9.19b–31 *'He Is God's Son'*

Session 5—The Spirit Surprises

Readings: Acts 9.32—12.25 (pages 116–47)

Acts 9.32–42 Back to Peter
Acts 10.1–16 *Peter's Vision*
Acts 10.17–33 Peter Goes to Cornelius
Acts 10.34–48 *Telling the Gentiles about Jesus*
Acts 11.1–18 Controversy and Vindication
Acts 11.19–30 Taking Root – and a Name! – in Antioch

Acts 12.1–5   Herod Kills James
Acts 12.6–19   *Peter's Rescue and Rhoda's Mistake*
Acts 12.20–25   Herod's Vanity and Death

Leading the Sessions

The group sessions (60 minutes) will feature these movements:

- Gathering
- Attending to the Word in the Text
- Engaging the Word in Context
- Responding to the Word in the World
- Closing

Gathering

In addition to welcoming one another to the study, spend time at the start of each session centering in prayer and clearing the way for meaningful encounter with the Bible. Consider establishing a pattern of praying together, including both speech and silence. One suggestion: Read aloud these words of the Risen Christ from Acts 1.7–8: *'It is not for you to know times or seasons . . . But you shall receive power when the Holy Spirit comes upon you; and you shall be my witnesses'* (RSV). Follow that with a brief time of silent reflection; then invite God's presence to undergird the group's study of God's Word.

Attending to the Word in the Text

Each session will highlight three scripture passages for the group to hear read aloud. Discussion of the scripture text will be guided by some basic questions of interpretation: What was the biblical writer's intent or purpose? What does the passage reveal about the acts of the spirit in animating the witness of the early church?

Engaging the Word in the Context

Wright's brief commentary sections provide the basis for this part of the session. For the most part, the questions will explore Wright's comments about the two or three highlighted scripture passages the group just discussed. When appropriate, the group may discuss other of Wright's commentary sections. Keep in mind that, in this case, the idea of 'context' refers both to Wright's insights and to the group's thoughts about the biblical texts under discussion – both have value. So the questions here will invite engagement with Wright's and each other's comments.

Responding to the Word in the World

Encountering God's word in scripture ideally should lead to engaging in God's work and purpose in the world. The questions in this section focus on making connections between the gospel expressed in the Bible and the gospel expressed in persons' faith and life. This is a place where attentive listening is key – be alert to when to insert follow-up or clarification questions of your own, or when to offer encouragement to those who are speaking.

Closing and Prayer

Once again, as the session closes, consider establishing a pattern of praying together, including both speech and silence. One suggestion: Name and lift up the concerns and joys of the group and then close by saying aloud, *Lord in your mercy, hear our prayers*, or by praying together the Lord's Prayer.

The Session Guides

SESSION 1
THE SPIRIT ARRIVES

Reading Selections: Acts 1.6–8; Acts 2.5–13; Acts 2.42–47

Introduction

[In the book of Acts,] Luke is keen that we latch on to two things which are fundamental to his whole book and indeed his whole view of the world. First, it is all based on the resurrection of Jesus. In the last chapter of his gospel, Luke described some of the scenes in which Jesus met his followers after being raised from the dead: it really was him, he really was alive, richly alive, in a transformed body that could eat and drink as well as walk and talk. . . . The second thing he wants us to latch onto, indeed is so eager to get to that he puts it here, right up front, is the presence and power of the holy spirit. He will have much more to say about this in due course, but already here he insists that the spirit is present when Jesus is teaching his followers about what is to come and, above all, that they are about to discover the spirit as a new and powerful reality in their own lives. (page 3)

Gathering

Welcome and then center the group with a brief prayer, closing by reading aloud, for example, a verse from Psalm 19: *Let the words of my mouth and the meditation of my heart be acceptable to you, O Lord, my rock and my redeemer* (Psalm 19.14 NRSV). Or recite together these words of the Risen Christ from Acts 1.7–8: 'It is not for you to know times or seasons . . . But you shall receive power when the Holy Spirit comes upon you; and you shall be my witnesses' (RSV).

Attending to the Word in the Text

Hear read aloud, one at a time, the selected scripture passages for this session. After hearing each selection, discuss the related question below.

Acts 1.6–8

What presumptions about God's mission in the world does Jesus correct or clarify in his answer to the question of those gathered: 'Is this the time when you are going to restore the kingdom to Israel?' What are Jesus' followers to be witnesses to?

Acts 2.5–13

The opening verses of Act 2 are full of the spectacular. What is Luke's purpose in describing the scene with such attention to the dynamic details? What boundaries or barriers does the spirit in Acts 2 begin to break down?

Acts 2.42–47

In Acts 2, Luke identifies the 'four marks of the church' – teaching, fellowship, communion and prayer – and that these all must go together for the church to be truly the witness that it is called to be. What did these four practices look like in the church in Acts? What do they look like today?

Engaging the Word in Context

How does Wright describe 'God's rescue plan' as it is expressed in Peter's preaching in Acts 2 (see pages 30–33)? How would you describe it in your own words?

Responding to the Word in the World

'Again and again in Acts we find opposition, incredulity, scoffing and sneering at what the apostles say and do, at the same time as great success and conviction. And again and again in the work of the church, to this day, there are always plenty who declare that we are wasting our time and talking incomprehensible nonsense' (page 22). Wright notes that the challenge of this text is that it invites congregations to ask the hard question of whether the energy or life of their witness would cause the world to take any notice at all. What is your congregation doing that might cause anyone to look on with amazement?

Closing and Prayer

Name and lift up the concerns and joys of the group, and then close by saying aloud, *Lord, in your mercy, hear our prayers.*

SESSION 2
THE SPIRIT ANIMATES

Reading Selections: Acts 3.1–10; 4.1–12; Acts 5.1–11

Introduction

Up to now, in Acts, the whole story has taken place in Jerusalem, but not in or around the Temple. Now we find that the believers were regularly going to worship in the Temple, even though (as we saw at the end of the previous chapter) the most important things they did (their teaching, fellowship, bread-breaking and prayer) happened elsewhere. But the demonstration of the power of Jesus' name took place, not in the Temple, but outside the gate. God is on the move, not confined within the institution, breaking out into new worlds, leaving behind the shrine, which had become a place of worldly power and resistance to his purposes. This theme will come to a head four chapters from now. Whereas Luke's gospel began and ended in the Temple, what he is telling us now is that the good news of Jesus, though beginning in Jerusalem, is starting to reach outside to anyone and everyone who needs it. (page 39)

Gathering

Welcome and then center the group with a brief prayer, closing by reading aloud, for example, a verse from Psalm 19: *Let the words of my mouth and the meditation of my heart be acceptable to you, O Lord, my rock and my redeemer* (Psalm 19.14, NRSV). Or recite together these words of the Risen Christ from Acts 1.7–8: 'It is not for you to know times or seasons. . . . But you shall receive power when the Holy Spirit comes upon you; and you shall be my witnesses' (RSV).

Attending to the Word in the Text

Hear read aloud, one at a time, the selected scripture passages for this session. After hearing each selection, discuss the related question below.

Acts 3.1–10

According to Wright, what counts in this story is the power of Jesus' name. Why is that such an important theme in Acts? What would it take to reclaim that power today? What might happen if we did? When have you experienced that happening?

Acts 4.1–12

The trouble the disciples find themselves in here is the result of their proclamation of Jesus' resurrection – 'a radical, dangerous doctrine'. Why is preaching the resurrection such a threat to those in power and to the status quo? How have you found the resurrection still a troublesome word to proclaim, even now?

Acts 5.1–11

This story is difficult to hear: a swift and violent judgment that, as Wright points out, occurs infrequently in the Bible. Nonetheless, here it is. What do you think Luke intended to convey? What do you think of Wright's commentary (see pages 60–63)?

Engaging the Word in Context

Peter's prayer for boldness in Acts 4.29–30 was one that literally shook the place where he was speaking. Wright believes the church in every age must learn to pray with such confidence. What is the intent of Peter's prayer? Where or how might this prayer be appropriately prayed in your life, or in the life of your congregation?

Responding to the Word in the World

The thorny issue in the story of Ananias and Sapphira, says Wright, is the lie. 'Lying is, ultimately, a way of declaring that we don't like the world the way it is and we will pretend that it is somehow more the way we want it to be. At that level, it is a way of saying that we don't trust God the creator to look after his world and sort it out in his own time and way.' Where do you see Christians or churches today getting caught in the lie – found to be acting in ways that reveal our mistrust of God?

Closing and Prayer

Name and lift up the concerns and joys of the group, and then close by saying aloud, *Lord, in your mercy, hear our prayers.*

SESSION 3
THE SPIRIT DISTURBS

Reading Selections: Acts 5.27–42; Acts 7.1–16; Acts 7.35–53

Introduction

One of the fascinating things about Acts is that nobody knew what to call the new movement. Even the angels seem to have had trouble with it. It wasn't called 'Christianity' for quite some time; indeed, it's only in chapter 11, when the movement has reached some non-Jews up north in Syria, that anyone calls the followers of Jesus 'Christians', that is, 'Messiah-people'. . . . Here, for the only time, but significantly, it is referred to as 'this Life'. 'Go and stand in the Temple,' said the angel, 'and speak to the people *all the words of this* Life.'

It's a strange way to put it but we can see what was meant. What the apostles were doing was quite simply to *live* in a wholly new way. Nobody had lived like this before; that, indeed, was one of the extraordinary challenges which impinged on people as the gospel set off around the wider world. (pages 67–68)

Gathering

Welcome and then center the group with a brief prayer, closing by reading aloud, for example, a verse from Psalm 19: *Let the words of my mouth and the meditation of my heart be acceptable to you, O Lord, my rock and my redeemer* (Psalm 19.14, NRSV). Or recite together these words of the Risen Christ from Acts 1.7–8: 'It is not for you to know times or seasons. . . . But you shall receive power when the Holy Spirit comes upon you; and you shall be my witnesses' (RSV).

Attending to the Word in the Text

Hear read aloud one at a time the selected scripture passages for this session. After hearing each selection, discuss the related question below.

Acts 5.27–42

Compare the account in Luke 20.1–7 of the chief priests and scribes questioning Jesus' authority with this account of Peter's authority questioned before the Assembly. How is the issue of authority the same or different in both accounts? What is at stake for the religious establishment in this question? What is at stake for the early believers/church in this question?

Acts 7.1–16

Why is Stephen's 'run-up', as Wright calls it – his appeal first to God's covenant with Abraham – such an important part of his overall sermon? How have you understood the connection between the story of Israel (the Old Testament) and the story of Jesus (the gospels)? How important is that connection?

Acts 7.35–53

As Wright observes, Stephen closes his speech by accusing his listeners of idolatry – their idol, the Temple! As outrageous a denunciation as this was, it challenges the church today to consider our own tradition, and 'whether we ourselves might be in the wrong place within it'. Thoughts?

Engaging the Word in Context

In his commentary on Acts 5.27–42, Wright says, 'Shall we obey God, or shall we obey human authorities? It is the question which Jesus still poses, both to those outside the faith (was he from God, or was he a deluded fanatic?) and to those inside the faith (shall we compromise our allegiance to him by going along with human instructions that cut against the gospel, or shall we remain loyal even at the risk of civil disobedience?)' (page 72). Where do you see evidence today of the church's continued struggle with this question?

Responding to the Word in the World

The crisis described in the opening verses of Acts 6 was one prompted by people from diverse ethnic and cultural backgrounds learning to relate to each other as a family of faith. This crisis resulted in two things: the intentional delegation of ministry tasks and the prioritizing of the ministry of teaching and prayer. How does that crisis show up in our church today? What are the challenges of managing the division of ministry labor?

Closing and Prayer

Name and lift up the concerns and joys of the group, and then close by saying aloud, *Lord, in your mercy, hear our prayers.*

SESSION 4
THE SPIRIT SENDS

Reading Selections: Acts 8.26–40; Acts 9.1–19a; Acts 9.19b–31

Introduction

It was part of the agenda which Jesus set his followers, at the start of Acts, that they should be his witnesses not only in Jerusalem and Judaea, but in Samaria – and on, to the very ends of the earth (1.8). Like many things in Acts, they don't seem to have had much of a plan for how to achieve this, and they don't seem to have thought out in advance what such a plan might look like if they did; but it began to happen anyway, as we have seen, because of the persecution in Jerusalem and the scattering of people who were eager to talk about Jesus to anyone they met, whether they were proper Jews or not. (page 98)

Gathering

Welcome and then center the group with a brief prayer, closing by reading aloud, for example, a verse from Psalm 19: *Let the words of my mouth and the meditation of my heart be acceptable to you, O Lord, my rock and my redeemer* (Psalm 19.14, NRSV). Or recite together these words of the Risen Christ from Acts 1.7–8: 'It is not for you to know times or seasons. . . . But you shall receive power when the Holy Spirit comes upon you; and you shall be my witnesses' (RSV).

Attending to the Word in the Text

Hear read aloud one at a time the selected scripture passages for this session. After hearing each selection, discuss the related question below.

Acts 8.26–40

Though much of the focus of this narrative section is on the conversion of Saul, discussion will focus on three other key figures whom the Spirit sends into mission. In the story of the Ethiopian, the spirit sends Philip to be an interpreter of the gospel. What was the key to Philip's interpretation of the prophetic scroll the Ethiopian was reading? When have you found yourself interpreting the gospel for someone?

Acts 9.10–19a

In the story of Saul's conversion, the spirit sends Ananias to confirm Saul's encounter with Christ. As Wright observes, Ananias went where the spirit sent him, despite knowing it was 'ridiculously dangerous' and performed his task with 'grace, love and wisdom'. What clues in the story suggest the requirements for being as attuned to God's voice as Ananias?

Acts 9.19b–31

In the story of Saul's beginning ministry, the spirit sends Barnabas to vouch for Saul's authority as a witness for Christ, though a witness challenged by controversy and death threats. Enter Barnabas. How would you characterize Barnabas's value to Paul's missionary calling and work in Acts?

Engaging the Word in Context

In the Acts 8.4–25 story of Simon the magician, the problem hinges upon his desire for 'not the gift of the spirit itself, but the power'. What is the message of the story to the early church, especially since Simon is let off with a just warning? Where are the Simons among us now? How can or should the church respond to them?

Responding to the Word in the World

Wright notes that the Ethiopian was, as a eunuch, 'an outsider, forever to remain so within the Jewish system'. Who are the church's outsiders to its religious traditions today? What guidance does the story of Philip offer in reaching out to them?

Closing and Prayer

Name and lift up the concerns and joys of the group, and then close by saying aloud, *Lord, in your mercy, hear our prayers.*

SESSION 5
THE SPIRIT SURPRISES

Reading Selections: Acts 10.1–16; Acts 10.34–38; Acts 12.6–19

Introduction

One of the glories of Luke's writing is that he can take us, in a couple of strides, from the enormous, earth-shattering, history-changing moments like the conversion of Saul to a small, intimate scene: an upstairs room in a poor home, filled with the knitting and sewing that had occupied the good lady who has just died. . . . But there is no such thing as a small errand in the kingdom of God. If all we knew about Peter was that he had healed the disabled Aeneas, and had raised Dorcas from the dead, that would be enough to know that the power of God was working through him; and perhaps these apparently smaller stories were told here by Luke to remind anyone who might be disposed to think otherwise that Peter was where he was on proper business from the Lord, the gospel business of healing and encouraging and building up God's people. (pages 116–17)

Gathering

Welcome and then center the group with a brief prayer, closing by reading aloud, for example, a verse from Psalm 19: *Let the words of my mouth and the meditation of my heart be acceptable to you, O Lord, my rock and my redeemer* (Psalm 19.14, NRSV). Or recite together these words of the Risen Christ from Acts 1.7–8: 'It is not for you to know times or seasons. . . . But you shall receive power when the Holy Spirit comes upon you; and you shall be my witnesses' (RSV).

Attending to the Word in the Text

Hear read aloud, one at a time, the selected scripture passages for this session. After hearing each selection, discuss the related question below.

Acts 10.1–16

The text indicates that Cornelius, though not a Jew, was devoutly religious. What does that say about Luke's intended audience and what Luke wanted them to know about Cornelius? How is Luke's description of Cornelius important for understanding the contrast between a Roman centurion and a common fisherman and how it plays out in their encounter?

Acts 10.34–48

Here is an instance of the Spirit's appearance with the surprising addition of speaking in tongues. Wright suggests that its purpose is to confirm to Peter that '*un*circumcised people have been regarded by the holy spirit as fit vessels to be filled with his presence and voice'. What would you say the sign of speaking in tongues conveys in this passage? What other signs might convey to us this same confirmation – that all are welcomed, forgiven and transformed?

Acts 12.6–19

The comical nature of this story, says Wright, contributes to its authenticity. Particularly remarkable is the gathered disciples' initial shock that their prayers could have been answered. What message did Luke intend this story to send to the early church? In what ways do you see the church still caught off guard by the surprising acts of the Spirit?

Engaging the Word in Context

In commenting on the story of Peter and Cornelius, Wright contends that the point of the story was not to depict the elimination of all distinctions between peoples. The point is not that God accepts us as we are, but rather that God *invites us as we are* – to be followed by repentance, forgiveness, baptism and receiving the holy spirit. How does Wright's perspective inform your understanding of the story?

Responding to the Word in the World

This first half of the book of Acts is full of stories of conversions – Paul, Ananias, Peter, Cornelius, Lydia, Tabitha – always initiated by the Spirit. What insights or critiques do these conversion stories offer to our traditional notions of conversion? In what ways do we, as Christians or the church, still need to be converted?

Closing and Prayer

Name and lift up the concerns and joys of the group, and then close by saying aloud, *Lord, in your mercy, hear our prayers.*